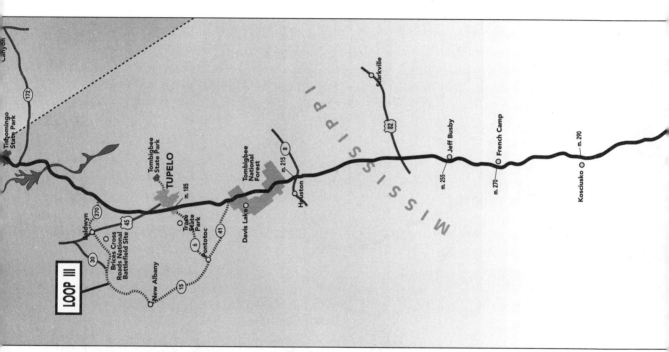

LOOP Ⅲ

Map Is Continued On Next Page

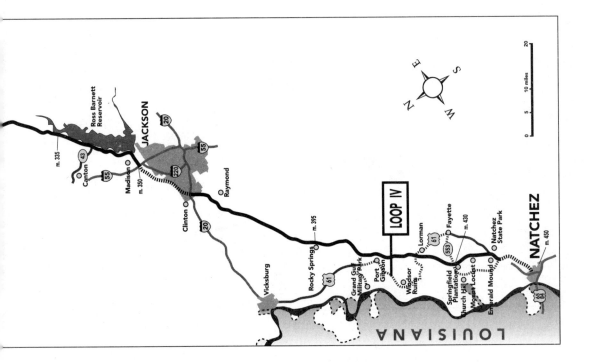

Traveling the Trace

CATHY AND VERNON SUMMERLIN

RUTLEDGE HILL PRESS ■ *Nashville, Tennessee*

Published in Nashville, Tennessee, by Rutledge Hill Press, 211 Seventh Avenue North, Nashville, Tennessee 37219. Distributed in Canada by H. B. Fenn & Company, Ltd., 1090 Lorimar Drive, Mississauga, Ontario L5S 1R7. Distributed in Australia by Millennium Books, 13/3 Maddox Street, Alexandria NSW 2015. Distributed in New Zealand by Tandem Press, 2 Rugby Road, Birkenhead, Auckland 10. Distributed in the United Kingdom by Verulam Press, Ltd., 152a Park Street Lane, Park Street, St. Albans, Hertfordshire AL2 2AU.

Typography by D&T/Bailey Typesetting, Inc., Nashville, Tennessee
Design and map by Bruce Gore, Gore Studio, Inc., Nashville, Tennessee

Mile markers on map are approximate.

Photograph Credits

Page xi © Bryan Curtis
Pages 37 (© Robin Hood), 40 (© David Wright), 42, 45 (© David Wright), 49, 51, 57 (© 1992 Bob Schatz) courtesy of Nashville Convention and Visitors Bureau.
Pages 67, 71 © Dana Hickman.
Pages 128, 131, 132 (top and bottom), 133, 134, 137, 138, 295 courtesy of Alabama Mountain Lakes Tourist Association.
Page 151 (bottom) courtesy of Tupelo Convention and Visitors Bureau.
Pages 165, 168 courtesy of Starkville Visitors and Convention Council.
Pages 177, 178 (top), 180 (top and bottom) courtesy of Kosciusko-Attala Chamber of Commerce, © Branning Photography.
Pages 183, 185 courtesy of Canton Convention and Visitors Bureau.
Pages 193, 200, 202 (top © Kathleen McClure), 202 (bottom), 203 (top and bottom from Mississippi Archives and History), 204 (© Kathleen McClure), 205 (© Kathleen McClure) courtesy of MetroJackson Convention and Visitors Bureau.
Page 266 (top) courtesy of Monmouth Plantation.
All other photographs are by the authors.

Library of Congress Cataloging-in-Publication Data

Summerlin, Cathy, 1953–
    Traveling the trace / Cathy and Vernon Summerlin.
      p.   cm.
    Includes index.
    ISBN 1-55853-340-0 (paperback)
    1. Natchez Trace—Guidebooks.   2. Natchez Trace National Scenic Trail—Guidebooks.   I. Summerlin, Vernon, 1943– . II. Title.
F217.N37S86   1995
917.62—dc20
                                      95-3793
                                       CIP

Printed in the United States of America

04 03 02 01 00 - 8 7 6 5 4 3

To our mothers, Bobbie McAllister and Georgia Summerlin

To my mom, who showed me the joys of traveling our mountain backroads as a child and for her boundless love and understanding.

A special remembrance for my grandmother who was always ready to grab her purse and go anytime we were going anywhere.

They taught me to seek the next horizon.

CSS

To Mom, who taught me the love and value of books, and for her encouragement and compassion.

A special remembrance of Dad for taking on the most difficult task of trying to prepare me for life, and instilling the thoughts that personal honor and integrity are life's greatest goals.

VSS

Contents

Acknowledgments

We thank all those who opened the doors of their homes and businesses to us, graciously sharing their time and knowledge and providing the information we needed for this book.

Special thanks to the Natchez Trace Parkway unit of the National Park Service for answering our questions and supplying the materials essential to portray accurately the many facets of the Trace. Of the many helpful souls we encountered, we want to mention the special help we received from Assistant Superintendent Don Thompson, Superintendent Dan Brown, and Chief of Interpretation and Visitor Services Sara Amy Leach at the Tupelo Headquarters, and ranger Eric Chamberlain for sharing his unique perspective on Mount Locust.

In our travels we have met several people who stand out in their professions. As we traveled the Trace, we found many people who were eager to share their knowledge with us. We want especially to acknowledge Susann Hamlin of North Alabama Mountain Lakes Association, Lenore Barkley of Vicksburg Convention and Visitors Bureau, and Willa Sanders of Kosciusko-Attala Chamber of Commerce.

Mary Current, with Jackson's Convention and Visitors Bureau, was a wonderful and exuberant source of information, as were Ann Mohon in Natchez and Cindy Ford-Sanders in Nashville.

Special gratitude to Kathie German for keeping the home fires burning while we were on the road, and to Dana Hickman, Margaret Kyser, and Libby Oldfield for their patience and support.

We appreciate Judy Butler Criss for sharing her love and extensive knowledge of antiques, and to friends from Middle Tennessee State University's Historic Preservation Department for introducing us to the "mystery of history."

Thanks to Ron Pitkin and Larry Stone of Rutledge Hill Press for their faith in our book and to our editor, Amy Lyles Wilson.

Introduction

When we first set out to travel the Natchez Trace Parkway, one fine autumn day in 1991, we were immediately drawn both to its beauty and history. The Natchez Trace led us down the dusty roads of time to glimpse cultures ranging from prehistoric to Reconstruction, urban to rural, antebellum to modern. During that first trip, stopping to read the interpretative markers, we began to see a land spreading out before us much as it did when the Chickasaw used the Trace on the way to hunting grounds in Middle Tennessee.

Then we learned about the postriders who maintained communication between the last outpost of the United States at the western frontier town of Nashville, and the sophisticated river town of

Cathy and Vernon Summerlin in front of the Natchez Trace Parkway entrance.

Natchez with its vestiges of French, Spanish, British, and finally American settlement.

At Natchez and Nashville, Andrew Jackson and Rachel Donelson Robards met and began a love affair that would stretch through the years to become interwoven with the history of our young nation. Andrew Jackson traveled this road many times: coming home to Nashville with his young bride; completing negotiations with the Indians to open lands for expansion of settlement into the Southwest; and returning in triumph after the Battle of New Orleans.

Thieves and murderers also traveled the Trace, terrorizing hapless travelers as they returned overland from the markets at Natchez and New Orleans. With the arrival of the steam engine, the boisterous road settled peacefully into well-worn ruts awaiting rediscovery.

That was the Old Trace. As you travel the Trace today, slipping into those other times, you can easily forget that today's communities lie just beyond the trees sheltering the parkway from their presence. All the sites we describe are within 30 miles of the Natchez Trace, and each has something unique to offer travelers. We hope you will take time to visit, because you will be rewarded with some memorable experiences and beautiful sights.

In this book we bring you the very best the communities along the Natchez Trace Parkway have to offer in the way of museums, antiques malls, state parks, bed and breakfasts, restaurants, specialty shopping, and outdoor recreation. Nashville offers music from country to classical, bluegrass to blues. Jackson, Mississippi, has wonderful family museums and parks. Learn about Vicksburg's history while taking up blackjack. Rest your head in delightful bed and breakfasts in Natchez.

Several communities are joined here in what we call "loop tours." For example, in northeast Alabama you can visit the homes of Helen Keller and W. C. Handy, visit Mrs. Rosenbaum in her Frank Lloyd Wright home, record your own version of a Roy Orbison hit, eat crêpes for breakfast in your own private dining room at a Victorian bed and breakfast, and see tiny creatures that glow in the dark at the bottom of an ancient canyon.

Or perhaps you'd rather travel to the Tennessee corridor and sample great country barbecue while you listen to some music in a small old-time picking parlor, then travel to several antiques malls and specialty shops in a historic town that was the site of a major Civil War battle. How about having dinner on a riverboat, or a train, or overlooking the Mississippi? Visit an antiquarian bookstore, view a galaxy, meet a rising country-music star, or watch a touring Broadway production. Want to see a Picasso, bring a mule to market, or learn to weave baskets? Within these pages you'll find these experiences and many, many more.

The first chapter consists of the interpretive markers placed by the National Park Service at points of interest along the Natchez Trace Parkway. The subsequent chapters take you from Nashville to Natchez as the postriders did nearly two hundred years ago.

Each chapter begins with directions from the parkway to the community, followed by a brief history of the area. A narrative recounts the sites we recommend visiting. Places in boldface are those that we found to be exceptional in one way or another. At the end of each chapter are lists of places to eat, sleep, shop, and have fun. We have provided sources for additional information; we urge you to contact them for brochures and maps. Three special sections concentrate on outdoor recreation, and the closing chapter offers brief information of interest to cyclists traveling the Trace.

Whether you drive a car, bring your camper, ride a horse, float a canoe, or pedal your bike, we hope you'll be as enchanted with these national treasures as we are and return often to visit.

Although we tried to be as thorough as possible in our coverage of the Trace, we feel sure that we missed some noteworthy spots along the way. And we weren't able to include every place we toured—part of the fun is exploring and discovering on your own. So if you see a back road that strikes your fancy, take it!

Traveling the Trace

Natchez Trace Interpretive Markers

The following information comes from the large wooden signs and other interpretive markers erected by the National Park Service. (Note: Signs and markers along the Trace are updated and revised as necessary. The information here reflects the signs and markers as they appeared in 1994, with slight changes for clarity.)

For tourist information about the Natchez Trace Parkway, call 1-800-305-7417 or 601-680-4025.

407.7 GORDON HOUSE/FERRY SITE ■ One of the few remaining buildings associated with the Old Natchez Trace, this was the home of ferry operator John Gordon. In the early 1800s, Indian scout Gordon made an agreement with the Chickasaw chief George Colbert to operate a trading post and ferry on the Duck River. Military expeditions with Gen. Andrew Jackson kept Gordon away from home much of the time. His wife, Dorothea, supervised construction of the present house in 1817–18. John Gordon died shortly after its completion, but Mrs. Gordon lived here until her death in 1859.

Old Natchez Trace: The 500-mile-long Natchez Trace of the early 1800s, then known as Natchez Road, connected Nashville on the Cumberland River with Natchez on the Mississippi River. This historic wilderness road crossed the Duck River one-quarter mile south of here.

In 1800, stream crossings were critical to the operation of the Natchez Trace. Small trees would bridge small streams, but rivers

The Gordon House—Construction of the house began in 1817 and was completed in 1818. John Gordon operated a ferry across the nearby Duck River until his death in 1819.

Baker Bluff—A 2,100-foot trail leads from the scenic overlook to Jackson Falls.

were greater barriers. Large-scale bridge-building wasn't practical in the wilderness, and rivers like this could be forded only during dry periods. A ferry was the best solution. John Gordon opened a ferry here in 1803, sharing the profits with Chickasaw chief George Colbert, who by treaty controlled ferries on Indian land. Gordon's ferry crossed the Duck River for more than ninety years, until the opening of a bridge in 1896.

A ten-minute walk beginning at the Gordon House leads to a section of the original Natchez Trace and the Duck River Ferry site.

405.1 BAKER BLUFF ▪ The Family Farm Working in Harmony with the Environment. *The plaque is a depiction of what you see from the bluff of farm land, river, and fields. A trail leads from Baker Bluff to Jackson Falls.*

404.7 JACKSON FALLS ▪ A steep trail nine hundred feet long takes you to a clear pool at the base of these falls.

Duck River Overlook: A gentle one-fourth-mile trail leads to a viewpoint three hundred feet (thirty stories) above the Duck River. *(The overlook is north from the sign. Waterfall trail is a concrete sidewalk.)*

Jackson Falls—The trail descends nine hundred feet to the base of the cool cascade.

Jackson Branch: A stolen stream. This trail descends to Jackson Falls, a beautifully sculptured cascade that seems ageless. For thousands of years before the falls existed Jackson Branch flowed into this high valley isolated from the Duck River below. Then in a classic case of stream piracy, the Duck River captured Jackson Branch. The flooding river and other erosional agents wore away at the bluffs, cutting a new channel through faults in the rock. At the site of Jackson Falls the diverted stream slips down into the Duck River Valley abandoning its former course.

403.7 OLD TRACE WALK ▪ Preserved here is a 2,000-foot-long section of the old original Natchez Trace, which follows a ridge 300 feet above the Duck River. A ten- to fifteen-minute stroll will take you to the end of the trail and back and provide a change of pace from driving. As you walk the Old Trace, imagine the ordeal of the 1800s travelers who had to make 20 to 30 miles a day on foot or on horseback.

401.4 TOBACCO FARM ▪ You see here a typical early 1900s tobacco farm. A ten-minute loop walk takes you through a field to the barn where you see tobacco hanging to dry.

Old Trace: From here you may drive north on a narrow two-mile section of the old original Natchez Trace and meet the parkway on the other end. Your slower pace may take you back in time and let you enjoy views of the valley below.

400.2 SHEBOSS STAND ▪ Travel on the Natchez Trace was an adventure in the early 1800s. The 500-mile Trace transversed a sprawling wilderness where only Indians, outlaws, and wild animals were at home. Travelers needed a place to find food, supplies, and shelter. At government request the Chickasaw tribe permitted an establishment of inns or stands at one-day intervals through their lands, but only if Indians were the proprietors. One such stand, known as Sheboss, operated near here although the exact location is unknown.

Tobacco Farm—Tobacco is one of the few cash crops suited to the smaller homesteads that were once typical of much of this section of Middle Tennessee.

A widow Cranfield operated an inn here with her second husband, an Indian who spoke little English. According to legend, when travelers approached with questions about accommodations he would only point to his wife and say, "She boss."

397.3 OLD TRACE/LANDS OF THE CHICKASAW ▪ Before 1805 the Chickasaw owned all the land in this vicinity. Only the Natchez Trace, part of which remains here, made inroads into tribal territory. When the Indians ceded the land to the United States in the early 1800s the Natchez Trace became a boundary. The land behind you became government property under the 1805 treaty. In 1816 the tribe ceded a much larger tract including the land in front of you. Eventually the Chickasaw left their homeland. In 1837 the government removed them to the Indian Territory in Oklahoma over the tragic Trail of Tears. Despite the dissolution of their lands, the Chickasaw evolved a unique culture based on the American model. As hunting ranges shrank and the Chickasaw became farmers, they established their own schools, courts, and legislature.

During the Civil War the tribe joined the Confederacy. Tishomingo was the last of the Chickasaw war chiefs. Winchester Colbert was a mixed-blood governor of the Chickasaw Nation.

392.5 SWAN VALLEY OVERLOOK ▪ *From here you can see the water tower in Hohenwald, the highest town between New Orleans and Chicago. This is a grand vista.*

392.0 FALL HOLLOW WATERFALL ▪ *No interpretive marker but a path leads to an overlook of the waterfall and a steep trail takes you to the bottom of the falls.*

390.7 PHOSPHATE MINE ▪ From here north for approximately 40 miles the parkway passes through or near a geologic region of limestone rich in phosphate deposits. Abandoned mine shafts and limestone ledges on both sides of the parkway in this immediate area are silent reminders of mining activity. A five-minute walk to your right leads to an abandoned railroad bed and a collapsed mine shaft in a limestone outcrop.

Swan Valley—The rolling Tennessee countryside presents a seasonal show at the Swan Valley Overlook.

Fall Hollow—A steep 630-foot trail leads to the waterfall overlook at Falls Branch.

385.9 MERIWETHER LEWIS/1774 TO 1809 ■ Beneath this monument erected under the legislative act by the state of Tennessee, A.D. 1848, reposes the dust of Meriwether Lewis, captain in the U.S. Army, private secretary to President Jefferson, senior commander of the Lewis and Clark Expedition, and governor of the Territory of Louisiana.

In the Grinder House, the ruins of which are still discernible 230 yards south of this spot, Lewis's life of romantic endeavor and lasting achievement came tragically and mysteriously to its close on the night of October 11, 1809. The report of the committee appointed to carry out the provisions of the Monument Act contained these significant statements: "Great care was taken to identify the grave. George Nixon, Esq., an old surveyor, had become very early acquainted with the locality. He pointed out the place; but to

Meriwether Lewis Monument—The broken column symbolizes Lewis's untimely death while traveling from St. Louis to Washington. The circumstances of his death continue to generate controversy.

make assurance doubly sure the grave was reopened and the upper portion of his skeleton examined and such evidence found as to leave no doubt this was the place of interment."

Plainly visible though long deserted, here is a section of the Natchez Trace that evolved from buffalo and Indian trails into the first national highway of the Southwest. Cut and opened under authority of the U.S. government after treaties negotiated with the Chickasaw and Choctaw in 1801 and designed to meet early necessities of trade between Nashville and the country of the lower Mississippi, it is an abiding footprint of the bold, crude commerce of the pioneers. Yet it is not without military significance in the history of our country. Over it passed part of the Andrew Jackson army in his campaign against the Creek Indians in 1813 and again on his return from the battlefield of New Orleans in 1815. But before Talladega and New Orleans—before the soldiers of Jackson had given renown to the Natchez Trace—it received its immortal touch of melancholy fame when Meriwether Lewis, journeying over it on his way to Philadelphia to edit the story of his great expedition, met here his untimely death on the night of October 11, 1809.

Grinder House: Site and ruins of the Grinder House in which Meriwether Lewis met his death on the night of October 11, 1809.

Grinder House—Many believe Meriwether Lewis committed suicide while staying overnight at the Grinder House, while others remain convinced of foul play. Today the Grinder House contains interesting exhibits. The 2.3-mile Little Swan Trail is near the campground.

Inside the Grinder House are exhibits depicting the significance of the Trace through its history and its chronology beginning in 1765, including the creation of the parkway in 1938 by an act of Congress.

Metal Ford—Once the site of a natural crossing for the Buffalo River, Metal Ford is presently a favorite put-in for canoeists on the Buffalo.

382.8 METAL FORD STEELE'S IRONWORKS. ▪ Here, about 1820, stood a charcoal-burning furnace used to manufacture pig iron. All that remains of this pioneer enterprise are the slag pile and the evidence of a millrace used to bring water from the Buffalo River to operate the furnace's air blasting machinery.

On the banks of the Buffalo River is another plaque that reads, "A five-minute stroll beyond Metal Ford leads you beside the Buffalo River to the McLish stand exhibit and then back to this point by way of the historic mill trace."

381.8 NAPIER MINE ▪ Just a few feet to your left was an open pit mine that provided most of the ore for the nearby iron-making operations. John Catron, circa 1786 to 1865, was a principal promoter of the activities here in the 1820s and 1830s. Catron later became the associate justice of the U.S. Supreme Court. The mine took its name from Catron's predecessors, the Napiers.

Napier Mine—Napier Mine was in operation for nearly one hundred years and produced some of the highest grade iron ore in the area.

377.8 JACK'S BRANCH ▪ *Picnic area with restrooms, no marker.*

375.8 OLD TRACE DRIVE ▪ *One way to north, 2½ miles with overlooks. Not for travel trailers!*

367.3 DOGWOOD MUDHOLE ▪ A mile to the south, the Old Natchez Trace crossed a depression in the flat, dogwood-covered ridge. After heavy rains it became almost impassable for wagons. Its name, Dogwood Mudhole, recalls the ordeals of frontier travel. It shows too, how place names arising from local conditions of long ago are carried down through the years.

Jack's Branch—A grove of hardwoods shades the picnic area beside the stream at Jack's Branch.

365.1 AND 364.5 GLENROCK PICNIC AREA ▪ These trails lead to picnic sites by the stream below. They continue along the stream to Glenrock Branch Area on the parkway two-thirds of a mile to the south.

363.0 SWEETWATER BRANCH ▪ This small branch receives its name from the clean and fresh or sweet flavor of its water. Thousands of years of erosion and flooding have gradually built up the fertile bottom lands you see under cultivation near here. The branch is still carving and shaping the valley. You may follow the struggle of trees and other vegetation to gain a hold in the shallow rocky soil of the bottom in a fifteen-minute stroll along the nature trail.

352.9 McGlamery Stand ■ In frontier language a stand was an inn or a trading post, sometimes both, and usually located on a well-traveled route. Such a place was established on the Old Natchez Trace near here in 1849 by John McGlamery. Although the stand did not outlast the Civil War, the name did. The nearest village is known as McGlamery's Stand.

350.5 Sunken Trace ■ This early interstate road-building venture produced a snake-infested, mosquito-beset, robber-haunted, Indian-pestered forest path. Lamented by the pious, cussed by the impious, it tried everyone's strength and patience. When the trail became so waterlogged that wagons could not be pulled through,

Old Trace Drive—A one-way narrow, paved road leads travelers along a section of the Old Trace.

Dogwoods are among the earliest harbingers of spring, blooming from March to May.

Fields of goldenrod greet fall travelers along the Natchez Trace.

travelers cut new paths through the nearby woods. Here you see three cuts made to avoid mud into which oxcarts and wagons sank, making progress slow, dangerous, and sometimes even impossible.

346.2 HOLLY ▪ *Picnic area, no markers.*

343.5 CYPRESS CREEK ▪ *Picnic area, no markers.*

341.8 ALABAMA STATE LINE ▪ In 1663 King Charles II of England granted the colony of Carolina all land between thirty-one and thirty-six degrees north latitude from the Atlantic Ocean west in a direct line as far as the South Seas. The separation of North and South Carolina fixed the boundary between them at thirty-five degrees in 1735. North Carolina's release of land claims west of the Appalachian Mountains permitted establishment of the state of Tennessee with the same southern boundary. John Coffee, one of Andrew Jackson's generals at the Battle of New Orleans, supervised the surveys of the line between 1817 and 1822.

330.2 ROCK SPRING ▪ A nature trail offers you an opportunity to explore a small natural spring as it bubbles forth from the ground. Small fish dart about in the deep pools created as the stream wanders through the rich bottomland soil and limestone rock. Vegetation and trees change as you move through an abandoned field past the stream into a rocky hillside. After completing the twenty-minute walk you may decide to pull off your shoes and dangle your feet in the swift cool water.

The trails and stepping stones in the area lead you across Colbert Creek past Rock Spring and through the woodlands. Since 1977 numerous beaver dams have been built, then abandoned, by the beaver or destroyed by high water. Walk the trails and enjoy a changing environment of this once free-flowing, spring-fed stream.

327.3 COLBERT'S STAND ▪ George Colbert operated a ferry across the Tennessee River from 1800 to 1819. His stand, or inn, offered travelers a warm meal and shelter during their journey on the Old Trace. Colbert looked after his own well-being and once charged

Pickwick Lake, an impoundment of the Tennessee River near the site of Colbert's Stand, is known for small-mouth bass.

Andrew Jackson $75,000 to ferry his Tennessee army across the river. The site of his stand is a short fifty yards up the path. An additional twenty-minute stroll will take you along the Old Trace to the bluff overlook and back.

"Shrewd, talented, and wicked" thus a traveling preacher characterized George Colbert, the half-Scot half-Chickasaw chief who operated a stand here between 1801 and 1820. But for more than thirty years he helped negotiate with the United States for Chickasaw rights as the tide of settlement advanced from the east. His successful farm showed his people the way of the future. The short path will take you to the site of his stand and along the remnants of the Old Trace that it served.

Wilderness Haven: After a venison supper, one guest at Colbert's Stand spent the night in an outbuilding with "not less than fifty

Indians, many of them drunk." Here, and in about twenty other stands along the Trace, Kaintucks (men from Kentucky, Ohio, Indiana, and Tennessee who brought their wares to Natchez via the river), money-laden businessmen, Indians, and outlaws shared a spot of fellowship on a long, hazardous road.

320.3 Buzzard Roost Spring ▪ Originally called Buzzard Sleep, the name was changed to Buzzard Roost in 1801 by Levi Colbert, a renowned Chickasaw chief. The spring was a water source for the Colbert house, which also served as an inn and stand for travelers on the Old Natchez Trace. Travelers who stopped here remarked that it was a good place for they were well received, well fed, and kindly treated. *(Levi was a brother to George Colbert; they both ran the Colbert Ferry and their stands were about two hours apart by horseback.)*

317.0 Freedom Hills Overlook ▪ *Trail and overlook from highest point on the Trace in Alabama.*

313.0 Bear Creek Canoe Access ▪ No markers.

308.9 Mississippi-Alabama State Line

308.8 Bear Creek Mound ▪ The village site was occupied as early as 8000 B.C. by hunters who stayed only long enough to prepare their kill. From the time of Christ to A.D. 1000, migratory people of this area practiced limited agriculture. The nearby fields and streams offered an abundance of nuts, fruits, game, and fish. These people shaped this mound and built a crude temple to house sacred images.

308.4 Cave Spring ▪ The description of the ground surface and the type of rock indicate that this cave was the result of a solution activity. A long room and corridor were dissolved out of the rock by the underground water. The roof of the room eventually weakened and collapsed. Indians may have used this site as a source of water and stone. The water is now unsafe to drink and the cave is dangerous.

302.8 TISHOMINGO STATE PARK ■ From 1750 to 1836, Chieftain Tishomingo and his Chickasaw tribesmen traveled this famous trail over Saddleback Ridge into Freedom Hills, their hunting ground.

296.0 JOURDAN CREEK ■ *Picnic area, no markers.*

293.4 BAY SPRINGS LAKE ■ In the 1840s George Gresham erected a waterpowered sawmill and gristmill at the narrow rocky gorge on Mackey's Creek. Rock overhangs in the gorge provided shelters, which had been inhabited by Indians thousands of years before. In 1862, Gresham and two partners founded the Bay Springs Union factory. This company contained the original sawmill and gristmill, along with a mill for spinning cotton yarn and carding wool. This small industrial center included not only the mill but a cotton gin, blacksmith, post office, and general store. In 1885, the factory was destroyed by fire, never to be rebuilt.

293.2 TENN-TOM WATERWAY ■ In the mid-1770s Sieur de Bienville, the founder of Mobile, recommended to Louis XIV a waterway connecting the Tennessee and Tombigbee rivers. Later, American settlers also recognized the advantages of such a shortcut. Residents of Knox County, Tennessee, first approached Congress in 1810 with a proposal to connect the two rivers. The first survey was made by the Army Corps of Engineers in 1827. Serious consideration was delayed for more than one hundred years because of the expansion of railroads. Construction of the Tenn-Tom Waterway was started in 1972 and completed in 1985. The waterway provides shallow draft boats and barges operating in some 16,000 miles of other navigable inland waterways with access to the Gulf of Mexico at Mobile, Alabama, 412 river-miles to the south of the Bay Springs Lock and Dam. The junction of the waterway at the Tennessee River is 47 miles north of the lock and dam. The lock on the waterway is standard dimension, 110 feet wide and 600 feet long.

The Tennessee-Tombigbee Waterway has three main parts. The largest section from Demopolis, Alabama, north to Amory,

Tennessee Tombigbee Waterway—
One of the many locks located on
the Tenn-Tom.

Mississippi, utilized the Tombigbee River but changes and shortens the existing channel with dams, locks, and shortcuts. From Amory a canal section, using a chain of lakes, extends to the Bay Springs Lock and Dam. The final section cuts deeply through high ground to the Tennessee River. Its total length is 234 miles with the river section being 149 miles, the canal section 46 miles, and the divide cut section being 39 miles. The standard width is three hundred feet.

286. PHARR MOUNDS ■ The largest and most important archaeological site in northern Mississippi. Eight large dome-shaped burial mounds are scattered over an area of ninety acres (one hundred football fields). These mounds were built and used about A.D. 100–1200 by a tribe of nomadic Indian hunters and gatherers who returned to this site at times to bury their dead with their possessions.

Indian Mound—There are seven Indian mound sites along the Natchez Trace Parkway. While the majority are burial mounds, two are ceremonial mounds. One site is believed to have been occupied as early as 7000 B.C.

283.3 DONIVAN SLOUGH ▪ This woodland trail takes you through a lowland where rich soil and abundant moisture support a variety of large water-tolerant trees including tulip poplar, sycamore, and water oak. Bald cypresses thrive in the swampy backwaters of a slough or channel that winds through the bottomland. A twenty-minute walk lets you see these trees and the dramatic way the bald cypresses grow only in the wet slough.

278.4 TWENTYMILE BOTTOM OVERLOOK ▪ Twentymile Bottom, now cultivated, was typical of the many low areas along streams through which the Natchez Trace passed. In 1812, Rev. John Johnson stopped at Old Factors Stand near this bottom and wrote this account of bottomland travel: "I have this day swam my horse five times, bridged one creek, forded several others besides the swamp we had to wade through. At night we had a shower of rain. Took up my usual lodging on the ground in company with several Indians."

275.2 DOGWOOD VALLEY ▪ Flowering dogwood is a common small tree throughout the eastern United States from Maine and Michigan south to Texas and Florida. Here the Natchez Trace passes

An unusually thick stand of dogwoods caused early travelers to name this area Dogwood Valley. A 1,000-foot nature trail leads visitors along twelve interpretive sites.

through a small valley with an unusual stand of large dogwood trees. An easy fifteen-minute walk takes you along a sunken portion of the Old Trace and through the small wooded area named Dogwood Valley.

269.4 OLD TRACE AND CONFEDERATE GRAVESITE ▪ Much of the Old Trace had been abandoned by the start of the Civil War. However, the war did leave its mark on the Trace as it did upon the rest of the South. The soldiers marched, camped, and fought along portions of this historic old road. A five-minute walk on the Old Trace here takes you to the gravesites of thirteen unknown Confederate soldiers, a mute reminder of bygone days and of the great struggle out of which developed a stronger nation.

266.0 THE NATCHEZ TRACE HEADQUARTERS ▪ *Information Center, bookstore, restrooms, nature walk, and offices.*

263.9 OLD TOWN OVERLOOK/OLD TOWN CREEK ▪ In the early 1800s ordinary Americans could not be bothered with learning the names of Chickasaw villages on the Natchez Trace. One they called Old Town and passed the name on to the stream running through this valley. This is one of the sources of the Tombigbee River first called "River of the Chickasaw" and later the "Tombeckbee" by the French. Near here in 1795, the Chickasaw defeated the Creek in a battle described by Andrew Jackson as, "When the whole Creek Nation came to destroy your towns . . . a few hundred Chickasaw aided by a few whites chased them back to their nation, killing the best of their warriors and covering the rest with shame."

261.8 Chickasaw Village ▪ Here once stood an Indian village of several houses and a fort. During the summer the inhabitants lived in rectangular, well-ventilated houses. In the winter they lived in round houses with plaster walls. In times of danger, everybody—warriors, women, children—sought shelter in strongly fortified stockades. Original foundations of four of these structures are overlaid with concrete curb on the ground to your left.

The Chickasaw Nation: This tribe, population about 2,000, lived in the Chickasaw Old Fields, a small natural prairie near Tupelo, Mississippi. Although their villages occupied an area of less than 20 square miles, the Chickasaw claimed and hunted over a vast region in northern Mississippi, Alabama, western Tennessee, and Kentucky. The Chickasaw were closely related to the Choctaw, Creek, and Natchez, as well as some of the smaller tribes of the Mississippi Valley. De Soto's followers were the first Europeans to see the Chickasaw, with whom they fought a bloody battle in 1541. The Chickasaw, after ceding the last of their ancestral lands to the United States, moved in 1837–47 to Oklahoma to become one of the Five Civilized Tribes.

The English-French Conflict 1700–1763: England and France, after the founding of Louisiana, fought four wars for control of North America. The Chickasaw became allies of the British, who used them as a spearhead to oppose French expansion. This tribe, with British help, not only remained independent, but threatened French shipping on the Mississippi. The French conquered or made allies of all the tribes along the Mississippi except for the Chickasaw. They made great efforts to destroy this tribe, sending powerful forces against them in 1736 and 1740 and incited the Choctaw and other tribes to do likewise. The Chickasaw successfully resisted and remained a thorn in the side of France, until she in 1763, lost all her North American possessions.

The French-Chickasaw War in 1736: The Chickasaw threatened French communications between Louisiana and Canada, and urged the Choctaw to trade with the English. Bienville decided to destroy the Chickasaw tribe. In 1735, he ordered a column of French and Indians led by Pierre D'Artaguette from Illinois to meet him near Tupelo. Bienville, leading a French army joined by the Choctaw, proceeded via Mobile up the Tombigbee. Arriving at the Chickasaw villages on May 25, 1736, he saw nothing of D'Artaguette. D'Artaguette was dead. Two months earlier the Chickasaw had defeated and killed him and forced his followers to flee. Ignorant of D'Artaguette's defeat, Bienville attacked the fortified village of Ackia on May 26, 1736. Bloodily repulsed, he withdrew to Mobile, leaving the Chickasaw more dangerous than ever.

251.9 BLACK BELT ▪ Ages ago this area was under an arm of the ocean. Shells and other marine organisms were deposited to form the limestone seen here. Exposure of the limestone to all types of weathering gradually changed it into a heavy fertile soil of various colors. The dominant black soil, which before cultivation was prairie grassland, has given the area the name Black Belt, or Black Prairie. The Black Belt extends south beyond Columbus, Mississippi, then trends eastward across nearly all of Alabama. Formerly one of America's great cotton areas, it is now considered excellent pasture for livestock.

251.1 CHICKASAW COUNCIL HOUSE ▪ Westerly on the Natchez Trace stood an Indian village, Pontatock, with its council house, which in the 1820s became the capital of the Chickasaw Nation. The chiefs and the head men met there to sign treaties or establish tribal laws and policies. Each summer two or three thousand Indians camped nearby to receive an annual payment for lands they had sold to our federal government. After the treaty of 1832, the last land was surrendered. The council house disappeared but its memory remains here in the names of a Mississippi county and town that went west with the Chickasaw as a county and village in Oklahoma.

249.6 TOCKSHISH ▪ Named for a Chickasaw word meaning "tree root," Tockshish was a community of Indians and white men on the Natchez Trace to the northwest. John McIntosh, British agent to the Choctaw, first settled there before 1770. In 1801, McIntosh's was made the second post office between Nashville and Natchez and a relay station where postriders exchanged weary horses for fresh ones. The post office is gone—only the name recalls the time when hoof-beats marked the arrival of mailbags that had left Nashville five days before and were due in Natchez seven days later.

245.6 MONROE MISSION STATION ▪ At Monroe Mission Station northwest of here, the Chickasaw first received Christianity and education in 1822. Five years later, one hundred acres were under cultivation and eighty-one pupils were attending the school. Boys learned farming and carpentry, and girls learned spinning and weaving, in addition to classroom work. More than 150 persons were baptized in the church, a room not larger than sixteen feet square. In front was a large arbor, covered with brush and seeded with puncheons for summer meetings. Monroe and three other stations were the training centers for many who became leaders of the Chickasaw in Oklahoma.

243.3 HERNANDO DE SOTO ▪ Somewhere in this vicinity, the Spanish explorer Hernando de Soto crossed the animal path that later became the Natchez Trace. In 1539, he set out on a long arduous journey that took him across the southeastern United States. He crossed the Tombigbee River east of here in December 1540 and spent the ensuing winter among the nearby Chickasaw Indians. Later attacked by the Indians, de Soto and his army moved westward. He is credited with discovering the Mississippi River somewhere south of Memphis, Tennessee, in June 1541.

241.4 CHICKASAW AGENCY ▪ U.S. agents to the Chickasaw lived from 1802 to 1825 west of here on the Old Natchez Trace. That

Americans could peacefully travel the road through Indian lands was due in large measure to the agents. Their efforts to preserve harmony included such thankless tasks as collecting debts, recovering stolen horses, removing trespassers, and capturing fugitives. Winter was lonely but spring and summer brought thousands of Kaintucks on the long journey from Natchez to their Ohio Valley homes. Many expected the agency to supply medicine, food, or a good night's rest.

233.2 WITCH DANCE ■ The very name conjures visions of eerie midnights, swirling black capes, and brooms stacked against a nearby tree. The old folks say the witches gathered here to dance and wherever their feet touched the ground the grass withered and died, never to grow again. Impossible? Maybe so, but look around. Try to find a hidden spot where no grass grows.

232.4 BYNUM MOUNDS ■ In prehistoric times, raw materials and articles from distant areas reached the Indians of the Bynum site by trade along early trails that were the forerunners of the Natchez Trace. Spool-shaped objects made of copper filled with lead were found with Bynum materials. Flint for tools and weapons came from as far away as the region of Ohio. Green stone for polished celts (axes) was obtained from the Alabama-Tennessee Piedmont. Marine shells came from the Gulf Coast.

A Living from the Land: The Indians hunted, fished, and gathered wild berries, nuts, and fruit. They supplemented these activities by farming. Deer was the most common game animal. The Indians used the bones for tools and the skin for clothing. Cooking pots were made of clay mixed with sand or grit. The surfaces were decorated with the impressions of fabrics or cords. You may see specimens from the Bynum Mounds in the Parkway Visitors Center near Tupelo.

Summer Shelters: In summer the Indians probably lived largely out of doors under temporary brush lean-to shelters. Most of their time was spent caring for their crops and hunting and gathering wild plants, fish, and shellfish from the surrounding area. New homes were built as necessary for the winter months. Three permanent house foundations were discovered during archaeological excavations. These were built by placing timbers upright in a circular pattern, weaving willow or reed stems into them, and finally plastering mud on the outside. Roofs were thatched with grass and bark with a center hole for smoke to escape.

221.4 OLD TRACE ■ Preserved here is a portion of a nearly two-hundred-year-old road, the Old Natchez Trace. Maintaining this 500-mile-long wilderness road in the early 1800s was a difficult if not hopeless task. As you look down the sunken trench, note the large trees growing on the edge of the ten-foot-wide strip we see today. These trees are mute testimony to the endless struggle between man to alter and change and nature to reclaim, restore, and heal.

213.3 LINE CREEK ■ Unlike modern nations, Indian nations seldom recognized clear, exact boundaries to their lands. However, Chickasaw and Choctaw Indians came to accept as a dividing line the stream that flowed in this valley. It remained the boundary until both tribes moved to Oklahoma in the 1830s. Although the stream's course has been changed somewhat by a modern drainage canal, it is still called Line Creek. Near here Noah Wall and his Choctaw wife had a stand where food and shelter were provided.

203.5 PIGEON ROOST ■ Pigeon Roost Creek to your left is a reminder of the millions of migrating passenger pigeons that once roosted in trees in this area. The species has been completely destroyed. One mile east where the Natchez Trace crossed the creek, Nathaniel Folsom of New England and his Choctaw wife had a trading post before 1790. Their son, David, later operated it and accommodated travelers. When Rev. Thomas Nixon stopped here in 1815, David's wife prepared suitable nourishment and would have no pay. David Folsom, strong supporter of Christianity and Indian education, was elected chief of the northeast district of the Choctaw Nation in 1826.

Old Trace—Even today the Old Natchez Trace must be maintained regularly to prevent tree overgrowth.

201.3 BALLARD CREEK ▪ *Picnic tables, no interpretive marker.*

198.6 THE OLD NATCHEZ TRACE ▪ In the early 1800s many thoughtful Americans believed that isolation and the difficulties of communication would force the Mississippi Valley settlements to form a separate nation. Hoping to hold the frontier, Congress in 1800 established a postroute from Nashville to Natchez. The Trace, then a series of Indian trails, had drawn from the secretary of state the bitter comment, "The passage of mail from Natchez is as tedious as from Europe when westerly winds prevail." To speed the mail, President Jefferson ordered the army to clear out the trail and make it a road. Postriders carrying letters, dispatches, and newspapers helped bind the vast, turbulent frontier to the republic. However, their day passed. By the mid-1830s steamboats running from New Orleans to Pittsburgh robbed the Trace of its usefulness as a main postroad.

193.1 JEFF BUSBY PARK ▪ On February 15, 1934, while serving as U.S. congressman from Mississippi, Thomas Jefferson Busby (1884–1964) introduced a bill authorizing a survey of the Old Natchez Trace. Four years later, the historic road was designated a unit of the National Park System. This area is named in Jeff Busby's honor to commemorate his part in the parkway's establishment.

Little Mountain: On a clear day from here atop Little Mountain you can see about 20 miles. The ridges and valleys are part of a geological land form called the Wilcox series that extends northeast into Alabama. Some fifty million years ago the Wilcox existed as layers of sand and mud. Pressure of overlying sediments and early upheavals have resulted in those layers being tilted and converted into sandstone and shale. More resistant to erosion than the shale, the sandstone portions are the present-day ridges.

To your left is a one-half-mile-long loop nature trail that descends into a shady hollow. You can easily complete the loop in thirty minutes. However, the more time you allow the more you will see and hear. Walk gently and give the forest residents a chance to welcome you into their home. A one-half-mile-long side trail from the loop leads to the campground.

Little Mountain—A 1-mile trail guides visitors from the Jeff Busby Campground to the interpretive shelter atop Little Mountain.

Drane House—With parking just yards off the Trace, the Col. James Drane house was begun in 1846 and moved to this location in 1981. It has been furnished with antiques donated by friends of French Camp Academy.

184.8 YOWANI ■ *Picnic area, no marker.*

180.7 FRENCH CAMP/THE DRANE HOUSE ■ Construction of the Col. James Drane house began in 1846 using a waterpowered saw. The foundation and framing are secured with wooden pegs and the ceiling with squared nails. Moved to this location in 1981, the house is now owned and operated by the French Camp Academy. You are invited to visit the Drane house. The information station 175 yards to your right is in the 1840 Huffman log cabin. A sorghum mill adjacent to the cabin operates during the fall sorghum season. Open Monday through Saturday, 8:30 A.M. to 5 P.M. Restoration of the Col. James Drane home, which is listed on the National Register of Historic Places, has been funded with assistance of a matching grant-in-aid from the Department of the Interior National Park Service under the provisions of the Jobs Bill Program of 1983.

Louis LeFleur first traded with the Choctaw at a bluff now part of Jackson, Mississippi. About 1812, he established his stand nine hundred feet to the northeast on the Natchez Trace. Because of the storekeeper's nationality the area was often called "French Camp," a name retained by the present village. LeFleur married a Choctaw

French Camp Visitors Center is located in the Huffman log cabin, a fine example of a dog-trot cabin.

woman, and their famous son, who changed his name to Greenwood Leflore, became a Choctaw chief and a Mississippi state senator. The city of Greenwood and the county of Leflore are named for him.

A stone memorial marks a stage of the Natchez Trace at French Camp. The memorial was presented to the town by the Mississippi Daughters of the American Revolution, November 10, 1915, and reads: "The first highway was opened through the lower south by the Treaty of Dancing Rabbit Creek in 1830 between the American government and the Choctaw Indians. The surrounding country became a part of the state of Mississippi. Here Andrew Jackson's Tennessee and Kentucky commands rested on their way to join him in his coast campaign in the War of 1812, during which second struggle for American independence, Mississippi took a heroic part."

176.3 BETHEL MISSION ▪ About one-half mile northwesterly, Bethel, meaning "house of God," was opened in 1822 as one of thirteen Choctaw mission stations. Indians, slaves, and Squawmen labored hard during four weeks, frequently until ten at night by the light of the moon or large fires, to clear the forest and erect the buildings. The missionaries who took the gospel to the wilderness also taught farming, carpentry, weaving, and housekeeping as well as reading, writing, and arithmetic to Choctaw and half-breed children. In 1826, people moved from the Trace to new roads and Bethel was closed.

175.6 COLE CREEK ▪ Forests are fascinating places. Whole new worlds unfold to anyone who takes time to explore them. Across Cole Creek you will find a typical mixed hardwood forest. Here you can discover for yourself the many marvels in a bottomland forest, which are more intriguing than you might expect. Time means little in a forest, but a fifteen-minute adventure along this short trail will take you through the last days of a tupelo-bald cypress swamp and into the first stage of a mixed hardwood bottomland forest. Water tupelo thrives in lowlands and swamps because it can survive with its roots completely submerged underwater. The swollen base, called a buttress, helps support the tree. Bald cypress, another swamp lover, is

Cole Creek—Here you will find a 700-foot nature trail with ten interpretive stops describing the transition from swamp to mixed hardwood forest.

easily recognized by its knees. It was once thought that these knees were breathing organs but it is now believed they merely give additional support to the towering tree. As the swamp is filled, other species of trees are able to survive and reproduce. Beech, hickory, red oak, chestnut oak, ash, elm, and many others comprise the mixed hardwood forest that is taking over the area. Cole Creek will always be here but as the swamp fills in and the hardwood forest becomes established, the creek will be more and more limited to its banks. Someday the area will be a hardwood forest with a creek running through it, all evidence of the swamp erased.

164.3 HURRICANE CREEK ■ Plants need water much as men need money. Some are satisfied with little, some cannot flourish unless they have a lot, and the majority can live contentedly with just enough. From here a trail descends to the vegetation that thrives in the wet bottomland along Hurricane Creek. The path winds upward among plants growing in soil of medium dampness and on to the top of a dry hill before returning here. The differences in vegetation are due largely to the varying water content of the soil.

Kosciusko Museum Center—The volunteer staffed center welcomes more than 4,000 visitors per month from the United States and foreign countries.

160.0 MUSEUM/INFORMATION CENTER, KOSCUISKO

154.3 HOLLY HILL ■ *Picnic area, no marker.*

145.1 MYRICK CREEK ■ Meet the beaver, a member of the rodent family that has adapted itself to work and live both on the land and in the water. Beavers are large, weighing up to sixty pounds in Mississippi. Squat and with a low center of gravity, they are clumsy on land. The beaver has many special adaptations for life in the water. A powerful swimmer with webbed hind feet, the beaver's flat tail is a rudder that also serves as a prop when he sits up and a signal of danger when slapped. The prominent chisel-like cutting teeth are strong, sharp, and self-sharpening. Beavers can gnaw underwater without difficulty because their lips seal out the water. Hearing is keen, sense of smell is acute, and vision is supposedly excellent underwater, while only fair on land. The beaver's nose and ears contain valves that close when the animal dives and open when its head appears out of water. They have a natural instinct for keeping busy. They can fell trees, float logs to desired places through canals dug for the purpose, build lodges and dens with underwater entrances and tunnels, and construct dams to form ponds. One such dam in Mississippi measured 1,080 feet. The beavers' service to good conservation far outweighs the damage they do. Beavers usually pair in February and stay mated for life. Young beavers, called kits, are born in May, completely furred and with eyes open. The average litter is four. The diet of the beaver, mostly bark, changes with the seasons. Spring menu is sweet gum, pine, and hophornbeam. Summer menu is willow, cottonwood, and tender green plants. Fall menu is acorns, buttonbush, willow, and giant cane. Winter menu is ash, elm, and miscellaneous plants. Follow the nature trail to see beaver cut trees and build dams.

140.0 RED DOG ROAD ■ The road to your left, running to Canton, Mississippi, was opened in 1834 and named for a Choctaw Indian, Ofahoma, or Red Dog. Like other Choctaw, he had accepted the ways of his palefaced neighbors and had become a farmer. Red Dog, an important chief, was one of the signers of the Treaty of Dancing Rabbit in 1830, by which the tribe agreed to move to Oklahoma. Nearby is the community of Ofahoma, which for many years had a post office.

135.5 ROBINSON ROAD ■ The road crossing the parkway follows the Robinson Road, which was built in 1821, nearly all of it passing through the country of the Choctaw Indians. It joined Jackson and Columbus, Mississippi, center of the settlements on the Tombecbee. There it connected with Andrew Jackson's military road through Florence, Alabama, to Nashville. Designation of the Robinson Road as the mail route in 1822 drew much of the traffic from the northern Mississippi section of the Natchez Trace, which quickly lost importance. No longer was the Trace the only direct road through the wilderness from the East to the old Southwest.

128.4 UPPER CHOCTAW BOUNDARY ■ The line of trees crossing the parkway immediately to your left marked a section of the boundary accepted by the Choctaw Indians and the American commission under Andrew Jackson in the Treaty of Doak's Stand, October 20,

1820. You are on the Choctaw side of the boundary. The Choctaw reluctantly gave to the United States the land west of the line from White Oak Spring on the old Indian path, northwardly to a black oak standing on the Natchez Road, about forty poles eastwardly from Doak's fence marked "AJ" and blazed. The area surrendered by the Choctaw Nation amounted to some 5.5 million acres, about one-third of their land. Ten years later in 1830, the Choctaw were forced to give up all their lands. Other Indians were forced to do the same by 1834, thus clearing for white settlement all areas of the three states crossed by the Natchez Trace.

Doak's Stand: About 1812 William Doak established his stand, or tavern, on the Natchez Trace 5 miles north of the parkway at this point. The Treaty of Doak's Stand was signed there in 1820 because, "He conducted himself respectfully toward those who called at his house and made considerable improvement on the land." Doak was given sole right to purchase his land after it was opened for settlement. When the Robinson Road took traffic from the Natchez Trace, the stand was moved to the crossing of the Choctaw Boundary and the new road about one-half mile north of here.

Pearl River backwaters provide a habitat for mammals, birds, amphibians, reptiles, and fish.

122.6 RIVER BEND/PEARL RIVER ▪ In 1698, the French explorer Pierre LeMoyne Sieur d'Iberville sailed into the mouth of this river and found pearls. He named it "River of Pearls." The Natchez Trace, one hundred years later, avoided the marshy lowlands by following the ridge between the Pearl and the Big Black for 150 miles. The last 75 miles of the river course have served since 1812 as a boundary between Mississippi and Louisiana.

122.0 CYPRESS SWAMP ▪ Water tupelo and bald cypress trees can live in deep water for long periods. After taking root in summer when the swamp is nearly dry, the seedlings can stay alive in water deep enough to kill other plants. This trail leads to an abandoned river channel. As the channel fills with silt and vegetation, black willow, sycamore, red maple, and other trees will gradually replace the bald cypress and tupelo. There's no need to hurry, for the change will take several hundred years.

107.9 WEST FLORIDA BOUNDARY ▪ At the end of the French and Indian War in 1763, Great Britain gained control of the territory

Cypress Swamp is home to many creatures, including this relaxed resident.

between the Appalachians and the Mississippi River except for the New Orleans area. The northern boundary of West Florida was first established at thirty-one degrees north latitude. It was soon determined that settlement was too restricted. In 1764, Great Britain moved the boundary north to thirty-two degrees, twenty-eight minutes into the land of the Choctaw and Creek.

106.9 BOYD MOUNDS ■ Archaeologists tell us that there was a house here around A.D. 500 and that the pottery found in the mounds was made before A.D. 700. The population was probably continuous over centuries with customs being handed from generation to generation, relying on fields, forests, and streams for food. The simple social system was probably based on the family and close relatives. In this one-hundred-foot-long mound, archaeologists found the remains of forty-one burials. The mound is really three mounds in one. Differences in the types of pottery found in each indicate that the construction of the mounds was separated by a considerable lapse of time.

105.6 RESERVOIR OVERLOOK ■ This 50-square-mile reservoir is formed by an earth-filled dam. It is administered by the Pearl River Valley Water Supply District, an agency of the state of Mississippi. Information concerning recreational facilities may be obtained at the marinas. Access from the parkway is by way of state and county roads.

104.5 OLD TRACE AND BRASHEAR'S STAND ■ Two portions of the nearly two-hundred-year-old wilderness road, the Old Natchez Trace, are preserved here. Nearly 500 miles long, it grew from Indian trails to a national road and communications link between the old Southwest and the United States to the northeast. A five-minute loop walk to your left lets you see both sections and lets you stroll down a deeply eroded sunken part of the Old Natchez Trace.

102.4 MISSISSIPPI CRAFTS CENTER ■ *Exhibits, books, information, and restrooms. Sales and demonstrations of crafts are featured here.*

Mississippi Crafts Center at Ridgeland is a showplace for arts and crafts and frequently features craft demonstrations.

Ross Barnett Reservoir—This photo of Ross Barnett Dam shows a portion of the 3-mile earthen dam that impounds 50 square miles.

78.3 BATTLE OF RAYMOND ▪ By the Civil War, the Natchez Trace had lost its significance as a national road. One of the sections ran from Port Gibson toward Jackson but the route veered from the original Trace to reach Raymond. In the spring of 1863, Gen. U. S. Grant marched his men over this route after crossing the Mississippi and taking Port Gibson. On May 8, Grant's forces drew fire from a Confederate brigade, commanded by Brig. Gen. John Gregg, located on the southern edge of Raymond 3 miles east of here. After a day of bitter fighting, the Confederates retreated toward Jackson leaving their wounded in the county courthouse. This set-to convinced Grant of the need to take Jackson in order to assure the success of his forthcoming siege of Vicksburg.

73.5 DEAN'S STAND ▪ The Treaty of Doak's Stand in 1820 opened this land to white settlement. Land was quickly claimed and pioneer families established themselves in this wilderness. William Dean and his wife, Margaret, settled near here on the Old Natchez Trace in 1823. The Deans supplemented their farm income by offering lodging to travelers. The clientele was a cross section of the advancing frontier—the homeward bound boatman, the hurrying mail rider, the trader in land and horses, the fugitive, and the itinerant preacher. On the night of May 12, 1863, Gen. U. S. Grant made his headquarters here after the Battle of Raymond.

61.0 LOWER CHOCTAW BOUNDARY ■ The line of trees to your left has been a boundary for two hundred years. It was established in 1765 and marked the eastern limits of the Natchez District. This boundary ran from a point 12 miles east of Vicksburg, southward to the thirty-first parallel.

First surveyed in 1778, it was reaffirmed by Spain in 1793 and by the United States in 1801. Since 1820 it has served as the boundary between Hinds and Claiborne counties in Mississippi.

Red Bluff Stand: "John Gregg at the lower Choctaw line respectfully informs the public and travelers particularly that he keeps constantly on hand a large and general supply of groceries, ground coffee ready to put up, sugar biscuits, teas, cheese, dried beef or bacon, and every other article necessary for the accommodation of travelers going through the nation, on very reasonable terms. He is also prepared to shoe horses on the very shortest notice." Established in 1802, this hostelry on the Indian boundary was for several years the last place for a northbound traveler to secure provisions.

Rocky Springs—This rural community once contained a post office, a tavern, several stores, and artisans' shops. This safe is a remnant of the settlement that existed here from the late 1790s until the last shop closed in the 1930s. A campground and hiking trails greet visitors today.

54.8 ROCKY SPRINGS ■ At the end of this trail is evidence of a once thriving community, the town of Rocky Springs. First settled in the late 1790s, the town grew from a watering place along the Natchez Trace and took its name from the source of that water— the rocky springs. In 1860 a total of 2,616 people lived in this area covering about 25 square miles. The population of the town proper included three merchants, four physicians, four teachers, three clergy, and thirteen artisans; while the surrounding farming community included fifty-four planters, twenty-eight overseers, and more than two thousand slaves who nurtured the crop that made the town possible—cotton. Civil War, yellow fever, destructive crop insects, and poor land management brought an end to this once prosperous rural community.

Rocky Springs Methodist Church is the only structure still remaining in Rocky Springs today. The bricks used to build the church were baked in a nearby kiln in 1837.

52.4 OWENS CREEK ▪ The sounds of a busy woodland stream and the quiet murmur of a lazy waterfall have long been stilled here. Only after heavy rainfall does water fill the stream and set the waterfall singing. Over the years the water table has dropped several feet and the spring that feeds Owens Creek has all but disappeared. Little remains of a scene once familiar to residents of Rocky Springs.

45.7 MANGUM MOUND/GRINDSTONE FORD ▪ Indian burials and Grindstone Ford.

Grindstone Ford: This ford marked the beginning of the wilderness of the Choctaw Nation and the end of the old Natchez District. Nearby Fort Deposit was a supply depot for troops clearing the Trace in 1801–02, and troops were assembled here during the Burr conspiracy allegedly to separate the western states from the Union. The site takes its name from a nearby water mill.

The trail to your left takes you to the Old Trace and Grindstone Ford. Riverboatmen on foot or horseback crossed here, northbound, after floating cargo down the Ohio and Mississippi to New Orleans. Soldiers splashed across from the north to protect the Natchez District from British and Spanish threats. For postriders, Indians, bandits, and preachers, Bayou Pierre was the line between civilization and the wilderness.

Daniel Burnett's stand stood near here. Burnett was the speaker of the territorial house of representatives, a principal negotiator with the Choctaw, and a framer of the state constitution, but his stand was unpretentious. His guests supped on mush and milk in a room filled with their own gear and Burnett's supplies. From here you may follow their path along the Old Trace to Grindstone Ford.

Mangum Mound: Excavation of this site tells us much about the people of the late prehistoric period. The Plaquemine culture included the ancestors of the modern tribes of Mississippi and Louisiana. It was a society with elaborate, agriculturally oriented religious ceremonies. From the burials on this mound we have learned that there was a high infant mortality rate and upon the death of a chief, a brutal ritual was enacted in which his retainers were slain and buried with him.

41.5 Sunken Trace ▪ Preserved here is a portion of the deeply eroded or "sunken" Old Trace. Hardships of journeying on the Old Trace included heat, mosquitoes, poor food, hard beds (if any), disease, swollen rivers, and sucking swamps. Take five minutes to walk this sunken trail and let your imagination carry you back to the early 1800s when people walking 500 miles had to put up with these discomforts and where a broken leg or arm could spell death for the lone traveler.

18.4 Bullen Creek ▪ Before your very eyes an endless struggle is taking place. Trees are striving here for the essentials of life—water, sunlight, and space. Trying to get ahead, the hardwoods push upward, their crowns filling out all the overhead space, shutting out sunlight from young seedlings. Like their elders, this younger generation also has to fight for survival. The competition is keen and the hardwoods are winning over the pines. A fifteen-minute walk along this trail will take you from a mixed hardwood and pine forest (the loser) to a mixed hardwood forest (the winner).

Sunken Trace—Several segments of the Old Trace have been identified and preserved.

Mount Locust welcomes visitors to free tours and strolls about the grounds.

17.5 COLES CREEK ▪ *Picnic area, no marker.*

15.5 MOUNT LOCUST ▪ *(Enter to see the restored historic house that was one of the first stands in Mississippi. There is an interpretive program here, exhibits, walks around the area, ranger station, and restrooms.)*

12.4 LOESS BLUFF ▪ This bluff shows a deep deposit of wind-blown topsoil known as loess ("low-ess"). It was formed during the Ice Age when glaciers covered the northern half of the United States. At this time nearly continuous dust storms swept in from the western plains and covered this area with windblown dust to a depth of thirty to ninety feet. Here it rests on sands and clays of an ancient sea. It originally covered a vast region but in this area is now confined to a strip east of the Mississippi River from 3 to 30 miles wide extending from Baton Rouge into Tennessee. Where the Old Natchez Trace passed over loess it formed sunken roads, in places twenty feet deep.

12.1 TURPIN CREEK ▪ *Picnic area, no marker.*

Mount Locust originated as a sixteen-by-twenty-foot cabin in 1780. It became a family farm and eventually an inn.

Emerald Mound—Emerald Mound is the second largest mound in the United States. The Indians who built this mound and used it from A.D. 1250 to A.D. 1600 were ancestors of the historic Natchez. They are referred to as the Mississippians because they lived in the Mississippi River Valley.

10.3 EMERALD MOUND ▪ Before you is the second largest Indian temple mound in the United States. It was built and used between A.D. 1300 and 1600 by the forerunners of the Natchez Indians. These Indians used a natural hill as a base, which they reshaped by trimming the top and filling the sides to form a great primary platform, 770 feet long, 435 feet wide, and 35 feet high. At the west end still stands a thirty-foot secondary mound once topped by a ceremonial structure.

8.7 OLD TRACE EXHIBIT ▪ Across the parkway behind you is a portion of the Old Natchez Trace—a wilderness road that grew from wild animal and Indian trails. Traders, soldiers, Kaintucks, postriders, circuit riding preachers, outlaws, settlers, and adventurers trampled a national road. Here is the Natchez Trace: a bond that held the Southwest to the rest of the nation, a channel for the flow of people and ideas, a memorial to the thousands whose footsteps stamped into the American land.

8.1 TEMPORARY TERMINUS

2 Nashville: Athens of the South and Music City USA

Hunters may have visited what is now Nashville as early as 12,000 years ago drawn by the fertile valley and the animals attracted to the salt licks. By the mid 1700s the Cumberland basin was a shared hunting ground for Cherokee, Choctaw, Chickasaw, and Creek seeking buffalo, bear, turkey, deer, and geese.

According to William E. Beard in *Nashville, The Home of History Makers*, a group of nearly five hundred North Carolina settlers set out for the site on the Cumberland River bluff now known as Nashville in two groups in 1779. The first group to arrive was led overland by

Nashville—Here is the northern terminus of the Natchez Trace as it appears today.

James Robertson, crossing the frozen Cumberland River on Christmas Day. Col. John Donelson led the second group, which consisted of about thirty families with about thirty or so men to work the boats and defend them against Indians. Before they reached the settlement their provisions had been exhausted and they were forced to leave the boats periodically to hunt for game. The 1,000-mile river journey was marred by running aground on various uncharted shoals and rapids, Indian attacks, and a smallpox outbreak that caused the boat of one family and their friends to keep a "safe" distance behind the other flatboats to try to prevent further infection.

At the treacherous Muscle Shoals, Donelson described a "dreadful appearance to those who had never seen them before. The water . . . made a terrible roaring sound." It took the party three hours to traverse the swift shoals, which they believed to be about thirty miles long. The group, including Donelson's daughter, Rachel, continued the journey, arriving at the Cumberland settlement the following April. Rachel was later to become the wife of Andrew Jackson, the controversial seventh president of the United States.

On April 19, 1784, Fort Nashborough's name was changed to Nashville when the North Carolina legislature officially established the town. During the early 1800s Nashville prospered in its prime location on the Cumberland River at the edge of the western frontier. During this time, the Natchez Trace became an important route of commerce and communication. Later, with the development of the steamship, merchants proliferated along Market Street (2nd Avenue). As trade increased they built substantial brick warehouses that stand to this day, now housing specialty shops and restaurants.

One of the wealthy riverboat captains, Tom Ryman, was inspired to build the **Ryman Auditorium** in 1892 following a religious revival. Enrico Caruso and Sarah Bernhardt performed here long before WSM radio station began hosting a Saturday night show called the "WSM Barn Dance" in 1925. Two years later, following a classical music presentation, George Hay announced, "For the past hour, we have been listening to music taken largely from the grand opera. But from now on, we will present the **Grand Ole Opry**." By 1943, the Ryman had become the home of the Grand Ole Opry.

Statue of riverboat captain Thomas Ryan, who originally constructed Ryman Auditorium to house religious revivals for a frontier town.

Ryman Auditorium, the original home of the Grand Ole Opry.

One has to wonder what Donelson and Robertson would think if they could see the thriving capital of Tennessee today with its metropolitan area of approximately a half-million residents and visitors arriving daily from all over the world.

Visitors will find abundant opportunities to explore interests in history, nature, outdoor recreation, music, specialty shopping, fine dining, and the arts. In fact, Nashville is known as the Athens of the South not only because it is home to the only full-scale replica of the Parthenon in existence, but also because it has sixteen excellent institutions of higher education and six graduate schools in addition to two law schools and two medical schools.

Nashville is also known for its printing and publishing industry. Remnants of this past are preserved in Printer's Alley, but presently 15,000 jobs are directly related to publishing. The Tennessee Humanities Council gathers acclaimed writers from around the country to participate in the Southern Festival of Books each October. The festival features lively panel discussions, readings by authors, and book signings.

Nashville is likewise known as a center for the arts with eleven performing arts facilities. It is the home of the Nashville Symphony, Nashville Ballet, Nashville Opera Company, Tennessee Repertory Company, and the Leonard Bernstein Center for Education Through the Arts. The **Carl Van Vechten Gallery** at Fisk University has more than one hundred works of twentieth-century artists, known as the Stieglitz collection, donated by celebrated American artist Georgia O'Keeffe. Additional permanent collections may be seen at the Parthenon and Cheekwood as well as galleries at Vanderbilt and Belmont universities.

The Heart of Country Antiques Show is held at **Opryland Hotel** in late February and the Antiques and Garden Show is held at the

Opryland Hotel, a part of the Opryland Complex, displaying its Christmas spirit.

Nashville Convention Center in early February. Eighth Avenue South is considered Nashville's antiques district but several fine antiques malls and antiquarian bookstores are scattered throughout the city. You will also find museums, a botanical garden, historic homes, and specialty shops with items ranging from original artwork to country-western clothing, whimsical souvenirs to designer dresses. Nashville prides itself on catering to a wide range of tastes and interests.

Without a doubt, Nashville is best known by music fans the world over as Music City USA. Not only is Nashville home to the legendary Grand Ole Opry, the world's longest-running radio broadcast, but many fine, small clubs feature established entertainers, successful singers/songwriters, and up-and-coming performers in country, pop, bluegrass, blues, and jazz.

Musically minded visitors will find that the beautifully renovated historic Ryman Auditorium, **Starwood Amphitheater**, and Opryland's "Nashville On Stage" offer performances for audiences on a larger scale. In addition to attending Friday or Saturday night Grand Ole Opry performances, many visitors make arrangements to view tapings of such Nashville Network television shows as "Nashville Now."

Each June, Fan Fare offers fans from all over the world a chance to meet their favorite stars in a less formal setting, while Nashville's Summer Lights Festival features a variety of performing artists.

If country isn't your style, the Nashville Symphony showcases classical performers, and the **Tennessee Performing Arts Center** (TPAC) hosts special performances that include such touring Broadway productions as *The Phantom of the Opera*. Vanderbilt University hosts an acclaimed Great Performances series, ranging from modern dance to classical music. Special summer concerts in Centennial Park and Riverfront Park invite music lovers to enjoy a variety of classical, rhythm-and-blues, jazz, and rock.

Opryland theme park is dedicated to offering visitors some of the finest musical entertainment available in more than a dozen shows along with two dozen rides and many other attractions.

Branson and Las Vegas may have headliners but they can't offer the Ryman, the Grand Ole Opry, Tootsie's Orchid Lounge, or Music

The Hermitage, home of the seventh president of the United States, Andrew Jackson, was rebuilt in the Greek revival style in 1836 after a devastating fire.

Row. So let's get going because there are lots of sites you'll want to visit before you leave!

Although you may reach Nashville by various routes, we will begin our tour at the Hermitage, the home of Andrew Jackson, several miles east of Nashville via Interstate 40. To visit the Hermitage, take Exit 221 onto Highway 45 North. The entrance to the Hermitage is 3 miles north of the interstate. Begin your tour with a twenty-minute orientation film in the modern brick building that houses the museum, gift shop, and restaurant.

Jackson's story begins with the American Revolution. According to Gerald W. Johnson's *Andrew Jackson, An Epic in Homespun*, Jackson's parents were Irish immigrants who were linen drapers by trade. They found themselves in possession of uncleared acres on 12 Mile Creek, in North Carolina in 1765. Immigrants without money such as the Jacksons were forced to purchase uncleared lands such as this on the edge of a region known as the Waxhaws. Although his father managed to clear the land, raise one crop, and build a house, he died early in 1767 shortly before Andrew was born.

The remainder of the family came with his body to the Waxhaw churchyard and never returned to the hard-won frontier home. Mrs. Jackson's brother-in-law, George McKemey, gave the expectant widow and her sons refuge and Andrew was born in his home a few nights later. It was a hard beginning.

A few weeks later the family continued to the home of another brother-in-law, for whom Mrs. Jackson managed the household in return for a home for herself and her children. Andrew, nine years old when the Revolutionary War erupted, witnessed firsthand the devastation of war when his oldest brother Hugh, who had fought at the Battle of Stono, died of fatigue and exposure.

At fourteen, Andrew and his surviving brother, Robert, joined a band of patriot colonists known as the Waxhall Whigs. A British patrol surprised the band one night and the boys were captured. The commander of the patrol was not pleased to learn his men had captured only two children, who were not ordered to be shot or hanged as spies. Instead they were ordered to clean the officer's boots. When Andrew defied the order, the officer drew his saber and dealt Andrew a blow that left gashes in his hand and scalp. He then turned on Robert and delivered a wound from which the child never completely recovered.

The wounded children were marched off to the prison camp at Camden. Smallpox broke out in the prison but Jackson's mother, Elizabeth, managed to secure thirteen British soldiers to exchange for her sons and five other Americans. Robert died two days later and Andrew was deathly ill, but he managed to pull through. Once her son recovered, the indomitable Elizabeth traveled to Charleston with medicines and supplies for the prisoners there. She contracted ship fever, died, and was buried in an unmarked grave. Before his fifteenth birthday, Andrew found himself without family or material assets, but possessed of an intimate understanding of war and hardship. It is no wonder that soldiers in his command would later say he was as tough as old hickory: he had to be to survive.

At the Hermitage you'll learn how Andrew ventured to North Carolina to become an attorney, became an attorney general at age twenty-three, a congressman six years later, a senator in his thirties, and eventually the seventh president of the United States.

In 1788 Jackson moved to Nashville, still in its infancy as a frontier town. He and his friend John Overton were boarders in the widow Donelson's household while practicing law in Nashville. It is in this house that Jackson made the acquaintance of Rachel Donelson Robards, the lively young dark-haired, dark-eyed daughter of John Donelson, the leader of the flatboats that originally settled Nashville. Rachel was estranged from her husband, who in a jealous fit had sent for her family to come get her, saying he would live with her no longer in Kentucky. A reconciliation was attempted, but Robards again became jealous, this time of Andrew Jackson. Words were exchanged between the two men. Although the exact content of this discussion remains a mystery, Robards departed for Kentucky. Jackson and Overton found other lodgings in their attempt to calm the unfounded fears of Robards, but Jackson now seemed to feel a degree of responsibility for contributing to Rachel's unhappiness.

When it was decided that she would travel in the company of a Colonel Stark to stay with relatives in Natchez, Mississippi, Jackson accompanied them to provide additional protection for the young woman and the old man on the rough and dangerous journey. Later Jackson returned to Nashville where he was informed some months later that Robards had divorced Rachel. Jackson promptly returned to Natchez and wooed and won the lovely Rachel. In 1791 he married his "dearest love," believing she had been divorced by Robards.

Unfortunately for them both, Rachel had not been granted a divorce. They learned this two years after their marriage in Natchez and Rachel was ostracized by many for committing what was technically bigamy. Although they didn't want to lend credence to the illegitimacy of their first marriage, they remarried as soon as they were convinced that they had no other alternative, and they were scarred for the rest of their lives. Jackson forever remained ready to defend the honor of his wife, with his life if necessary.

In 1801 Jackson was called to national prominence as a government witness in the notorious treason trial of Aaron Burr in Richmond. As the most powerful leaders in Washington discovered, this was a man who adhered to his own set of beliefs about right and wrong, innocence or guilt. Jackson was no political puppet willing to

The Hermitage entry hall contains scenic French wallpaper recounting ancient legends.

do someone's bidding in exchange for future favors. When he became convinced of Burr's innocence he proclaimed this fact loudly. The horrified government counsel struck his name off their list and sent the frontiersman home.

Jackson purchased the Hermitage in 1804 and for the next fifteen years the family lived in a cluster of log homes. In 1809 one of Rachel's sisters-in-law gave birth to twin boys. The mother's health was poor and the demands of rearing two infants were great. She and her husband sent one of the boys to the Hermitage and a legal adoption took place. A few years later a second nephew came to the Hermitage to live, and many stories are told of the tolerance and kindness the formidable Jackson displayed whenever in the company of his family.

When war broke out in 1812, Jackson's young friend Thomas Hart Benton arrived at the Hermitage with the announcement of a call for volunteers. Jackson mustered 2,500 volunteers in mid-December and proceeded rapidly to Natchez with Benton as his aide-de-camp. There they received orders to halt until quarters could be prepared for the troops before they proceeded to New Orleans.

While Jackson waited in Natchez, it became evident that New Orleans was not threatened, and the government in Washington sent word for Jackson to discharge his troops on the spot, because the emergency was over. Whether the government realized the troops were five hundred miles from home is unclear. At any rate, an enraged Jackson fired off blistering letters to all concerned and with his personal voucher to the merchants of Natchez raised rations enough to return the men to Tennessee. It was on this march that his admiring troops gave him the name Old Hickory. The government refused to honor Jackson's vouchers and he faced financial ruin. It took Benton's political savvy—and a trip to Washington—to obtain payment.

Jackson's friendship with Benton was marred by his involvement in a duel between one of his captains and Tom Benton's brother, Jesse. When Thomas Benton returned and learned of Jackson's role as second to the captain against his brother, angry words were exchanged between the two friends and Jackson swore to horsewhip Tom Benton on sight. They managed to avoid each other for some time but eventually the brothers and Jackson encountered each other in a tavern in Nashville. Jesse Benton fired at Jackson, damaging his left shoulder. Doctors in Nashville recommended amputation but Jackson refused. Thomas left middle Tennessee, supposedly bitter over the loss of his friendship with Jackson.

Soon after this brawl, word was received of a massacre of four hundred people at Fort Mims in southern Alabama by the Creek Indians, who were following the war cries of Tecumseh and his brother, the Prophet, for a general Indian uprising. The legislature in Nashville passed a war bill and the weakened Jackson managed to ride with his men, his left arm bound tightly to his chest. His tenacity in the face of pain, lack of provisions, and threats of mutiny led his men to a definitive victory at the Battle of Horseshoe Bend, essentially the end of the Creek War.

It was the battle against the British in New Orleans, however, that made Jackson a national hero. On January 8, 1815, 10,000 members of the army that defeated Napoleon met Jackson's 5,500 men. At day's end, the remnants of the British army retreated to the fleet, and Jackson returned to a hero's welcome.

As it turned out, a treaty of peace had been signed with Great Britain two weeks before the battle, but the beleaguered Americans remained thrilled with their hero. New Orleans lay at Jackson's feet. It was not nearly so kind to Rachel when she came to join him. Although she was overweight and no longer the great beauty she had been in her youth, even that city of sophistication was forced to see that their hero saw her as more beautiful than the prettiest among them and felt for her a love that endured.

Jackson returned to the Hermitage in poor health, but between 1819 and 1821 he built a conservative brick home for Rachel. Some visitors considered it an unusually simple home for such a hero, but many famous men, including the French general Lafayette, paid their respects to Jackson here.

In 1824 he was narrowly defeated in a run for the presidency, instigated by his trusted friend and former quartermaster, Major Lewis. None of the four candidates that year had a clear majority so the election went to the House of Representatives. Although Jackson had the most votes, the election went to John Quincy Adams when one of the contenders, Henry Clay of Kentucky, endorsed him.

The election of 1828 was one of the meanest in American history, but Jackson won by a landslide. According to Gerald Johnson's *Andrew Jackson, An Epic in Homespun*, the pro-Adams press called Jackson a murderer, illiterate, drunken, lewd, and a homicidal maniac. Then they started on Rachel, calling her an adulteress and finally even attacking the memory of Jackson's late mother. The story is told that Old Hickory sat down and cried like a child at these cruel attacks. Although the intellectual community and business interests firmly supported Adams, the common people continued to trust in their hero's integrity and elected Jackson by more than two to one.

His victory was not to be a sweet one, though, for his beloved Rachel suffered a sudden attack of angina that lasted nearly three days. Her husband remained at her bedside. When she regained consciousness she admonished him to get some rest. He dutifully went to the room next door intending to sleep, but her scream brought him to her side only to discover she was gone from him forever. She died in 1828, the day before a celebration dinner in Nashville for the president-elect, many say as a result of being used to viciously attack her husband in every city and town throughout the land. A messenger from the Hermitage turned Nashville's celebration into mourning. A heartless New York newspaper even suggested a scornful epitaph.

The grieving Jackson assumed his duties in the White House. He was reconciled with his friend Thomas Hart Benton, by that time a senator from Missouri. He opposed the United States Bank, promoted passage of a law to remove the Indians beyond the Mississippi, and redirected expansion toward the Southwest (the present southeastern United States). He was called "the terrible old man at Washington." His presidency, like the man himself, was controversial. He was looked at by some as an "atrocious saint," by others as an "urbane savage," but he was reelected by a large majority.

In 1832 he met South Carolina's famous Ordinance of Secession with his own Nullification Proclamation and a quiet assemblage of troops awaiting an overt act that never came. His administration inherited a public debt of $48 million dollars, paid it off, and accumulated a surplus in the treasury.

Gerald W. Johnson tells us as Martin Van Buren assumed the presidency and Jackson left office at age seventy, Jackson commented to his friends that he'd only left two things undone: he hadn't shot Henry Clay or hanged John C. Calhoun.

The Hermitage was remodeled extensively in the Greek Revival fashion after a disastrous fire in 1834. In the spring of 1837 Jackson returned to the Hermitage and settled down to the life of a farmer in order to clear up debts he'd contracted during his presidency. Nashville was no longer an uncivilized frontier town and many of his old friends were gone. He occasionally fired off an editorial letter to the country and maintained an active interest in politics. Although he died a relatively poor man, at the end of his life his farm was free of encumbrances and he was able to visit Rachel's tomb every day at sunset.

Soon after you return to the interstate, you'll pass the Percy Priest Dam on your left. The Opryland Complex is about 4 miles farther west. Watch for the signs for Briley Parkway and the Opryland Exit on your right. **Opryland Theme Park**, the present home of the **Grand Ole Opry**, broadcast studios, and the impressive

Andrew and Rachel Jackson are buried in this monument commissioned by Jackson in 1831.

Opryland Hotel are delighted to welcome you. In addition to the great country music you expect to hear, you'll find thrills a plenty riding Chaos and Grizzly River Rampage while at the park. For those of a more sedate persuasion there are daily shows featuring country music stars, refreshments, a host of slightly less thrilling rides, and lots of benches where you can sit and rest while you enjoy the beautiful landscaping.

Admission to the park includes all the rides but not all the shows. If you plan to go to the Grand Ole Opry, get tickets as soon as you get in town because they do sell out! Better yet, the ticket office advises ordering by phone well ahead of your trip.

If you still haven't found an amusement that suits you, visit Opryland Hotel's Cascades and sip the cool beverage of your choice while you enjoy the lush surroundings and cascading indoor waterfalls. For those of you preferring luxury accommodations, the Opryland Hotel Grand Terrace rooms put you comfortably in the middle of the action. The hotel is at present actually a sprawling complex of 1,891 rooms, but Opryland is always striving to be bigger and better so who can say what size it will be when you visit?

If you don't stay here, you must at least go see the incredible gardens inside the hotel. The Conservatory is a two-acre tropical garden with curving walkways and wrought-iron benches that beckon you to explore its many lovely nooks and crannies. In the Cascades flowering bouganveilla climb toward the one-acre glass roof that's approximately fifty feet above where you're sitting. We enjoyed a champagne toast amid the lush beauty of the Cascades. Try it yourself!

Opryland Hotel's newest landscaping marvel will be the Delta. It will be as large as the Conservatory and the Cascades combined and include a river system with guided boats to transport you through yet another botanical wonderland.

The Opryland Hotel is next door to the Opryland Theme Park, the Grand Ole Opry, The Nashville Network Studios, the *General Jackson* **showboat,** and all the attractions that have grown up in this area since the Opryland theme park opened in 1972. The *General Jackson* offers daily morning, lunch, evening, and Southern nights—as well as special theme—cruises on the Cumberland River.

Opryland Hotel Cascades—Here you see just one of the hotel's lovely indoor gardens.

Alternative choices for accommodations in this area include the nearby **Ramada Inn** at 2401 Music Valley Drive and the Holiday Inn Express Music Valley.

The **Tanglewood Lodge** is located five minutes from Opryland across the Cumberland River. The accommodations here are located in a century-old log home surrounded by patios and porches set amid seven acres. One double room with private sitting area and private bath is available. The owners tell us most of their visitors are tourists doing the country-music scene. A full breakfast is served and ranges from waffles and bacon to pork apple pie and egg casserole or country ham and biscuits.

There are several excellent campgrounds in the immediate vicinity including the **Nashville KOA**, at 2626 Music Valley Drive, which features free live country-music shows in its own 750-seat arena.

Continue to Nashville on Interstate 40 and exit on Broadway. You're now within sight of downtown Nashville. You will notice that intersecting street signs are frequently numbered streets like 8th Avenue, 2nd Avenue, etc. These streets are bisected by Broadway into north and south divisions so if you are searching for a site on 2nd Avenue North it will be to the north (or left as you're heading east on Broadway) while 8th Avenue South destinations will involve a right (or southerly) turn. Broadway becomes West End Avenue as it leaves the downtown area. The Broadway/Printers Alley/Historic Second Avenue District is several blocks east. There are several ways to visit downtown Nashville sites.

The **Nashville Convention and Visitors Bureau,** at 161 Fourth Avenue North, is a great place to obtain information on all sites in Nashville. Be sure you leave with the City Walk brochure to direct you along the painted green lines that travel 2 miles and more than two hundred years. The tour begins at the reconstructed Fort Nashborough site on 1st Avenue North. You will continue to Historic Market Street, Printers Alley, historic 5th Avenue (which was the center of Nashville's civil rights movement), the Arcade, the Tennessee State Capitol, the **Tennessee State Museum**, the **Hermitage Hotel**, the Ryman Auditorium (former home of the Grand Ole Opry), and Hatch Show Museum and Print Shop.

The Nashville Trolley offers another method to visit points of interest including hotels, nightclubs, restaurants, Music Row, lower Broadway, 2nd Avenue and Riverfront Park. A trolley passes by each stop every ten to twelve minutes for carfree, carefree visitors. A three-day pass entitling you to unlimited rides is available for less than $5 (one day's parking fee in downtown area garages): otherwise the fare is around 85 cents for each ride.

For more extensive touring, we suggest **Country and Western/ Gray Line Tours** or **Grand Ole Opry Sightseeing Tours**. Nashville Carriage Service provides evening visitors with rides in beautiful horse-drawn carriages built at the Amish Carriage Shop in Lyles, Tennessee. The tours begin at Riverfront Park and last about twenty-five minutes.

Fort Nashborough in Riverfront Park on 1st Avenue is a reconstruction of the original Cumberland settlement. Although the area around the Cumberland settlement was known by wilderness travelers as the Big Salt Lick, Fort Nashborough was the original name given to the two-acre settlement. The name commemorates a Revolutionary officer, Brig. Gen. Francis Nash of North Carolina. Nash had been a friend of one of the sponsors of the settlement, Col. Richard Henderson. Henderson proposed honoring the memory of his old friend who had died for his country.

William Beard tells in *Nashville, The Home of History Makers*, that Fort Nashborough may have succumbed to an attack of Cherokee warriors in 1781 but for the efforts of Mrs. Charlotte Reeves Robertson, wife of Gen. James Robertson, and the settlers' dogs. Two Indians appeared, fired shots and withdrew, luring the men from the fort in hot pursuit. Unfortunately, the remaining seven hundred Indians lay in ambush along what is now 4th Avenue, and ran forward to cut off the white men from the fort. Mrs. Robertson saw the crisis unfold and ordered the dogs to be set loose to assist the beleaguered settlers. The dogs jumped into the fray, snapping and snarling at the Indians. They were able to create enough confusion to allow Robertson and most of his men to reach the fort, although not without casualties.

Historic Market Street, now known as 2nd Avenue, is the site of several specialty shops and a variety of restaurants. The **Old**

Nashville comes alive at night with fine restaurants and varied entertainment.

The old 2nd Avenue district is Nashville's newest hot spot.

Spaghetti Factory offers a great, inexpensive dinner amid lavish decor. Youngsters will enjoy it too. A variety of specialities are well represented by other restaurants in the area. Mere Bulles offers a more upscale dining experience. The **Wildhorse Saloon** has a restaurant featuring soups, salads, barbecue buffet (at lunch), and grilled sandwiches, but the biggest attraction is the boot scootin' going on. There's a 3,000-square-foot dance floor that's ringed with seats on two levels, three bars downstairs, three bars upstairs, and a large stage for live performances. Free line dancing lessons start at 5:30 every evening, so newcomers can become comfortable with the latest line steps. The Wildhorse is a venture of Gaylord Entertainment, the owners of Opryland and The Nashville Network, and is also the setting for TV tapings and concerts.

The **Hard Rock Cafe,** at 100 Broadway, is one of several Hard Rocks around the world. Nashville manager Jeff McKewan explained to us that the first restaurant opened during the 1970s in the middle of the financial district in London, which is a distinctly upscale area. They were determined to serve working class patrons equally as well as the upper class patrons; hence their slogan to "serve all." With this philosophy in mind, they do not accept reservations, and have open hiring policies that seem to attract an unusual number of extremely

Known for rock-and-roll memorabilia, Hard Rock Cafe came to Nashville in 1994.

nice employees of all ethnic backgrounds. But judge for yourself: we've never seen a more pleasant group, beginning with the young man who greeted us at the entrance. Our server, Trish Brantley, told us the employees sponsor a group called the Ambassadors, which has brought together orphans and senior citizens for picnics in the park and trick-or-treated for canned goods for the Second Harvest Food Bank, a local group dedicated to feeding the hungry.

They begin serving delicious pig sandwiches (the most popular sandwich on the menu), salads, pasta dishes, burgers, and blue-plate specials at 11 A.M. daily. There's also a heaping helping of rock-and-roll memorabilia on the walls ranging from Chet Atkins to Prince and Springsteen. Four display cases contain costumes worn by Doug Green of Riders in the Sky, Hank Williams, Bob Dylan, and Elvis. We were also surprised to find a diaper-changing station—in the men's room. Now that's what we call an attitude that refuses to accept stereotypes! Stop in for a snack or a specialty drink.

Many Nashville restaurants serve locally brewed Market Street Beer. If you're a beer connoisseur you can visit the brewery, take a tour, and sample the wares just up 2nd Avenue at **The Market Street Brewery and Public House.** They mix a variety of barley malts or wheat malt to produce several different beer styles including pilsner, golden ale, and bock. Hops are added for aroma and bitterness. The beer is brewed, then cooled and fermented after the addition of yeast. One unusual selection adds blackberries to wheat malt.

The Market Street Public House usually has about five varieties of draft beer to accompany your salad, étouffée, or sandwich and fries. The Public House is located in the 107-year old Greenbriar Distillery. Buster Williamson, vice president of the brewery, told us the lovely Victorian woodwork and stained glass that is especially evident in the tasting room overlooking the Cumberland River is original.

For those of you interested in riding the rails while dining, consider the **Broadway Dinner Train** departing at the foot of Broadway. Your ticket price includes a two-and-a-half-hour, 35-mile train ride and a four-course dinner. Each table seats four; passengers are boarded at 6:30 P.M. by confirmed reservation only.

At the foot of Broadway you will also see the Nashville Trolley stop and boarding for Opryland's River Taxis at the Riverfront Park dock. You can travel round-trip to Opryland on the river taxi, either inside (where a bar serves beer and wine coolers) or on the upper deck in open air. A bus will shuttle you from the river taxi landing at the other end of the trip to the Opryland complex.

As you can see, there's a lot to do in the District so plan to spend at least one day visiting downtown sites. If you are driving to the downtown area you may want to look for parking south of Broadway. It's less expensive and during pleasant weather and daytime hours gives you a chance to enjoy stretching your legs.

The restored **Hermitage Hotel** on 6th Avenue North is the last of Nashville's grand hotels and one of your choices for downtown accommodations. It was built in 1910 in the beaux-arts style and offers excellent accommodations and a hotel dining room, featuring Continental cuisine. It has its own garage and also is served by the Nashville Trolley.

In 1920 this historic hotel was the site of the headquarters for both sides in the struggle for (and against) women's suffrage. In that year, the Tennessee legislature's ratification of the Nineteenth Amendment gave women all over the country the right to vote. The

Opryland's River Taxi offers a thirty-minute ride up the Cumberland River to Opryland.

Hermitage Hotel is near TPAC, the **Tennessee State Museum**, and the Tennessee State Capitol. The Tennessee State Museum is located on Fifth Avenue between Union and Deaderick. No admission is charged for visiting exhibits tracing Tennessee history from prehistoric and historic Indian cultures through the Civil War and the early 1900s. Mastodon jaws, fishhooks made from deer toe bones, and tools of Ice Age hunters represent Tennessee's earliest history. One section displays fine examples of furniture made in Tennessee in the early nineteenth century, while another is devoted to Andrew Jackson.

The struggle for ratification of the amendment granting women the right to vote is represented. Tennessee became the thirty-sixth and final state required to ratify the amendment in a joint session of the Tennessee legislature.

Another area recounts the history of Fisk University, one of our nation's earliest black universities. It was founded in October 1865 under the auspices of the American Missionary Association and the Freedmen's Bureau. It was named to honor Union general Clinton B. Fisk, a dedicated supporter of education for blacks. The famous Fisk Jubilee Singers toured Europe in 1874 and raised $50,000 used to purchase a twenty-five-acre campus in Nashville and erect Jubilee Hall, a National Historic Landmark. Fisk University also is home of the Van Vechten Gallery and the one hundred works of art from the Alfred Stieglitz collection, including Renoir, Toulouse-Lautrec, Renoir, Picasso, and of course, O'Keeffe.

Fisk is located at the corner of Jackson Street and D. B. Todd Boulevard. Fisk is also home to the Aaron Douglas Gallery and its collection of African Art, including ceremonial objects, masks, and musical instruments. Both museums are open daily except Mondays and university holidays, without admission fees. The Tennessee State Museum is open daily except Mondays, New Year's Day, Easter, Thanksgiving, and Christmas.

The Tennessee State Capitol was constructed in 1859 and became the first state capitol in the South to fall to the Union army. Military governor Andrew Johnson used the building as the seat of government for Union occupation. Visitors may observe the legislature in session from the visitors gallery. Several areas have been restored to their nineteenth-century appearance. The capitol is open Monday through Friday from 9 A.M. to 4 P.M. Self-guided walking tour brochures are available at the information desk on the first floor.

Nashville's **Union Station Hotel**, on Broadway just east of the I-40 bridge, features distinctive historic accommodations in the old railroad station. Seven floors have been restored and converted to elegant headquarters for your stay in Nashville. Downstairs, Arthur's Restaurant features upscale Continental dining.

Downtown accommodations also include the **Nashville Stouffer Hotel**, a AAA four-diamond facility that is connected directly to both the Nashville Convention Center and the Church Street Centre shopping mall. Here you'll find twenty-four-hour room service, an indoor pool, and a health club. The Stouffer is also convenient to downtown attractions. The Ryman is one block east, 2nd Avenue North with its specialty shops and restaurants is three blocks east, Printers Alley is northeast about three blocks between 3rd and 4th avenues North, lower Broadway is four blocks southeast, and Tennessee Performing Arts Center and the Tennessee State Museum are two blocks north.

Union Station, once a bustling railroad station, has been restored to house a fine restaurant and hotel.

As you travel down Broadway, you may want to turn south on Fourth Avenue to visit the **Cumberland Science Museum and Sudekum Planetarium** on Ridley Boulevard. Turn right on Oak Street and follow the signs that direct you to take a left on Bass before reaching the parking lot directly in front of the museum. Inside children and adults will find a great way to spend a few hours having fun while learning about the world around them and how their bodies work. You'll find hands-on exhibits ranging from technology and the environment to physics and health.

The Curiosity Corner is specially designed for children kindergarten through third grade. A country store lets you be the shopkeeper, ringing up your customers' purchases on an old-fashioned cash register, taking orders by phone, or "sewing" calico into the

Cumberland Science Museum will intrigue children and adults alike.

latest fashions on a treadle sewing machine. Sign up for a deep sea mission—your position could be in life support, operations, plankton, or marine-mammal labs. Test your reaction time, trade facial features with your partner, or learn about recycling. Seasonal features have ranged from dinosaurs to space exploration and rain forests to the deep seas. The kinetic roller coaster is a perennial favorite.

Shows at the Sudekum Planetarium let visitors of all ages experience the thrill of space flight. The museum gift shop offers science games and books, jewelry, and souvenirs; the Skyline Room invites hungry explorers to sample vending-machine snacks while enjoying a panoramic view of Nashville.

Eighth Avenue South is Nashville's equivalent of an antiques row. Most of the shops are in a two-block area south of the intersection with Wedgewood. Their specialties range from fine European antiques to art deco, American primitives to 1950s furniture, and lava lamps to 78-rpm country-western recordings. Nearby Douglas

Corner is another popular destination for musically inclined visitors with an interest in up-and-coming performers/songwriters. Douglas Corner, like the Bluebird Cafe on 21st Avenue South, has been featured in many country-western videos.

Every fourth weekend antiques hunters can visit one of the South's finest flea markets at the Tennessee State Fairgrounds, the **Nashville Flea Market.** No admission is charged and you can easily spend a morning or afternoon browsing among the displays of dealers from all over the Southeast and occasionally New England and the Ohio Valley as well. Booths are located indoors and outdoors so foul weather should not foil your desire to go treasure hunting.

To visit the flea market, turn east (a left-hand turn if you're heading south) off 8th Avenue South onto Wedgewood. Continue on Wedgewood until you see the parking lots for the fairgrounds. Parking can be at a premium on weekends but patience and an eagle eye can usually net you a spot in one of the free lots or along the streets leading up the hill to the fairgrounds. Just follow the crowds up the hill—you can't miss it. Bring your own shopping bag and wear comfortable shoes!

Another major area with concentrations of points of interest is Music Row off Broadway along 16th and 17th avenues (named Music Row East and Music Row West, respectively) between Demonbreun and Wedgewood. There are several choices for accommodations in this area. We had a particularly pleasant experience with the helpful staff at the **Shoney's Inn** on Demonbreun. The rooms are not luxurious but you will find them clean, tidy, and reasonably priced. There are several suites, including one Jacuzzi suite if you want to splurge a bit while watching your budget. There's also a Shoney's Restaurant next door for breakfast or a late-night snack. The streets outside are usually full of tourists visiting attractions like the nearby **Country Music Hall of Fame**, Studio B, and countless recording studios and gift shops. The Nashville Trolley runs by the door to take you downtown. The Quality Inn on Division is also near Music Row.

The Country Music Hall of Fame is a museum dedicated to recording the development of country music, past and present.

The Country Music Hall of Fame takes an intimate look at the music industry. One display features hit songs scribbled on napkins and pieces of notebook paper like Ed and Patsy Bruce's "Mamas Don't Let Your Babies Grow Up To Be Cowboys." This display reminds us that many a hit was scribbled between carrying trays of food to waiting patrons by part-time waiters and waitresses who were on their way to stardom as well as weary musicians on backroad buses with high hopes of writing the next big hit.

Some exhibits use vintage film and television clips to review the history of country music while others explore the range of "country" music including bluegrass, cajun, cowboy, honky tonk, and swing. Of course, you'll also find memorabilia of the stars like the cigarette lighter found in the wreckage of the airplane crash that took the life of the legendary Patsy Cline, Minnie Pearl's straw hat, Bill Monroe's mandolin, Willie Nelson's blue bandanna and tennis shoes, and one of Elvis's Cadillacs.

Several displays invite museumgoers to test their knowledge by matching songs and songwriters or naming the most successful song in country-music history (so far it's "The Tennessee Waltz" by Pee Wee King and Redd Stewart). One section focuses on Johnny Cash's life and career. Did you know he started his first band while stationed in Germany in the Air Force in the early 1950s? Remember his first hit? Different artists' lives are featured periodically.

A gift shop offers a large collection of CDs and tapes, straw hats, T-shirts, and a Nashville monopoly game with penalties like IRS audits and rewards that advance you to the Bluebird Cafe. Admission is charged and includes a visit to Studio B, where visitors will see displays and original recording equipment. Although this studio is no longer used, greats like Elvis and Roy Orbison recorded here.

Barbara Mandrell Country is just around the corner on Division. Mandrell's fans will find information about the star including her early life, a life-size model wearing her wedding gown, an awards room, and a videotape tour of her fantastic "log home." If you don't already know about her career, you'll learn she was in a band that was performing in Las Vegas when she was only twelve years old and is a former beauty queen. Downstairs musically inclined visitors may want to visit the sing-along recording studio for a unique souvenir. If you can't carry a note in a bucket, how about a photo from Amazing Pictures? They'll put your face on the body of your dreams with "startling realism."

In addition to several other popular tourist attractions including the Country Wax Museum, Music Row also contains industry giants like Warner Brothers, MCA, RCA, and Tree Publishing that produce, promote, publish, and record most of the world's country music.

We invite bed and breakfast travelers to visit **Ms. Richie** (pronounced "Ricky") at 1614 19th Avenue South. The accommodations in her 1920s Georgian-style bed and breakfast include antiques filled queen-size bedrooms in the main house and a queen-size bed with a twin loft up the spiral staircase, living room with fireplace, kitchen, bath, private phone line, and cable TV in the stone cottage out back. The house was built by Nashville stonemason David Johnson, who constructed buildings at nearby Vanderbilt and Peabody

Elvis's gold piano is but one of the many artifacts you'll find at the Country Music Hall of Fame.

Ms. Richie's Bed and Breakfast offers comfortable accommodations in the main house or the guest home.

campuses as well. Breakfast choices include fresh orange juice, fresh fruit, stuffed French toast (raisin bread stuffed with almonds and cream cheese), pure maple syrup, and cinnamon spiced, baked oatmeal topped with ice cream or yogurt. Cottage guests may choose to have their breakfast delivered in a basket or join the other guests and their hostess at the dining room in the main house.

Nestled unassumingly on 19th Avenue South in the wedge between the union of West End Avenue and Broadway, the **Midtown Cafe** serves the best crab cakes and Caesar salad in Nashville, according to many. Don't let the name or the location fool you, for this little gem is an upscale restaurant offering the likes of lemon artichoke soup, delicious breads, and seafood dishes served by candlelight on sparkling white linens. Lunch and dinner are served and reservations are recommended.

Nearby the **South Street Smokehouse Crab Shack** and Authentic Dive Bar on 20th Avenue South gives you chance to sample seafood a little less elegantly.

Art collectors should stop by the **Local Color Gallery** at 1912 Broadway, just a few blocks northwest of Music Row. The gallery showcases more than one hundred local artisans with a wide variety of styles and mediums. In addition to oils, acrylics, watercolors, and multimedia, Local Color offers unusual designs in jewelry, pottery, sculpture, weaving, clothing, furniture, and neon sculpture.

If you're interested in vintage records, don't miss **The Great Escape** just down the street. They have selections ranging from '50s rock-and-roll to Motown and Windham Hill artists.

While you're in this vicinity you may want to visit the Belmont/Vanderbilt/Hillsboro Village area as well. **Belmont Mansion** on Belmont Boulevard just off 21st Avenue South was the home of one of Nashville's most colorful women. Adelicia Acklen was one of the wealthiest women in the United States during the Civil War. An astute businesswoman, she managed to convince both Confederate and Union troops that she would donate her cotton crop to their respective causes if they would help her get it past the blockades at New Orleans. With both sides helping her she managed to run the blockades and transport her cotton to England. There she sold it for slightly less than $1 million and proceeded to take the grand tour of Europe while both armies were forced to settle their differences without benefit of the proceeds of her cotton crop. The Italianate mansion is open for tours and admission is charged.

As you near Vanderbilt University on 21st Avenue South watch for the campus eatery known as **San Antonio Taco Company** on the left. The parking is atrocious but the chicken fajitas, chips, chili con queso, and guacamole are terrific. Service is typical for a college hangout. You fill out your choices on a tear-off menu found on pads lining the wall leading up to the cash register, pay a usually harried cashier (this is a very popular spot), and mill around getting salsa and condiments until they holler out that your order is ready. You'll probably want to send someone in your group outside to grab a table if the day is nice. They serve cold beer and great lemonade. If teens are in your group be a pal and take them to San Antonio Taco—we're pretty sure it'll be a big hit.

The campus of Vanderbilt University is on your right as you travel south on 21st Avenue. The Blair School of Music features concerts by internationally known instructors in an intimate and pleasant setting. The Langford Auditorium is the usual site of Vanderbilt's

Great Performances series. Specialty shopping and two of Nashvillians' favorite restaurants are located just a few blocks farther south on 21st Avenue South at Hillsboro Village.

The **Pancake Pantry,** at 1724 21st Avenue South, has had locals lining up on the sidewalks for breakfast on weekend mornings for more than thirty years. No stranger to change, they even offer a low-fat breakfast if you're so inclined. They also serve lunch and dinner at reasonable prices.

We think you'll agree with the ever-increasing numbers of devoted patrons that Randy Rayburn's **Sunset Grill** at 2001-A Belcourt Avenue just off 21st Avenue South deserves the consistent awards of excellence it receives year after year. Nashvillians not only dine here to see and be seen but to experience the ever-changing lunch and dinner menu with selections like VooDoo Pasta (wonderful), Rosemary Chicken (delicious), and Sunset Caesar Salad (not to be rivaled). One of the co-authors of the famous T-Factor diet, dietician Jamie Pope, assisted in the development of the Lean Style items. Attention has been given to every detail from the coffee and wine list to the artwork on the walls. Lunch entrées start at $5 and are seldom more than $8. On a pleasant day you can eat on the patio. No smoking is allowed inside the dining room. Reservations are accepted for lunch and dinner.

The best hamburger and fries in town are yours if you locate **Brown's Diner** on the right just before 21st Avenue crosses Blair. This is a much beloved, well, sort of classic dive also frequented by Vanderbilt students. It is usually lots less boisterous (and therefore not as appealing to the younger set) than San Antonio. Although it's a neighborhood hangout, lots of new faces peer into the dim interior each day for lunch and dinner so step inside and get ready for a plate of burger heaven.

If you continue on 21st Avenue South you'll eventually come to a 957-acre state natural area that is probably the most photographed in Tennessee, a wonderful antiquarian bookstore, the finest small music club in Nashville, a very good antiques mall, and one of the best caterer/picnic/lunch sources in Nashville. We think you'll find it well worth the ten-minute drive to visit the Green Hills area. During peak times traffic does become congested so try to travel this road after 9 A.M. and avoid the 4 to 6 P.M. onslaught of Green Hills, Brentwood, and Franklin commuters.

I'll start with **Dad's Old Bookstore** because it's closest to downtown Nashville and because Ed Penny and his shop are such delights. Ed had his turn at being a successful songwriter (in this town that means you've had releases on major labels) and now he's the proprietor of a quite remarkable shop. Not only does he feature old (and current) books of all sorts, but he also has a wonderful collection of authenticated autographs that usually range from Franklin Delano Roosevelt to W. C. Handy, Father of the Blues. The really wonderful part is that they're all for sale! The bookstore is in a small shopping center just across from the truly outstanding **Davis-Kidd Booksellers**.

Although Davis-Kidd does not offer rare books, it is Nashville's premier bookstore and frequently has signings by noted authors so they, too, offer autographed volumes. But we must warn you, bibliophiles (present company included) have been known to disappear into these two shops for hours that stretch dangerously close to days! Davis-Kidd has tried to anticipate this sort of patron and although they simply cannot provide overnight accommodations, they are happy to supply benches for resting while you browse and food and entertainment in the Second Story Cafe.

Behind Grace's Plaza, which houses Davis-Kidd and several other specialty stores, you'll find lots of people enjoying meat-and-three for under $5 at the **Sylvan Park** tucked in the bend of Bandywood Drive (there are other Sylvan Parks around town). Not fancy by any means, this is an unusually nice little restaurant for home-style cooking and it's open on Saturdays too. Arnold's, Hap Towne's, and Mack's also feature meat-and-three, but the decor tends to early linoleum and formica with accumulated years of use. We believe evidence of hard use, much like the numbers of yellowed calendars hanging on the walls, directly corresponds to the "tastes good" quotient. We, therefore, tend to seek out places like Hap Towne's whenever possible. So do droves of struggling songwriters and musicians, successful businessmen and women, and hard-working day laborers.

They offer carryout if the lack of interior designer influence spoils the ambience for you. These three restaurants are scattered on the perimeter of the downtown area and are open weekdays only.

Once you tear yourself away from Davis-Kidd, Dad's, and Sylvan Park, several other enticements await you. One of the most inviting for music fans is the **Bluebird Cafe.** Watch for the Bluebird sign on the left as you continue south on 21st Avenue. The Bluebird may be small but it has helped launch some of the biggest careers in Nashville. Not that long ago unknown Garth Brooks performed for appreciative audiences here on Friday and Saturday nights, as did Mary Chapin Carpenter and too many others to name. You may very well hear someone at the Bluebird who soon will be receiving prime air time on the radio back home. If you're interested in being on the cutting edge of country music "fandom," this is one of the best places in Nashville. We strongly suggest you make reservations.

Almost next door, the **Green Hills Antique Mall** has dealers that do their absolute best to offer you some of the finest collections in the Nashville area.

Across the street you can sample award-winning lunch fare or carryout items at **Clayton Blackmon.** Their pimento cheese is absolutely the best we've ever eaten. They also feature express lunches with a variety of deli sandwiches, pasta salads, low-fat and regular chicken salads, fried chicken breasts, unusual vegetable selections like bistro carrots, and a variety of desserts including Red Velvet Cake. There's not a huge sign announcing their location, so watch carefully for the next-to-last shopping center on the right before the traffic light at Hobbs and 21st (which is now called Hillsboro Road).

Next, let's visit **Radnor Lake State Natural Area** on Otter Creek Road, off Hillsboro Road. The 957-acre site contains an 85-acre lake, the result of impoundment in 1914 by L&N Railroad to furnish water for steam engines and livestock at the nearby railroad yards. The lake was immediately discovered by migrating birds and four years later an L&N official stopped all hunting and agreed to declare the area a wildlife sanctuary.

The site was purchased in 1973 by the Tennessee Department of Conservation at the behest of thousands of citizens who wished to

Radnor Lake State Natural Area is an exquisite wildlife sanctuary.

protect Radnor from the threat of development. Today wildlife is abundant and hundreds of species of wildflowers, ferns, shrubs, and trees flourish in the protected habitat. Because Radnor functions primarily as a nature sanctuary, activities here must be low impact.

Hiking on 6 miles of trails is encouraged and pets may be walked on leashes along Otter Creek Road. As you can well understand, off-trail hiking, hunting and fishing, boating and swimming, jogging, bicycling, and horsebacking on the trails are viewed as adverse activities and therefore prohibited. Radnor is better suited to quiet reflections, photography, and leisurely strolls to enjoy its scenic beauty.

At this point you may return to Nashville by traveling north via Franklin Road or Hillsboro Road. If you head north on Franklin Road watch for a sign on your right for another historic home open for tour, **Travellers Rest.** This was the home of Judge John Overton from 1789 to 1733. The Federal-style two-story frame dwelling features double galleries or porches and an extensive collection of pre-1840 Tennessee furniture. The guided tour includes the historic house, eleven acres of grounds, and the outbuildings.

A southerly turn on Franklin Road will take you to Franklin and Brentwood. As you travel south on Franklin Road watch for Murray Lane and the **English Manor Bed and Breakfast.** Owner Willa Dean English prides herself on making her guests feel at home. She has six bedrooms, one double, the rest are queens and kings with private baths, televisions, and ceiling fans. She has a large garden room across the back where breakfast is served. Guests will find menus offering choices of eggs, sausage, French toast, fruit, gravy, and biscuits. Ms. English treats her guests every night to turn-down services, including a box of her homemade chocolate fudge.

A southerly turn on Hillsboro Road will lead you past the Old Hickory Boulevard intersection. A right turn here will take you to the Warner Parks and the northern terminus of the Natchez Trace Parkway. Hillsboro Road will also eventually take you to the intersection of Highway 96 West to reach the entrance to the Natchez Trace Parkway outside of Franklin. A northerly turn on Hillsboro Road returns you to Nashville via Green Hills.

For those of you deciding not to visit the Green Hills area we will resume our tour on Broadway near 21st Avenue South and Music Row. If you decide to omit the 21st Avenue/Green Hills area, proceed westward on West End. Centennial Park, on your right, is the site of the Tennessee Centennial Exposition of 1897. Prior to that it was the site of the West Side race course. A replica of the Parthenon was built for the exposition and retained to serve as an art museum in response to community interest. Within the Parthenon, a forty-two-foot re-creation of Athena, the goddess of wisdom, was produced by Nashville sculptor Alan LeQuire. The Cowan Collection of nineteenth- and twentieth-century American painters is permanently housed here. A gift shop at the Parthenon's galley-level entrance offers a wide range of gifts including original artwork, clothing, and reproductions of Greek antiquities. Admission is charged for the **Parthenon** only.

Outside, large open spaces accommodate kite flyers and frisbee tossers, as well as statewide craft fairs held in May and October. Picnic tables and benches beckon to passersby to stop and enjoy the gardens as well as their lunches. The Art Center at the rear right of the park behind the Parthenon also houses art and craft displays.

The **Hog Heaven Barbeque Shack** is on the west side of the park next to McDonald's. They have some really tasty sandwiches if you decide to linger for a leisurely lunch. Save some crusts for the ducks on the pond!

East of Centennial Park visitors will find several shops and restaurants on and around Elliston Place. **Rotier's Restaurant** has been serving Vanderbilt students great cheeseburgers for years at very reasonable prices. They also serve a fresh vegetable plate. Across the street, the small but worthwhile **Calypso Cafe** features Caribbean fare.

If you're traveling with teens, continue a few blocks down Elliston Place to **T.G.I. Fridays** on your left. It's a good lunch or dinner choice. They have twenty or thirty variations of burgers, are frequented by many Vanderbilt students, and the decor is kind of fun. The decibel range is toward the upper end of the scale usually on weekend nights especially, so don't plan on an intimate dining experience here.

For a real sweet treat, we suggest you continue on Elliston to the **Soda Shop** on the right a few blocks down. Amid '50s style decor that is not a cutesy recreation but the well-worn real McCoy, chocolate malts and ice cream sodas are served up with traditional meat-and-three selections from an always reliable menu. If you only visit one meat-and-three restaurant while in Nashville, make it the Soda Shop. The cherry sodas are personal favorites but a wedge of apple pie topped with vanilla ice cream is also delicious.

Next door to the Soda Shop, one of Nashville's two fine antiquarian bookstores awaits you. **Elder's Book Store** is a treasure trove for book collectors of all types, but particularly historians. There are several other specialty shops in the area including a good record store and a vintage clothing shop.

Across the street, Mosko's Luncheonette makes really tasty chicken-salad, turkey, and Philly sandwiches but all their deli selections are good and they include low-fat alternatives. Just off Elliston Place at 217 Louise Avenue, **Jimmy Kelly's** has been serving steaks and seafood since 1934. Third generation restaurateur Mike Kelly was recently favorably reviewed by the *New York Times*. The cozy atmosphere is almost as noteworthy as the plate of famous corn cakes served with every meal. A Faucon salad is a perfect light accompaniment but delicious Chateaubriand, lobster tails, and filet mignon await patrons with heartier appetites.

If none of these choices appeal to you, visit **Houston's** at 3000 West End or the **Tin Angel** at 3201 West End, both local favorites for casual dining. Houston's features a varied menu including prime rib, soups, and a great grilled chicken salad. The Tin Angel offers delicious pasta dishes and healthy, creative, modern cuisine. One of their most popular dishes is Good and Good for You.

As visitors continue on West End there are a couple of shops along the way that may be of interest. The **American Artisan** is on the left in a shopping center across from Saint Thomas Hospital. It offers an unusually fine selection of arts and crafts from all across the country including jewelry, pottery, glassware, and wooden items. Many an unusual present for a wedding or birthday has come from this shop.

West End Avenue has now become Harding Road. The intersection of Harding Road and White Bridge Road will take you to a good lunch choice for those with small children. Turn right onto White Bridge Road and **Dalt's** is on the right in Lion's Head Shopping Center. Dalt's welcomes youthful patrons while serving their parents from adult menus as well. On the left side of White Bridge a very tasteful Thai restaurant, the Orchid, waits to serve you lunch or dinner.

If the opportunity for an afternoon walk in the woods appeals to you continue on Harding Road and watch for a sign directing you to an entrance to the Warner Parks nearby on the left. This approach takes you through the community of Belle Meade, the site of many of the finest homes in the metropolitan area. Be sure to observe the posted speed limits. Belle Meade has its own police force, and they intend to keep the streets safe for the many joggers who take advantage of the pleasant surroundings leading to the park.

The original northern terminus of the Natchez Trace is in the parks. These 2,665 acres make up one of the largest municipally operated parks in the United States. The Works Progress Administration had a hand in the construction of more than 28 miles of roads and rustic picnic shelters. There are bridle paths and a nine-hole golf course. Admission to the parks is free, from daybreak until 11 P.M. daily.

The Iroquois Steeplechase is held here each year on the second Saturday in May. If you're in town, bring a lawn chair and come early. The Nature Center can give you information about the park's busy activities schedule and is the starting point for the trails system.

The Edwin and Percy Warner parks also serve as informal laboratories for naturalists. One of the oldest and longest continually operated Eastern Bluebird research projects was started here in 1936. Visitors will find a variety of clean, appealing spots for picnicking, bird watching, bike riding, hiking, playing ball, and enjoying the beautiful middle Tennessee countryside. Of course, springtime and autumn are especially lovely but the parks are pleasant spots for nature lovers year-round.

Continuing on Harding Road, the signs to **Belle Meade Mansion** should appear on your left. On a site originally known as Dunham Station, a trading post in the Cumberland settlement, Belle Meade became one of Tennessee's greatest plantations and one of our country's earliest thoroughbred horse nurseries. The plantation was established by John Harding and inherited by his son, William Giles Harding. Docents in period costume will lead you on a one-

Belle Meade Mansion, the queen of Tennessee plantations, was once a famous thoroughbred horse farm.

hour tour that will show you where a daughter of the household, Selene, etched her name in the glass window in the office, proving to her girlfriends that the fine engagement ring she'd received from William Hicks Jackson was definitely a diamond. During the owner-ship of Gen. William H. Jackson, Belle Meade was to achieve its greatest fame.

In addition to the 1853 Greek-revival mansion, the thirty-acre site includes a carriage collection in the carriage house, stables, and a 1790 log cabin that was the original family home. Admission is charged.

Each fall, usually in September, the two-day **Belle Meade Fall Fest** is held on the grounds. A sale of donated items, fine antiques, crafts, food, and a host of children's activities highlight the weekend.

West End eventually becomes Harding Road.

The 106 Club is tucked away on your left and is actually an upscale dinner club serving an appreciative public a varying menu including tasty seafood selections and rack of lamb. The intimate set-ting offers entertainment on a baby grand piano every evening.

As you near the division of Harding Road, the Sportsman's Grille on the left offers cold beer and good hamburgers. Across the street you'll find **Finezza Trattoria** featuring Italian-style family din-ing, delicious gnocchi, Pescato Finezza (fried, herbed, bread-encrusted orange roughy served on a bed of caramelized onions topped with lemon sauce and black olives with pasta on the side), and Genoa salad (romaine with feta cheese and black olives) with a delicious house dressing.

Harding Road splits into Highway 100 and Highway 70. You may reach several excellent restaurants, Bellevue Mall, and Jim and Shirley Ruppert's "homestay" accommodations, **Rose Garden**, by bearing to the right at this junction. Highway 70 is also known as Old Harding Road. The Rupperts offer an entire downstairs living area with private entrance, bath, fireplace with comfortable seating area, stocked kitchen, and a sleeping area with a queen-size bed, a daybed, and a twin. Additional amenities include their prize-winning roses, which line the walk to the hot tub on the patio, an entertainment center complete with VCR and current popular video titles, a desk with private phone line for working guests, and access to Westside Athletic Club facilities, including exercise equipment, indoor and outdoor tennis courts, twenty-five-meter all-season pool, indoor track, and massage by appointment. They often host visiting parents of Vanderbilt students who love being able to spend time with their children in these "home away from home" facilities. Depending on the season, you may be greeted with Mama Lee's Gourmet Hot Chocolate, fruit tea, or hot apple cider. Jim is a New Mexico native and serves huevos rancheros as a breakfast specialty. The Rupperts are gourmet cooks and also offer pecan Belgian waffles, spinach quiche, crêpes with fruit filling, a hearty Continental, or a traditional ham-and-eggs breakfast to their guests. Although this is not a historic home, there are many special touches that make it a delightful stop.

Bellevue also offers a great spot for barbecue pork or chicken and great tasting country style vegetable selections at the **Country Cabin Barbecue** on Old Harding Road. Proceed on Harding to Bellevue Mall, one of Tennessee's largest shopping centers.

If you bear to the left at the intersection you'll proceed on Highway 100 toward the northern terminus of the Natchez Trace. **The Corner Market**, in a small shopping center on your left, offers a great selection of gourmet deli sandwiches, soups, fresh fruits, and specialty items. A good picnic lunch source is on the right at the junction. Something Special offers dinners that are a far cry from the usual carryout fare. Their baked chicken breasts and miniature lemon blueberry loaves are especially tasty. Continuing west, you'll pass the sign for the entrance to **Cheekwood Botanical Gardens and Museum of Art** on the left. This once was a private estate designed to support an elegant lifestyle. The fifty-five-acre site is now home to a variety of gardens including wildflowers, perennials, roses, and herbs, water gardens, greenhouses, a library, gift shop, and the Pineapple Room restaurant. The chicken-salad sandwiches make excellent picnic lunches or stay inside and try the shrimp salad in avocado while overlooking lush green vistas. The three-story Georgian mansion on the property hosts major traveling exhibitions and

The elegant Cheekwood Mansion is home to fifty-five acres of botanic gardens and an art museum.

a permanent nineteenth- and twentieth-century American art collection. Included in the private collection are works of Will Edmondson, born in Davidson County of former slave parents. He believed he was called by God to carve stones and began producing primitive limestone carvings in 1931. His work was photographed by Louise Dahl-Wolfe for *Harper's Bazaar* and Edmondson became the first black man to have a one-man exhibit at the Museum of Modern Art in New York. Admission is charged.

Additional entrances to the Warner Parks also appear on your left including the Visitors Center, the Steeplechase site, and golf course.

Farther west on Highway 100, visitors will find an entertaining dinner at **Chaffin's Barn Dinner Theater** featuring an all you can eat country style buffet including salads and desserts and theater productions suitable for the whole family.

You'll soon cross the Harpeth River, designated a state scenic river. Some historians believe the Harpeth was named for the notorious criminals, Big and Little Harpe, who once terrorized travelers on the Natchez Trace. A canoe access is located on the left

The Harpeth River, a placid waterway near the terminus of the Natchez Trace Parkway, is ideal for canoeing.

side of the bridge after you cross it. The put-in here on the left just past the bridge is easy for canoeists interested in a pleasant, primarily Class I float trip. The closest take-out is in Bellevue, 2.9 river-miles away.

Along Highway 100 on your right, a local dining tradition for more than thirty-five years awaits you at the **Loveless Cafe.** The Loveless has even been visited by *People* magazine and the *Today Show* due to its sometimes celebrity clientele, mouthwatering breakfasts, and great fried chicken. They're open for breakfast, lunch, and dinner (closed Mondays) if you're interested in homemade biscuits, preserves, country ham, or southern fried chicken.

The northern terminus of the Natchez Trace Parkway on your left is scheduled for completion in the summer of 1996. Until then the temporary terminus is on Highway 96 about eight miles west of Franklin. To reach the temporary terminus, proceed on Highway 100 until you intersect Highway 96. Turn east (or right) on Highway 96 and continue until you see the impressive preformed concrete bridge that spans Highway 96. The entrance to the parkway is just past the bridge on the right.

ACCOMMODATIONS

English Manor Bed and Breakfast Inn—6304 Murray Ln., Brentwood, TN 37027-6210, 615-373-4627, or 615-373-4640.

Hermitage Hotel—Sixth Ave. N. and Union, Nashville, TN; 615-244-3121.

Nashville KOA Campground—2626 Music Valley Dr., Nashville, TN 37214; 615-889-0282.

Opryland Hotel—2800 Opryland Dr., Nashville, TN 37214; 615-883-2211.

Ramada Inn—2401 Music Valley Dr., Nashville, TN 37214: 615-889-0800.

Ms. Rickie's Bed and Breakfast—1614 19th Ave. S., Nashville, TN; 615-269-3850.

Rose Garden—6213 Harding Rd., Nashville, TN 37205; 615-356-8003.

Shoney's Inn—I-40 and Demonbreun (Music Row area), Nashville, TN; 615-255-9977, 800-222-2222.

Shoney's Inn—Briley Pkwy. and McGavock Pike (Opryland), Nashville, TN; 615-885-4030, 800-222-2222.

Stouffer Hotel—611 Commerce St., Nashville, TN; 615-255-8400, 800-468-35713.

Tanglewood Lodge—P.O. Box 160531, Nashville, TN 37216-0531; 615-262-9859.

Union Station Hotel—1001 Broadway, Nashville, TN; 615-726-1001.

ATTRACTIONS

Barbara Mandrell Country—1510 Division St., Nashville, TN; 615-242-7800; Daily, 9 A.M.–5 P.M., Sept.–May; 9 A.M.–7 P.M., June–Aug.; Admission.

Belle Meade Mansion—5025 Harding Rd., Nashville, TN 37205; 615-356-0501; Mon.–Sat., 9 A.M.–5 P.M.; Sun., 1–5 P.M.; Admission for one-hour tour.

Belmont Mansion—1900 Belmont Blvd., Nashville, TN; 615-269-9537; Mon.-Sat., 10 A.M.–4 P.M.; closed Mondays, Sept.–May; Admission.

Cheekwood Botanical Gardens and Museum of Art—1200 Forest Park Dr., Nashville, TN 37205-4242; 615-356-800; Mon.–Sat., 9 A.M.–5 P.M.; Sun., 1–5 P.M.; Admission.

Country Music Hall of Fame—4 Music Sq. E., Nashville, TN 37203; 615-

255-5333; summer, daily, 8 A.M.–7 P.M.; Sept.–May, 9 A.M.–5 P.M.; closed Thanksgiving, Christmas, and New Year's; Admission.

Cumberland Science Museum and Sudekum Planetarium—800 Ridley Blvd., Nashville, TN 37203; 615-862-5160; June–Aug., Mon.–Sat., 9:30 A.M.–5 P.M.; Sun., 12:30–5:30 P.M.; Sept.–May, closed on Mondays; Admission.

The Hermitage—4580 Rachel's Ln., Hermitage, TN 37076; 615-889-2941; Daily, 9 A.M.–5 P.M.; closed Thanksgiving, Christmas, and the third week in January; Translations available in Chinese, French, German, Japanese, Russian, and Spanish; Admission.

The Parthenon—Centennial Park, Nashville, TN 37201; 615-862-8431; Tues.–Sat., 9 A.M.–4:30 P.M.; Sundays, April 1–Sept. 30, 12:30–4:30 P.M.; Admission.

Radnor Lake State Natural Area—1050 Otter Creek Rd., Nashville, TN 37220; 615-373-3467; summer, 7 A.M. to sundown; winter, 8 A.M. to sundown; Free.

Ryman Auditorium—116 Fifth Ave. N., Nashville, TN 37219; 615-254-1445; Museum, daily, 8:30 A.M.–4 P.M., except Thanksgiving and Christmas; Shows at 8 P.M.; call for information; Admission.

Tennessee State Museum—505 Deaderick St., Nashville, TN 37243-1120; 615-741-2692; Mon.–Fri., 10 A.M.–5 P.M., Sun. 1–5 P.M., except state holidays; Free.

Travellers Rest—636 Farrell Pkwy., Nashville, TN 37220; 615-832-2962; June–Aug., Mon.–Sat., 10 A.M.–5 P.M.; Sun., 1–5 P.M.; Sept.–May, 9 A.M.-4 P.M.; closed Mondays; Admission.

Van Vechten Gallery—Fisk University, 1000 17th Ave. N., Nashville, TN 37208-3051; 615-329-8543; Tues.–Fri., 10 A.M.–5 P.M.; Sat. and Sun., 1–5 P.M.; Closed Mondays and university holidays; Donations suggested.

Warner Parks—Highway 100, Nashville, TN; 615-352-6299; Free.

✂ ENTERTAINMENT

Ace of Clubs—114 Second Ave., Nashville, TN 37201; 615-254-2237; open at 5:30 P.M., Mon.–Fri.; Sat., 8 P.M.; shows begin at 9 P.M.; Close 2 A.M.; Rock music.

Bluebird Cafe—4104 Hillsboro Rd., Nashville, TN; 615-383-1461; Reservations suggested; Cover charge after 9 P.M., except Sunday; Variety, writers showcase.

Boardwalk Cafe—4114 Nolensville Pike, Nashville, TN; 615-832-5104; Reservations suggested; Open daily; Live music six nights; Variety, writers showcase.

The Captain's Table—Printer's Alley, Nashville, TN 37201; 615-256-3353; four shows nightly, Mon.–Sat.; Country.

Country and Western/Gray Line Tours—2416 Music Valley Dr., Nashville, TN 37214; 615-883-5555, 800-251-1864.

Douglas Corner Cafe—2106A 8th Ave. S., Nashville, TN 37203; 615-298-1688; Variety, writers showcase.

Earnest Tubb Record Shop Midnight Jamboree—2414 Music Valley Dr., Nashville, TN 37214; 615-889-2472; Sat., 11:30 P.M.; Live country radio.

The General Jackson *Showboat*—2802 Opryland Dr., Nashville, TN; 615-889-6611; Morning, noon, and evening cruises; variety.

Grand Ole Opry —2804 Opryland Dr., Nashville, TN 37214; 615-889-3060; Show times vary; Generally, Fri. and Sat., 6:30 and 9:30 P.M.; Admission.

Grand Ole Opry Tours—2810 Opryland Dr., Nashville, TN 37214; 615-889-9490.

Music City Blues Hotline—A nonprofit organization affiliated with the National Blues Foundation; call 615-292-5222 for a recording giving you current information about local club performances, festivals, and jam sessions.

Opryland Theme Park—2802 Opryland Dr., Nashville, TN 37214; 615-889-6611; 3–10 p.m.; Sat. and Sun., late March–May 1; daily, May–Sept. 30; Sat. and Sun., during Oct.; call for Christmas schedule; Admission; Variety.

Station Inn—402 12th Ave. S., Nashville, TN 37203; 615-255-3307; Tues.–Sun., evenings; Bluegrass.

Starwood Amphitheater—3839 Murfreesboro Pike, Antioch, TN 37013; 615-737-4849, 800-333-4849.

Tennessee Performing Arts Center (TPAC)—505 Deaderick St., Nashville, TN 37219; 615-737-4849, 800-333-4849.

☙ RESTAURANTS

Broadway Dinner Train—P.O. Box 25085, Nashville, TN 37202-5085; 615-254-8000, 800-274-8010.

Brown's Diner—2102 Blair Blvd., Nashville, TN; 615-269-5509, Mon.–Sat., 11 A.M.–midnight; Sun., noon–10 P.M.

Calypso Cafe—2424 Elliston Pl., Nashville, TN; 615-321-3878;
   Mon.–Sat., 11 A.M.– 9 P.M.; Sun., noon–8 P.M.

Chaffin's Barn Dinner Theater—8204 Hwy. 100, Nashville, TN; 615-
   646-9977; Tues.–Sat., 6 P.M.; show begins at 8 P.M.

Clayton-Blackmon—4117 Hillsboro Rd., Nashville, TN; 615-297-7855;
   Mon.–Fri., 7 A.M.–6 P.M.; Sat., 8 A.M.–6 P.M.

The Corner Market—6051 Hwy. 100, Nashville, TN; 615-352-6772;
   Mon.–Fri., 8:30 A.M.–7 P.M.; Sat., 10 A.M.–7 P.M.; Sun., noon–5 P.M.

Country Cabin Barbecue—7093 Old Harding Rd., Bellevue, TN; 615-
   662-1553; Mon.–Thurs., 11 A.M.–9 P.M.; Fri., until 10 P.M.; Sat.–Sun.,
   7 A.M.–10 P.M.

Dalt's—38 White Bridge Rd., Nashville, TN; 615-352-8121; Mon.–Fri.,
   11 A.M.–11 P.M.; Sat. and Sun., 10 A.M.–12 A.M.

Demos' Steak and Spaghetti House—300 Commerce St., Nashville, TN; 615-
   256-4655; daily, 11 A.M.–11 P.M.

Elliston Place Soda Shop—2111 Elliston Pl., Nashville, TN; 615-327-1090;
   Mon.–Sat., 11 A.M.–8 P.M.

Finezza Trattoria—5404 Harding Rd., Nashville, TN; 615-356-9398;
   Mon.–Thurs., 5–10 P.M.; Fri. and Sat., to 11 P.M.; Sun., to 9 P.M.

The Gerst Haus—228 Woodland St., Nashville, TN; 615-256-9760;
   Mon.–Sat., 11 A.M.–11 P.M.; Sun., 3 P.M.–11 P.M.

Hap Towne's Restaurant—493 Humphreys St., Nashville, TN; 615-
   242-7035; Mon.–Fri., 11 A.M.–2:45 P.M.

Hard Rock Cafe—100 Broadway, Nashville, TN; 615-742-9900; daily,
   11 A.M.–2 A.M.

Hog Heaven—115 27th Ave. N., Nashville, TN, 615-329-1234; Mon.–Sat.,
   11 A.M.–9 P.M.; Sun., until 6 P.M.

Houston's—3000 West End Ave., Nashville, TN; 615-269-3481;
   Sun.–Thurs., 11 A.M.–10:30 P.M.; Fri. and Sat., to midnight.

Jimmy Kelly's—217 Louise Ave., Nashville, TN; 615-329-4349; Mon.–Sat.,
   5 P.M.–midnight.

Loveless Cafe—8400 Hwy. 100, Nashville, TN; 615- 646-9700; Mon.–Sat.,
   8 A.M.–2 P.M., 5 P.M.–9 P.M.; Sun., 8 A.M.–9 P.M.

Market Street Brewery and Public House—134 Second Ave. N., Nashville, TN;
   615-242-8223.

Midtown Cafe—102 19th Ave. S., Nashville, TN; 615-320-7176;
   Mon.–Thurs., 11 A.M.–10 P.M.; Fri., to 11 P.M.; Sat., 5:30–11 P.M.;
   Sun., 5–10 P.M.

The Pancake Pantry—1724 21st Ave. S., Nashville, TN; 615-383-9333; Mon., 7 A.M.–3:30 P.M.; Tues.–Sun., 7 A.M.–7:30 P.M.

The Pineapple Room at Cheekwood—1200 Forest Park Dr., Nashville, TN; 615-352-4859; daily, 11 A.M.–2 P.M.

The Old Spaghetti Factory—160 2nd Ave. N., Nashville, TN; 615-254-9010; Mon.–Fri., 11:30 A.M.–2 P.M., 5–10 P.M.; Sat., 4:30 P.M.–11 P.M.; Sun., 4–9:30 P.M.

106 Club—106 Harding Pl., Nashville, TN; 615-356-1300; Sun.–Thurs., 5:30–10 P.M.; Fri. and Sat., until midnight.

The Orchid—73 White Bridge Rd., Nashville, TN; 615-353-9411; daily, 11 A.M.–3 P.M., 4:30–10 P.M.; Sun., 4–9 P.M.

Rio Bravo Cantina—3015 West End Ave., Nashville, TN; 615-329-1745; Mon.–Thurs., 11 A.M.–11 P.M.; Fri. and Sat., to midnight; Sun., to 10 P.M.

Rotier's—2413 Elliston Pl., Nashville, TN; 615-327-9892; Mon.–Sat., 9 A.M.–10:30 P.M.; closed Sun.

San Antonio Taco Co.—416 21st Ave. S., Nashville, TN; 615-327-4322; daily, 11 A.M.–1:30 A.M.

South Street—Original Smokehouse Crab Shack and Authentic Dive Bar; 907 20th Ave. S., Nashville, TN; 615-320-5555; Mon.–Sat., 11 A.M.–1:30 A.M.; Sun., 5:30–11 P.M.

Sunset Grill—2001-A Belcourt Ave., Nashville, TN; 615-386-3663; Mon.–Fri., 11 A.M.–2:30 P.M., 5 P.M.–1:30 A.M.; Sat., 5 P.M.–1:30 A.M.

Sylvan Park—Bandywood Dr., Nashville, TN; Mon.–Sat., 10:30 A.M.–7 P.M.

T.G.I. Friday's—Elliston Pl., Nashville, TN; 615-329-9575; Mon.–Sat., 11 A.M.–1 A.M.; Sun., 10 A.M.–1 A.M.

Tin Angel—3201 West End Ave., Nashville, TN; 615-298-3444; Mon.–Thurs., 11 A.M.–11 P.M.; Fri., until midnight; Sat., 5 P.M.–midnight.

12th and Porter—114 12th Ave. N., Nashville, TN; 615-254-7236, Mon.–Thurs., 11 A.M.–2 P.M., 5:30 P.M.–1 A.M.; Fri. and Sat., until 2 A.M.

Wildhorse Saloon—120 2nd Ave. N., Nashville, TN; 615-251-1001; daily, 7 A.M.–2 P.M., 5 P.M.–10 P.M.

✌ SHOPPING

American Artisan—4231 Harding Rd., Nashville, TN; 615-298-4691; Mon.–Sat., 10 A.M.–6 P.M.; Sun., 1–5 P.M.

Antique Merchants Mall—2015 8th Ave. S., Nashville, TN; 615-292-7811;
    Mon.–Sat., 10 A.M.–5 P.M.; Sun., 1–5 P.M.
Art Deco Shoppe and Antique Mall—2110 8th Ave. S., Nashville, TN; 615-
    386-9373; Mon.–Sat., 10 A.M.–5 P.M.; Sun., 1–5 P.M.
Cannery Antique Mall—2112 8th Ave. S., Nashville, TN; 615-269-4780;
    Mon.–Fri., 9 A.M.–5 P.M.; Sat., 10 A.M.–4 P.M.
Dad's Old Bookstore—4004 Hillsboro Rd., Nashville, TN; 615-298-5880;
    Mon.–Sat., 10 A.M.–6 P.M.; Sun., 12–5 P.M.
Davis-Kidd Booksellers—4007 Hillsboro Rd., Nashville, TN; 615-385-2645.
Downtown Antique Mall—612 8th Ave. S., Nashville, TN; 615-256-6616;
    Mon.–Sat., 10 A.M.–6 P.M.; Sun., 1–6 P.M.
Elder's Book Store—2115 Elliston Pl., Nashville, TN; 615-327-1867;
    Mon.–Fri., 9 A.M.–5 P.M.; Sat., 9 A.M.–2:30 P.M.
European Antique Furniture Import—217 Broadway, Nashville, TN; 615-
    242-2220; Mon.–Sat., 10 A.M.–5 P.M.; Sun., 1–5 P.M.
The Great Escape—1925 Broadway, Nashville, TN; 615-327-0646;
    Mon.–Thurs., 10 A.M.–9 P.M.; Fri.–Sat., 10 A.M.–10 P.M.; Sun.,
    1–6 P.M.
Green Hills Antique Mall—4108 Hillsboro Pike, Nashville, TN; 615-
    383-4999; open daily; Mon.–Sat., 10 A.M.–5 P.M.; Sun., 1 P.M.–5 P.M.
Local Color Gallery—1912 Broadway, Nashville, TN 37203; 615-321-3141;
    Mon.–Sat., 10 A.M.–5 P.M.
Whiteway Antique Mall—1200 Villa Pl., Nashville, TN; 615-327-1098;
    Mon.–Sat., 10 A.M.–5 P.M.; Sun. 1–5 P.M.

❧ SPECIAL EVENTS

Nashville Flea Market—Tennessee State Fairgrounds; 615-862-5016; held
    fourth weekend every month except Dec.; Sat. 6 A.M.– 6 P.M.; Sun.,
    7 A.M.–5 P.M.; no admission.
Great Performances at Vanderbilt—Langford Auditorium; 615-322-2471, 800-
    737-4849; ongoing series.
January: Heart of Country Antiques Show—Opryland Hotel.
May: Annual Tennessee Crafts Fair—Centennial Park, 615-665-0502; Run-
    ning of the Iroquois Steeplechase—Percy Warner Park, 615-322-7450.
June: Summer Lights—Downtown Nashville 615-726-1875; International
    Country Music Fan Fair—Tennessee State Fairgrounds and Opryland,
    615-889-7503 for info and tickets.

September: Italian Street Fair—Riverfront Park, 615-255-5600; Annual
    African Street Festival—Tennessee State University Campus, 615-
    256-7720 for info; Belle Meade Fall Fest—Belle Meade Plantation,
    615-356-0501.
October: Southern Festival of Books—Legislative Plaza, 615-329-7001;
    Oktoberfest—Historic Germantown; Native American Indian Associa-
    tion Annual Pow Wow, 615-726-0806.
November: A Country Christmas—Opryland Hotel, 615-872-0600.
December: Trees of Christmas—Cheekwood, 615-353-2150; Twelfth Night
    Holiday Celebration—Travellers Rest, 615-832-8197.

✍ FOR MORE INFORMATION

Nashville Area Chamber of Commerce—161 Fourth Ave. N., Nashville, TN
    37219; 615-259-4700.
Nashville Convention and Visitors Bureau—161 Fourth Ave. N., Nashville, TN
    37219; 615-259-4730.
Tennessee Tourist Development—P.O. Box 23170, Nashville, TN 37202; 615-
    741-2158; ask for free vacation guide.

3 *Franklin: Where Past and Present Converge*

The exit from the Natchez Trace to visit Franklin comes just before you cross the unique bridge over Highway 96. This bridge—1,610 feet long, 33 feet wide, and 160 feet above the valley—was made of precast concrete sections formed at another location and transported to the site. The two main piers contain stairwells for inspecting the piers, arches, and road-support structures. The bridge has been written about extensively and has been featured in *National Geographic*.

A visitors center, extra parking for bikers, picnic areas, and a nature trail are in the works, although completion dates are unknown. For now, walk across the bridge to the viewing station on its north

The Highway 96 Bridge spans a deep valley west of Franklin.

A view from the bridge looks toward Fernvale and Lyric Springs Bed and Breakfast.

side. The northern terminus of the Natchez Trace Parkway, 5 miles
north, is expected to open in the summer of 1996.

Exit the Natchez Trace on Highway 96 to visit Franklin,
approximately 8 miles east. Traveling an equal number of miles in
the opposite direction will bring you to Patsy Bruce's **Lyric Springs
Country Inn,** at 7306 South Harpeth Road in Fernvale (see chapter
4 for additional information).

According to information unearthed (literally) by archaeologists,
Williamson County has been inhabited for more than 10,000 years.
The earliest inhabitants occupied two Paleoindian sites. Nineteen
early Archaic sites have been discovered in Williamson County, usually at locations that once were camps along rivers and streams;
remains of mussel-refuse heaps are usually found at these sites. The
largest number of sites are associated with the late Archaic period,
from 3000 to 500 B.C. Some of the Indian artifacts discovered in
Williamson County sites are in the Smithsonian Institution. Indian
settlements in Williamson County had disappeared by the early
1500s, but the area remained a hunting ground shared by the Creek,
Chickasaw, and Cherokee.

The first white settlers, who entered the area from the Cumberland settlement at Fort Nashborough, had to face the constant threat
of Indian attacks. Despite numerous hardships, settlers—many of
them Revolutionary War veterans claiming land grants as compensa-
tion for their military service—by the early 1800s were pouring into
the area. Franklin was incorporated in 1799 and prospered as the
seat of one of the richest counties in the state.

During the Civil War, the area was occupied by Federal troops at
Fort Granger, just across the Harpeth River from Franklin. With so
many Confederate sympathizers in Franklin, the long occupation led
to espionage and counterespionage, skirmishes and strife, but nothing
prepared the community for the carnage that resulted from the Battle
of Franklin.

Confederate general John Bell Hood was infuriated by the
Union troop movement under cover of night, which allowed them
to slip past his forces spread out on both sides of the road leading
from Spring Hill to Franklin. After a furious march, the forces

Carter House National Monument, open to the public, was in the middle of one of the bloodiest conflicts of the Civil War.

clashed near the **Carter House.** The Confederates were poorly positioned, and at the end of that fateful November day in 1864, 6,000 Confederates lay dead. Among the mortally wounded were five Confederate generals, who legend tells us lay before burial on the porch of the Carnton Mansion, and young Capt. Tod Carter, who was brought to his family's home on Columbia Pike, where he died three days later.

After the war, the area prospered as an agricultural community, enjoying slow but steady growth. In the 1970s, Williamson County became the fastest-growing county in the state. The **Franklin and Williamson County Heritage Foundation** set out to preserve the best of the area's rich heritage; today the foundation continues its valiant efforts amid the ever-increasing pressures that result from such rapid and sustained growth.

Franklin's historic downtown has undergone an impressive restoration and revitalization. The fifteen-block downtown area is listed on the National Register of Historic Places. Several historic sites are on tour year-round, and special tours of private homes are conducted by the Heritage Foundation in May and during the candlelight tour each December.

Downtown Franklin streets are lined
with antiques shops, restaurants, and
businesses preserving the look of an
old southern town.

With a population just over 22,000, Franklin retains its small-
town charm, but due to its proximity to Nashville offers specialty
and antiques shopping usually associated with larger communities.
More than a dozen antiques shops and malls offer a wide variety
of collections for antiques enthusiasts. Specialty shops line both
sides of Main Street, and several restaurants accommodate a range
of palates.

Franklin is situated around a courthouse square, and the numbered streets are divided by Main Street into northern and southern
portions. Follow the signs to historic downtown Franklin at the
intersection of 96 and Hillsboro Road. You may also proceed
straight on Bridge Street to visit **Winchester Antique Mall,** where
Kim Tuzzio will be happy to help you with a wide selection of
antiques and collectibles. After you've visited this mall, drive along
Bridge Street to the **First Avenue Antique Mall,** which specializes in
furniture and accessories. The next traffic light is the intersection
with Main Street, and two Franklin landmarks are located side by
side after you make a left turn.

Dotson's Restaurant may not look like much from the outside,
but inside you'll find delicious country-style cooking. The vegetable
plates are excellent, and the coconut pie defies description. Next

door, "Mr. Earl" at Earl's Fruit Stand has been providing Franklin with fresh produce and live plants for years, but his most loyal patrons are the kids who come in droves every year to see Pumpkin-land. He creates corridors through the middle of his shop with pumpkins decorated and dressed to resemble celebrities and politicians of the day. Dolly Parton's been here, so have George Bush, Barney, and Bill and Hillary Clinton. Each year a new cast of characters appears around October 1.

About 1 mile north of Earl's on Main Street you'll find the **Battleground Antique Mall.** The dealers specialize in American primitive, French, and English furniture, Civil War artifacts, and collectibles.

If you proceed on 1st Avenue and do not turn at the intersection with Main, you'll come to Franklin's oldest antiques mall, at the corner of 1st and 2nd avenues South. **Franklin Antique Mall** offers a wide range of collections including furniture, glassware, wicker, and collectibles. First Avenue turns into Margin Street, and **Rebel's Rest,** at 212 South Margin, offers the largest selection of Civil War artifacts for sale and display in the area. To tour the museum, there's a nominal fee, which is applied toward your purchases, ranging in price from $1.50 to $1,000-plus.

If you turn west at 1st Avenue onto Main Street you'll want to visit the Heritage Foundation Tourist Information Center, in the 1815 brick building that was once the office of Dr. Daniel McPhail, an early Franklin resident. This building served as Gen. John M. Schofield's command headquarters before the Battle of Franklin. The folks here will happily supply you with maps, brochures, and directions; additional information is available at the modern City Hall building on the square. If the Civil War is of special interest, be sure and request the self-guided driving tour for the Battle of Franklin.

Park your car along Main Street (or in the free parking located in lots behind the shops on both sides of Main) and browse your way up and down both sides. You'll find antiques at **Antiques on Main** (we once found a signed Stickley desk here), exquisite handmade gold and platinum antique jewelry at **Walton's,** and a variety of gift items at the many specialty shops lining the street. (**Peggy's,** featuring

A monument to the soldiers who died during the bloody Battle of Franklin stands in Franklin's downtown square.

flowers, gifts, and linens; and **Magic Memories,** with unusual cards and gifts from lace to lockets, are two favorites). Quilters will find countless yards of fabrics from the Stitcher's Garden at 413 Main Street, which draws quilting enthusiasts from near and far. (In fact, one day we met a lady from Alaska who was stocking up from the incredible palette this specialty shop offers.) We've never seen another shop quite like it. For Every Child has a nice selection of children's clothes, and the Five Points Drug Store has a soda shop.

The **Franklin Cinema** offers a somewhat unusual theater venue. Geared toward adults, it serves cold beer, soft drinks, popcorn, hot dogs, and nachos to patrons gathered around tables in club chairs (toward the front of the larger screen) and sitting in standard seats (in the smaller theater).

If you've worked up an appetite, Main Street offers several restaurants. **Hunan** Chinese Restaurant has a great lunch menu. **H.R.H. Dumplin's** has chicken and dumplings. **Choices** features tasty crab cakes and Caesar salads, along with steak and other seafood. Don't miss the Sunday buffet! Also worth noting: **Merridee's** has a wonderful bakery, with great chicken-salad sandwiches.

When you reach the traffic light at the five points intersection on the west end of Main Street, you'll need to bear slightly to the left to visit the **Carter House** at 1140 Columbia Avenue. On the way you'll pass the **One Stop Market,** an excellent choice for carryout barbecue. You'll also see **Red Carpet Antiques** and the **Bunganut Pig Restaurant,** across the street from the Carter House in Carters Court.

According to Virginia Bowman's *Historic Williamson County,* the Carter House was built by Fountain B. Carter between 1829 and 1830 and was severely damaged during the Civil War. It was the scene of several skirmishes, but the major damage was sustained during the Battle of Franklin on November 30, 1864.

As mentioned earlier, Union general John Schofield had managed to slip his troops past Gen. John B. Hood's Confederates during the night of November 29, 1864. Schofield attempted to reach the Union fortifications at Nashville but was unable to cross the Harpeth River speedily. Continuing preparations to cross the Harpeth near the northern edge of town, Schofield left Gen. Jacob Cox to hold Hood at the southern end of town until the army could cross the river to the safety of Nashville. Cox established his communication center near the Carter House and dispelled the Carter family's fears for their safety throughout the early part of the day by his belief that a battle was not imminent. Later that afternoon, when Hood's intention to attack became apparent, it was too late to escape, so Carter's seventeen servants and family members and five members of another family hid in the basement. Above and around them, the battle raged.

South of town on Winstead Hill, Capt. Tod Carter looked anxiously toward Franklin—and home. With daybreak, unbelievable scenes lay before the horrified citizens of Franklin. Thousands of dead and wounded men, dead and injured horses, overturned wagons, swords, muskets, and pistols lay scattered in every direction.

Gen. Thomas Benton Smith himself rode up to the house and asked that Fountain Carter be informed that his son lay grievously wounded on the battlefield. The young captain's father and sisters found him face down by his horse, but still alive. His wounds were dressed and he was placed in bed, where he lived for forty-eight hours. The Carter House is open daily. Admission is charged.

The **Magnolia House Bed and Breakfast** is a few blocks south of the Carter House, at 1317 Columbia Avenue, and within walking distance of downtown Franklin. The house was built in 1905 on property that once was part of the Carter farm. It features three upstairs guest rooms with double or queen-size beds, private baths, and ceiling fans. Breakfast fare frequently includes Tennessee country ham, cheese grits, and homemade biscuits. Reservations for holidays and special events require a two-night minimum stay.

From the Carter House, continue down Columbia Pike to Winstead Hill Overlook, General Hood's command post during the battle. Hood, a deeply troubled man during the hours leading up to the battle, had had his left hand paralyzed in the Battle of Gettysburg and his right leg amputated at the hip due to a wound received at Chickamauga. Some historians say he was in constant pain, others that he was pursuing his own personal demons when he drove his nearly exhausted Army of Tennessee in pursuit of General Schofield and Nashville, Louisville, and Cincinnati.

Perhaps this black sheep of a respectable Kentucky family, an

Winstead Hill was Confederate general Hood's command post during the Battle of Franklin.

Magnolia House Bed and Breakfast, close to the Carter House, welcomes out-of-town guests.

Carnton Plantation served as a hospital during the Battle of Franklin and is said to be visited by ghosts.

unaccomplished West Point student and an unsuccessful suitor, saw the chance to have all his past defeats set to rights in one glorious battle. Perhaps the effects of chronic pain caused him to ignore the advice of General Cleburne, a man as much beloved by his men as Hood was disliked by his. Regardless of his reasons for placing his men in such jeopardy, Hood's dreams of glory, the lives of generals Cleburne, Granbury, Strahl, and Adams, and the hopes of the Confederacy ended on the battlefield at Franklin.

The dispirited remnants of Hood's Army of Tennessee discovered the next morning that Schofield had successfully evacuated the remainder of his troops and the battle had gained absolutely nothing for the Confederates, despite six thousand casualties.

To visit historic **Carnton Plantation,** proceed from the Winstead Hill Overlook north toward Franklin. Turn right before you reach the bottom of Winstead Hill onto the Mack Hatcher Bypass. Turn left at the Lewisburg Pike intersection and watch for signs for Carnton on your left.

Carnton Plantation was built in 1826 by Randall McGavock, whose family was from Virginia and who had been educated in Pennsylvania and sent to Middle Tennessee by his father in 1796 to lay claim to lands in the new western frontier. In 1824 he was elected mayor of Nashville. He named his Williamson County home Carnton after his family's ancestral home in Ireland. The McGavocks forged alliances with the wealthiest and most powerful families in Middle Tennessee, including General Harding of Belle Meade.

Carnton was designed to be a place of elegance and grace, but it was forced into service as a hospital following the Battle of Franklin. Virginia Bowman tells us in *Historic Williamson County* that more than three hundred wounded filled the house to overflowing. Every piece of white linen, damask, and cotton in the house was torn for bandages. Even family members' clothes were used. In the columned back gallery, awaiting burial, reposed the bodies of four generals: Patrick Cleburne, John Adams, Hiram Granbury, and Otho Strahl.

Corpses of soldiers hastily buried in shallow graves were reinterred in a two-acre cemetery donated in 1866 by John McGavock, the son of Randall McGavock. With 1,500 graves, this is the largest private Confederate cemetery in existence. Tours are available daily. Admission is charged.

On your way back to Franklin on Lewisburg Pike, watch for the **Country Charm Antique Mall** on your right. A right turn on Margin Street and a right turn at the traffic light on Murfreesboro Road (also known as 3rd Avenue South) will take you to Interstate 65, which leads to Nashville, two additional antiques malls, and a good Mexican restaurant. **Harpeth Antique Mall** and **Heritage Antique Gallery** are in Alexander Plaza, a shopping center on your left before you reach the I-65 access. Don't let the location fool you. Harpeth has more than eighty dealers and an excellent selection of furniture, art, pottery, books, prints, linens, and Depression glass. Heritage specializes in English, French, and American antiques and occasionally has some very unusual pieces. These two make the short drive worthwhile.

Camino Real offers Mexican food at reasonable prices, great margaritas, and a live mariachi band on Tuesday evenings. The restaurant is small and simple, the servings are generous, and the service is prompt. Because it's very popular with locals, there's often a wait during prime dinner hours, so you may want to eat a little early or a little late.

For a change of pace, equestrians especially should continue 13 miles east on Highway 96 to the community of Triune and artist Susan Freeman's **Xanadu Farm Bed and Breakfast Cottage.** Like Freeman's artwork, Xanadu is "just a tad bit different." There are no doilies or demitasse cups here, but she offers a cowboy country cottage and a comfortable stall for your horse. Negative Coggins papers are required. There's a stocked one-and-a-half-acre pond for fishing, trails for walking, and a resident zebra named Zelvis. Although Susan's artwork, if a wee bit tongue in cheek, is nonetheless wonderful, she candidly says her cooking isn't; however, she'll stock your refrigerator with pastries, fruit, juice, and cereals to suit your needs, and she invites you to rustle up some grub in the kitchen.

Carnton Graveyard is the largest private Confederate cemetery in existence.

❧ ACCOMMODATIONS

Holiday Inn—Hwy. 96 and I-65, Franklin, TN 37064; 615-794-7591.

Inn Towne Bed & Breakfast—1022 West Main St., Franklin, TN 37064; 615-794-3708.

Lyric Springs Country Inn—7306 S. Harpeth Rd., Franklin, TN 37064; 615-329-3385 or 800-621-7824; One cabin on the river is also available.

Maxwell's Best Western—Hwy. 96, Franklin, TN 37064; 615-790-0570.

Namaste Acres Bed & Breakfast—5436 Leipers Creek Rd., Franklin, TN 37064; 615-791-0333.

Xanadu Farm—P.O. Box 152 (8155 Horton Hwy.), Triune, TN 37014; 615-395-4771.

❧ ATTRACTIONS

Carnton Plantation—1345 Carnton Ln., Franklin, TN 37064; 615-794-0903. Admission. April–Oct., Mon.–Sat., 9 A.M.–5 P.M., Sun., 1–5 P.M.; Nov.–March, Mon.–Sat., 9 A.M.–4 P.M., Sun., 1–4 P.M.

The Carter House—1140 Columbia Pike, Franklin, TN 37064; 615-791-1861; Admission; April–Oct., Mon.–Sat., 9 A.M.–5 P.M., Sun., 1–5 P.M.; Nov.–March, Mon.–Sat., 9 A.M.–4 P.M., Sun., 1–4 P.M.

Franklin Cinema—419 Main, Franklin, TN 37064; 615-790-7122.

Rebel's Rest—S. Margin & 2nd Ave., Franklin, TN 37064; 615-790-7199; Mon.–Sat., 10 A.M.–6 P.M.; Sun., 1–5 P.M. Civil War relics for sale and on display.

❧ RESTAURANTS

The Bunganut Pig—1143 Columbia Ave. at Carters Ct., Franklin, TN 37064; 615-794-4777; Mon.–Thurs., 11 A.M.–11 P.M.; Fri. and Sat., 11 A.M.–12 A.M.

Camino Real—548 Alexander Plz., Franklin, TN 37064; 615-790-3104; Sun.–Thurs., 11 A.M.–10 P.M.; Fri.–Sat., 11 A.M.–10:30 P.M.

Choices—4th & Main, Franklin, TN 37064; 615-791-0001; Mon.–Sat., 11 A.M.–2 P.M.; Mon.–Thurs., 5:30–9 P.M.; Fri.–Sat., 5:30–10 P.M.; Sun., 10:30 A.M.–2 P.M.

Dotson's Restaurant—99 E. Main, Franklin, TN 37064; 615-794-2805; Mon.–Sat., 6 A.M.–8:30 P.M.; Sun., 7 A.M.–2:30 P.M.

Five Points Drug Store—Fifth & Main, Franklin, TN 37064; 615-790-7790.

H.R.H. Dumplin's—428 Main, Franklin, TN 37064; 615-791-4651;
  Mon.–Sun., 11 A.M.–2 P.M.
Hunan Chinese Restaurant—413 Main, Franklin, TN 37064; 615-790-6868.
Merridee's Breadbasket—110 4th Ave. S., Franklin, TN 37064; 615-
  790-3755; Mon.–Sat., 7:30 A.M.–5 P.M.
One Stop Market—901 Columbia Ave., Franklin, TN 37064; 615-
  794-3881; Mon.–Fri., 6 A.M.–8 P.M.; Sat., 8 A.M.–6 P.M.; Sun.,
  11 A.M.– 6 P.M.

ᔛ SHOPPING

Antiques on Main—334 Main, Franklin, TN 37064; 615-794-8580;
  Mon.–Sat., 10 A.M.–5 P.M.; Sun., 12:30–5 P.M.
Battleground Antique Mall—232 Franklin Rd., Franklin, TN 37064; 615-
  794-9444; Mon.–Sat., 10 A.M.–5 P.M.; Sun., 1–5 P.M.
Country Charm Mall—301 Lewisburg Ave., Franklin, TN 37064; 615-
  790-8908; Mon.–Sat., 10 A.M.–6 P.M.; Sun., 12–5 P.M.
First Avenue Antiques—1007 1st Ave. N., Franklin, TN 37064; 615-
  791-8866; Mon.–Sat., 10 A.M.–5 P.M.; Sun. 1–5 P.M.
Franklin Antique Mall—251 2nd Ave. S., Franklin, TN 37064; 615-
  790-8593; Mon.–Sat., 10 A.M.–5 P.M.; Sun., 1–5 P.M.
The Galloping Goose—405 Main, Franklin, TN 37064; 615-794-8514.
Harpeth Antique Mall—Alexander Plz., Franklin, TN 37064; 615-790-7965;
  Mon.–Sat., 9 A.M.–6 P.M.; Sun., 1–6 P.M.
Heirloom Antiques—125 S. Margin St., Franklin, TN 37064; 615-
  791-0847; Mon.–Sat., 9:30 A.M.–5 P.M.
Heritage Antique Gallery—Alexander Plz., Franklin, TN 37064; 615-
  790-8115; Mon.–Sat., 10 A.M.–6 P.M.; Sun., 1–6 P.M.
Magic Memories—345 Main, Franklin, TN 37064; 615-794-2848;
  Mon.–Sat., 10 A.M.–6 P.M.
Patchwork Palace—340 Main, Franklin, TN 37064; 615-790-1382;
  Mon.–Sat., 9:30 A.M.–5 P.M.; Sun., 12:30–4 P.M.
Peggy's Place—348 Main, Franklin, TN 37064; 615-790-6408; Mon.–Sat.,
  9:30 A.M.–6 P.M.; Sun., 12–4 P.M.
Red Carpet Antiques & Interiors—915 Columbia Ave., Franklin, TN 37064;
  615-794-7003; Mon.–Sat., 10 A.M.–5 P.M.; Sundays and evenings by
  appointment.
Tennessee Treasures—125 S. Margin St., Franklin, TN 37064; 615-
  794-9731; Mon.–Sat., 9:30 A.M.–5 P.M.; Sun., 1–5 P.M.

Watson's Antique & Estate Jewelry—410 Main, Franklin, TN 37064; 615-790-0244; Sat.–Mon., 10 A.M.–5 P.M.

Winchester Antique Mall—113 Bridge St., Franklin, TN 37064; 615-791-5846; Mon.–Sat., 10 A.M.–5 P.M.; Sun., 12:30–5 P.M.

SPECIAL EVENTS

April: Main Street Festival—Last weekend in April.

May: Franklin Rodeo; Heritage Foundation Town & Country Tour.

August: Franklin Jazz Festival.

October: Pumpkin Fest.

November: Christmas at Fox Hollow (Tom T. & Dixie Hall's)—Eleven days after Thanksgiving.

December: Carter House Candlelight Tour of Homes; Dickens of a Christmas.

FOR MORE INFORMATION

Heritage Foundation—209 E. Main, Franklin, TN 37064; 615-790-0378.

Williamson County Tourism—P.O. Box 156 (City Hall), Franklin, TN 37065; 615-794-1225 or 800-356-344; Ask for self-guided tour of historic downtown Franklin, driving tour of the Battle of Franklin, driving tour of Brentwood and Franklin and scenic parkway through Williamson County, and brochure of special events.

Downtown Franklin Association—231 2nd Ave., Franklin, TN 37065; 615-790-7094.

4 Leipers Fork: Small Town, Big Heart

The rural community of Leipers Fork is less than a mile from the Natchez Trace Parkway exit milepost 429.0. It's a good stopping point for antiques shopping, barbecue, bed and breakfast accommodations, and gas for your car.

As you exit the Natchez Trace Parkway, you will make an easterly turn to visit "the Forks." When you reach the stop sign you should turn right to reach the nearby **Namaste Acres Bed and Breakfast.** This modern Dutch Colonial home has facilities that include an outdoor swimming pool and hot tub, queen-size rope bunk beds, a clawfoot tub, and an indoor "outhouse" in the Old West style Tennessee bunkhouse, and a private entrance to a large suite with private bath, VCR, and phone in the more modern Leipers Loft. All rooms have thermostat controls.

One of the most unusual features about Namaste is its proximity (within walking distance) to a 27-mile bridle and hiking trail on the Natchez Trace. Your hosts have facilities for horses, and about 40 percent of the visitors bring their four-legged friends along for the ride. A full breakfast is served and ranges from French toast and sausage to breakfast casseroles and fresh fruit.

If you're interested in visiting Leipers Fork, exit the Trace, then turn right back under the Trace. In one-half mile you'll come to a stop sign; turn left and Green's Grocery will soon be on your right. The building has been a landmark since its construction in 1914. Inside is a picking parlor for listening to professional songwriters.

Namaste Acres Bed and Breakfast offers boarders quick and easy access to the Garrison Creek horse and hiking trail.

Garrison Creek horse and hiking trail is 27 miles long, running parallel to the parkway from Garrison Creek comfort station to Highway 50 near the Gordon house.

Owner Aubrey Preston says, "This is a listening room atmosphere. We have the world's best songwriters performing the original versions of their songs. Be assured, you'll see something pretty amazing!" Open only on Tuesday and Friday nights. Dinner served at 6 P.M. and music lasts from 7:15 P.M. until 10 or later. Cover charge ranges from $7 to $20, depending on performers. Call for reservations between noon and 3 P.M. on Tuesdays. No smoking inside but there is a smoking section on the porch.

Green's Grocery is just across the road from the home of statesman Thomas Hart Benton, who lived in the area from 1799 to 1815. As mentioned earlier, Benton was a close associate of Andrew Jackson until a quarrel developed between them. Benton later became an influential senator from Missouri and a staunch Jackson ally. All that remains of his home are the foundations and chimney stack.

Also nearby are the homes of country-music stars Eddie Rabbit and Wynonna and Naomi Judd. Many country-western stars make their homes in Williamson County, as do music-industry executives, songwriters, and musicians. The community has welcomed them quietly, for the most part, respecting a universal need for privacy. One obvious exception during the Christmas holidays is Wynonna's house on Old Hillsboro Road. She goes all out with Christmas lights and decorations, so fans have no problem locating her brilliantly illuminated farmhouse, barn, and pasture.

Your next stop, also on the right, is **Marty Hunt's Leipers Fork Antiques.** Not only does Marty usually have an interesting and varied collection, but she's also a wealth of information about the community. She and her husband host the annual community flea market each fall in their pasture down the road.

The Country Boy Restaurant is pleased to serve you breakfast, lunch, and dinner—if you can find a parking space among all the pickup trucks. The Country Boy breakfast (country ham, eggs, biscuits, and gravy) and the western omelet (with country ham, grilled onions, peppers, and cheese) are such crowd-pleasers that they're served all day.

Across the road at **Puckett's Grocery,** you can order the best hamburgers in Williamson County. The secret of their goodness may lie in the fact that the beef is ground fresh daily on the premises.

There's a small seating area in the rear of the market, or you can get your burgers to go.

The West Fork of the Harpeth River flows through the valley and may be of interest to fishermen and canoeists. The put-in on Southall Road is 6 river-miles from the take out on Highway 96 west of Franklin. The river is shallow in spots, Class I throughout most of its length, and is best run November through early June.

If you continue through Leipers Fork on Highway 46, you will intersect Highway 96. Turn east to go into Franklin or west to return to the Natchez Trace. We recommend you reenter the Trace at milepost 429.0 to view the next 8 miles of scenic Tennessee hills and the bridge over Highway 96.

One of the area's best-known bed and breakfasts, **Lyric Springs Country Inn,** is about 8 miles west of the intersection of Highway 96 West and the Natchez Trace Parkway. Owner Patsy Bruce, the co-writer of "Mamas, Don't Let Your Babies Grow Up to Be Cowboys," has filled this lovely inn with music memorabilia and antiques.

The fifty-acre site lets visitors take a dip in the swimming pool or wet a line in the stocked pond or the South Harpeth Creek just across the road. Patsy will lend you bicycles to travel the back roads or point out the hiking trails on the property. A barn is also available for guests' horses. There's a pool table in the Old West "saloon," which is part of the original hundred-year-old structure. Lyric Springs offers three attractive guest rooms with private baths; we found the Waltz, with its outdoor balcony, especially pleasant. The inn offers gourmet dinners as well as breakfast. The menu varies, but

Leipers Fork Antiques and Collectibles invites visitors to browse.

Lyric Springs Country Inn overlooks a creek and pond stocked with trout amid fifty acres.

grilled steaks, filets, shrimp, and chicken dishes are popular. Breakfast ranges from German apple pancakes to Southwest frittatas and a country breakfast.

This picturesque inn has been featured in national magazines and is a favorite getaway spot for locals as well as travelers. To visit Lyric Springs proceed west on Highway 96 after passing the landmark bridge at the Natchez Trace. Just before you intersect with Highway 100, you'll see the entrance to the lovely rural community of Fernvale on your left. Drive through Fernvale until you reach South Harpeth Road, turning across the valley on your right.

ACCOMMODATIONS

Lyric Springs Country Inn—7306 S. Harpeth Rd., Franklin, TN 37064; 615-329-3385.

Namaste Acres Bed and Breakfast—5436 Leipers Creek Rd., Franklin, TN 37064; 615-791-0333.

RESTAURANTS

Country Boy Restaurant—4141 Old Hillsboro Rd., Franklin, TN 37064; 615-794-7680; Mon.–Fri., 6 A.M.–8 P.M.; Sat., 7 A.M.–8 P.M.; Sun., 7 A.M.–7 P.M.

Green's Grocery—3302 Bailey Rd., Franklin, TN 37064; 615-790-0117; Tues. & Fri., 6 P.M.–10 P.M.

Puckett's Grocery—4142 Old Hillsboro Rd., Franklin, TN 37064; 615-794-1308; Mon.–Sat., 6 A.M.–8 P.M.; Sun., 8 A.M.–7 P.M.

SHOPPING

Marty Hunt's Leipers Fork Antiques—4149 Old Hillsboro Rd., Franklin, TN 37064; 615-790-9963; Wed.–Sat., 10 A.M.–5 P.M.; Sun., 1–5 P.M.

FOR MORE INFORMATION

Williamson County Tourism—P.O. Box 156 (City Hall), Franklin, TN 37065; 615-794-1225 or 800-356-3445.

Loop Tour I:

Columbia/Lawrenceburg/Waynesboro/ Hohenwald/Centerville/Lyles

Highway 7 is the perfect place to begin a loop tour. Exit the Trace onto Highway 7 and turn east toward Columbia ("Mule Capital of the World"), approximately 18 miles away. If you prefer, you may reverse this loop trip and turn west to Lyles. Either way, we will bring you back to this spot, because you won't want to miss the many sites and sights along the Trace.

Columbia and Spring Hill offer you a tour of many outstanding antebellum homes and other sites to visit, as well as the modern Saturn plant. This area is steeped in Civil War history, from **Rippa**

Athenaeum was established in 1835, and it later served as a private school for young women. It is open to the public at select times.

The courthouse in Columbia dominates the town square on a hill overlooking the downtown area.

Villa—where General Hood slept as the Union army walked by the front door up the road to Franklin and where he held his last council meeting before the Battle of Franklin (see chapter 3)—to the Columbia Athenaeum, where living and social skills were taught before the war.

Maj. Nathaniel Cheairs and his family lived in the earliest structure, which later became the kitchen while Rippa Villa was being built. The walls were erected and dismantled three times before they were "perfect." It is this mindset toward perfection that made Rippa Villa such a magnificent home when the large house was completed in 1855.

Unfortunately, a few years later Major Cheairs raised the Third Tennessee Infantry to fight in the Civil War. He was defeated and captured at Fort Donelson in 1862 and spent the remainder of the war as a prisoner in Ohio. He returned home with a pardon "for his Confederate sins" (the defeat at Fort Donelson) and lived until 1914. Rippa Villa has changed hands several times since then and is now owned by the Saturn Corporation.

President James K. Polk's home, at 310 West 7th Street, was built in 1816 by his father, Samuel Polk. Young James was twenty-one then and a student at the University of North Carolina. He returned home to begin his law career and in 1824 was elected to the state legislature and later to the U.S. House of Representatives. After seven terms in Washington, he returned to Tennessee to serve a two-year term as governor. In 1845 Polk moved into the White House as the eleventh president of the United States and returned to Columbia four years later.

During your tour of the home, you will see many furnishings that were used by Polk here and in the White House, in addition to items from his law office and his father's family. An especially rare item is the inaugural Bible used by Polk. An outstanding collection of portraits, pieces of four china services from the White House, and silver, crystal, candelabra, and many personal articles can be viewed.

Also on the tour are Greenway Farm, St. John's Church, Hamilton Place, Scott-Matthews-Wendt Home, Rattle and Snap, Persimmon Ridge, and others. Contact Columbia's chamber of commerce

The Federal style James K. Polk home built in 1816 is the only surviving home in Tennessee of the eleventh president of the United States. It is open to the public year-round.

for the historic driving tour brochure, and be sure to ask about **Mule Day.**

Mule Day is more than half a century old and the grandest celebration in Columbia. In the 1840s Columbia became a crossroads for mule traders, and by 1934 Columbia's Market Day was an official festival, touted as "1,000 girls and 1,000 mules."

Will Rogers said, "What the thoroughfare of Wall Street will do to you if you don't know a stock, Columbia will do to you if you don't know a mule." Today a good mule will cost you $1,500 to $5,000.

To see all the sights in Columbia and tour the Saturn Plant will take all day. Contact Maury County Chamber of Commerce for walking and driving tours.

There are many motels and restaurants in Columbia. **Sam's Hill** is a good choice if you are looking for a fun sports-bar setting. **Albert's** offers an award-winning Jack Daniel's steak.

Continuing our loop, leave Columbia, and head south on Highway 43 through Mt. Pleasant into Lawrence County, which features

Lawrenceburg's town square is surrounded by antiques shops and other businesses.

"Life in the Slow Lane." Before reaching the county seat of Lawrenceburg, you will pass near an Amish community in Ethridge on Edan Road (west of Highway 43). More than two hundred highly productive families have lived here since 1944. Avoiding modern conveniences, they thrive in a simple, rural setting. We stopped and bought honey, homemade peanut brittle, and hand-woven baskets and were very pleased with the asking prices.

Also in Ethridge is Granny's Network, a privately owned ten-watt TV station operated from Granny's basement. Granny is Sarah Evetts, who has become known across the country through appearances on many national network programs and talk shows. You can stop and be on her TV show and then get a tape of yourself appearing with Granny.

Farther south on Highway 43, you will arrive in Lawrenceburg. On the square you will see a life-size bronze statue of David Crockett, and a block to the south you can see where he lived and worked. There is a replica of his office and a historical marker showing where he lived for about six years.

Davy was a pioneer, soldier, politician, trapper, and industrialist who was born in upper East Tennessee in 1786. In 1817 he moved to Lawrence County and settled on Shoal Creek, where he set to work building and operating a grist mill, powder mill, and distillery. After the flood of 1821 washed it all away and left him financially ruined, he moved to West Tennessee, where he was elected to Congress. He died in March 1836 fighting for freedom at the Alamo.

David Crockett State Park, located on 950 acres just west of Lawrenceburg toward the Trace on Highway 64, was dedicated to his memory in May 1959. Here you can visit Davy's reconstructed distillery and mills.

The park has one hundred campsites in two campgrounds equipped with water, electricity, tables, and grills; these are available on a first come, first served basis. Modern bathhouses and dump stations are convenient.

A park restaurant with a seating capacity of 240 tops a hill overlooking Crockett Lake. The forty-acre lake has year-round fishing with a permit. You can fish from a rowboat or the bank, or even rent

David Crockett lived in Lawrenceburg for six years and the state park is dedicated to him.

There really are some covered bridges left in the world! Here is one inside David Crockett State Park.

a pedal boat at the dock. Other features include a swimming pool with bathhouse, concession stand, minibike trails, bike trails, hiking trails, tennis courts, amphitheater, and an interpretive center.

Another monument in Lawrenceburg is just one of two in the United States dedicated to the Mexican War. It was erected in 1849 to perpetuate the memory of the Lawrenceburg Blues and Capt. William B. Allen.

Around the Public Square and Historic District you will find antiques shops. **Carriage House II, Heirlooms,** and **Flea Market Shop** are on the square, and the **Dig Store** is on Military Avenue.

The Golden Panda came highly recommended as the place to eat. **David Crockett Park Restaurant, Rick's Barbeque,** and **Kuntry Kitchen** were runners-up.

The Amish have roadside stands with their hand-crafted and homemade goods on Buffalo Road (Highway 242) northwest of Lawrenceburg.

From Lawrenceburg we head west on Highway 64, our destination Waynesboro. In 15 miles we pass Laurel Hill Lake and Wildlife Management Area to the north and soon thereafter go under the Trace.

Laurel Hill is a nice place to picnic or wet a hook. You can rent a boat or fish from the bank for bass, walleye, bream, catfish, and

David Crockett Museum is a few blocks from downtown.

Buffalo River is Middle Tennessee's most popular canoe stream. One of the many access points to the Buffalo is north of Waynesboro.

crappie. Like other Wildlife Management Areas in Tennessee, Laurel Hill is a good place for a family outing.

The Natchez Trace Motel, in a little town called Ovilla, is on Highway 64 less than a mile west of the Natchez Trace Parkway.

Waynesboro, 12 miles to the west, was the location of Davy Crockett's first political address and the historic hideout for Natchez Trace bandits.

We found good dining at Emerald's, on the corner of the square. Specializing in pizza, it has a very nice atmosphere and a broad menu that features steak and chicken, burgers and fries. O'Henry's Restaurant is on Highway 64. Sims Motor Lodge and Restaurant, also on 64, offers you a place to eat and sleep.

Behind Emerald's, at 128 High Street, you will find Williams and Walker's Something Old Shop. Besides a nice selection of antique furniture and reproduction Tiffany lamps, they have gifts, dolls, and custom framing.

The Green River, known for its smallmouth bass, runs through Waynesboro and empties into the Buffalo River.

Hohenwald, our next stop on the loop, is the highest town between New Orleans and Chicago, at an elevation near one thousand feet above sea level. From Waynesboro, go east on Highway 64 until you see Highway 99 splitting to the north for a scenic but curvy drive through the Buffalo River Valley. You may prefer to take High-

Waynesboro contains a variety of shops and restaurants.

way 13 North from Waynesboro until you turn east on Highway 48 into Hohenwald.

In 1806 settlers began building homes and raising families in this area. After the mysterious death of Meriwether Lewis, former governor of the Louisiana Territory and good friend and personal secretary to Thomas Jefferson, in 1809, the Tennessee legislature created Lewis County from the area surrounding his grave.

German immigrants created a town named Hohenwald (meaning "high forest") in 1878 and developed a thriving lumber industry. Sixteen years later Swiss immigrants built their "New Switzerland" just south of Hohenwald. In time the two towns merged under the name Hohenwald. Unlike many other frontier towns, Hohenwald was highly cultured and populated by a wide assortment of artisans and craftsmen. Since the 1890s Lewis County has continued to attract a high percentage of creative personalities.

The **Museum of Natural History** is not something you would expect to find in a small southern town. It contains an unusually large collection of exotic animals taken from Europe, Asia, Africa, and South America. There are also exhibits of the early settlers and artifacts of Meriwether Lewis. This is a worthwhile stop.

The **Hohenwald Depot,** built in 1896, is listed on the National Register of Historic Places and contains displays and photographs illustrating the county's history. This includes a labor force that

You will be surprised at the contents of the Lewis County Museum of Natural History in Hohenwald.

The restored Hohenwald Depot is a tourist information center and museum.

worked on the depot and was made up of prisoners captured from Nazi general Rommel's African Corps. Today the depot also serves as the tourist information center.

You will want to spend time browsing in **Theodocia's** and other shops along Main Street. People come from miles around to take part in the junk stores' "grab bag days." Bales of clothing are shipped to various stores in the city for grand free-for-all openings. In the pockets, purses, and other nooks and crannies, rings and other items of value have been found, but your chances of having such luck are about the same as your chances of winning the lottery. The main attraction is getting a great buy on clothes that range from average to designer. This has become an exciting event in Hohenwald.

Helen's Second Impression opens bales on Wednesday, Saturday, and Sunday. The process of pulling clothes from the bales is called digging, and as Helen says, "The big attraction is the great buys you can get. You get a clothes basket and get in there and dig for dear life!"

Lawson's, across the street on the corner of the next block, is another dig store. It opens its bales of clothes every Wednesday and Saturday.

From here, to get to Centerville, travel north on Highway 48 and turn right when you intersect Highway 100. If you want to return to the Trace from Hohenwald, it's 8 miles east on Highway 20, which takes you to Meriwether Lewis Park (milepost 385.9). Or 7 miles via Highway 412, which takes you to **Swan View Restaurant and Motel,** 1 mile from the Trace. The restaurant specializes in fresh catfish. Owner Dwight Henson promises, "The fish comes in twice a week and is never frozen." It also has a variety of other items, from steaks to seafood.

You can hike and bicycle at Meriwether Lewis Park. Thirty-two campsites have grills and picnic tables. A telephone is available at the ranger station. Things to see: a monument and exhibits, an old log house, and Pioneer Cemetery.

This is the site of Grinder's Stand, where Meriwether Lewis met his death. Was it murder or suicide? No satisfactory resolution has been reached.

The top half of the Meriwether Lewis monument seems to be missing, but in reality it was left incomplete to commemorate Lewis's premature demise. The monument reads: "Meriwether Lewis born near Charlottesville, Virginia, August 18, 1774, died October 11, 1809." There is more inscription around the monument, but most of it is very difficult to read. Lewis is the only person buried in Pioneer Cemetery.

The monument is on the Old Natchez Trace and marks the beginning of a 2.3-mile hiking trail that goes through the hardwood forest called Little Swan Trail. A marker on the Old Trace reads: "At the entrance to the cemetery, plainly visible through the long deserted road is a section of the Natchez Trace evolved from buffalo and Indian trails into the first national highway of the southwest. Cut and reopened under the authority of the U.S. government after treaties negotiated with the Chickasaw and the Choctaw Indians in 1801. Designed to meet early necessities of trade between Nashville and the country of the lower Mississippi, it is an abiding footprint of the bold, crude commerce of the pioneers. Yet it is not without military significance in the history of our country. Over it passed a part of Andrew Jackson's army in his campaign against the Creek Indians

A hiking trail at Meriwether Lewis runs 2.3 miles from the Lewis gravesite to the Little Swan picnic area.

in 1813 and again on his return from the battlefield of New Orleans in 1815. But before Talladega and New Orleans, before the soldiers of Jackson had given renown to the Natchez Trace, it received its immortal touch of melancholy fame when Meriwether Lewis, journeying over it on his way to Philadelphia to edit the story of his great expedition, met here his untimely death on the night of October 11, 1809."

Inside the reconstruction of Grinder's old stand is a museum with the chronology of the Natchez Trace, beginning in 1765.

Return to Hohenwald to go to Centerville via one of the routes previously described.

Centerville, the county seat of Hickman County, holds to tradition and maintains its small-town homeyness. A walk around the square offers you a variety of places to browse and dine. We found **Breece's** to be a favorite eating place of locals and tourists alike, with a very tasty meat-and-four that hardly leaves room for the wonderful desserts. Almost all their produce is home-grown.

You've heard Cousin Minnie Pearl talk about her home in Grinder's Switch; that's just a stone's throw from Centerville. Sarah Ophelia Colley Cannon, a.k.a. Minnie Pearl, was born in Centerville and incorporated Grinder's Switch into her act. The railroad switch got its name from the man who owned Grinder's Stand in what is now Meriwether Lewis Park.

One more bit of Hickman County trivia: "Let Me Call You Sweetheart" was written by Beth Slater Whitson, who was born in Hickman County in 1879.

When you are ready, head northeast on Highway 100 to Lyles. Norma Crow owns and operates **Silver Leaf Country Inn** 10 miles away. Dating back to 1815, this establishment, which is one of the oldest log homes in Middle Tennessee, offers you fine dining in a wooded setting. Norma serves lunch and dinner in addition to breakfast for her bed-and-breakfast guests. You need to make reservations.

Silver Leaf is full of antiques and collectibles. The inn has been written about in many magazines, including *Redbook* and *Southern Liv-*

ing, and her recipes are award-winning. You don't want to miss a chance to sample Norma's food, especially her desserts. You can sit and look down on the pond and perhaps see deer and turkey in the woods from one of her dining rooms.

Also in Lyles is **Rocking Horse Antiques and Collectibles,** across from the old post office.

From Silver Leaf on Mills Creek Road, go back to Highway 100, turn right toward Nashville, then east on Highway 7, and you are just 12 miles from the Trace, where you began this loop tour.

If you don't have time to make the loop but are looking for a place to stay, try **Ridgetop Bed and Breakfast.** It's set on 170 wooded acres and conveniently located 4 miles east of the Trace on Highway 412 toward Columbia. It offers hiking in the woods and along streams from the contemporary cedar home with antiques and a huge deck overlooking the woods.

Owner Kay Jones says she specializes in bicyclists making their way along the Trace. She also has a reservation service for bed and breakfasts along the Trace.

Likewise, if you don't want to leave the Trace for a tour, you can fill up with gas in Collinwood within sight of the Trace to the west of the parkway just beyond milepost 355. Collinwood has food at Pat's Place, Keith's Country Triangle Restaurant, and Old Depot Cafe.

ACCOMMODATIONS ▪ *Columbia*

The Richard Inn—2407 Hwy. 31 S., Columbia, TN 38401; 615-381-4500.

Econo Lodge—1548 Bear Creek Pike, Columbia, TN 38401; 615-381-1410.

Grinder's Switch Inn—107 N. Central Ave., Centerville, TN 37033; 615-729-5195.

Holiday Inn of Columbia—1208 Nashville Hwy., Columbia, TN 38401; 615-388-2720.

James Polk Motel—1111 Nashville Hwy., Columbia, TN 38401; 615-388-4913.

ATTRACTIONS ■ *Columbia*

Columbia Historic Driving Tour—P.O. Box 1076 (308 W. 7th St.), Columbia, TN 38402; 615-381-7176; Rippa Villa, President Polk's home, and 20 other sites.

Mule Day—308 W. 7th St., Columbia, TN 38402; 615-381-9557; Liars contest, mule sale, flea market, fiddlers contest, and the world famous mule parade held the first weekend in April (unless it's Easter, then it is held the next weekend).

RESTAURANTS ■ *Columbia*

Albert's—708 N. Main St., Columbia, TN 38401; 615-381-3463.

Chinese Panda Restaurant—100 Berrywood Dr., Columbia, TN 38401; 615-381-7733.

Lucille's Restaurant—822 S. Main St., Columbia, TN 38401; 615-383-3005.

Marion's Restaurant—104 W. 6th St., Columbia, TN 38401; 615-388-6868.

Sam Hill's—1144 Riverside Dr., Columbia, TN 38401; 615-388-5555.

SHOPPING ■ *Columbia*

High Attic Antiques—416 W. 15th St., Columbia, TN 38401; 615-381-2819.

Luna's Antiques—201 E. 9th St., Columbia, TN 38401; 615-388-7101.

Mule Town Antiques—1130 Carmack Blvd., Columbia, TN 38401; 615-381-2514.

Sewell's Antiques—217 Bear Creek Pike, Columbia, TN 38401; 615-388-3973.

FOR MORE INFORMATION ■ *Columbia*

Tourists Bureau—P.O. Box 1076 (308 W. 7th St.), Columbia, TN 38402; 615-381-7176.

ACCOMMODATIONS ■ *Lawrenceburg*

David Crockett Motel—503 E. Gaines, Lawrenceburg, TN 38464; 615-763-7191.

Granville House Bed & Breakfast—229 Pulaski St., Lawrenceburg, TN 38464; 615-762-3129.

Natchez Trace Inn & Motel—Rt. 6, Box 414, Lawrenceburg, TN 38464; 615-722-3010.

Parkview Motel—1105 W. Gaines, Lawrenceburg, TN 38464; 615-762-0061.

Villa Inn—2126 N. Locust Ave., Lawrenceburg, TN 38464; 615-762-4448.

RESTAURANTS ■ *Lawrenceburg*

Big John's Bar-B-Que—904 N. Military Ave., Lawrenceburg, TN 38464; 615-762-9596.

The Golden Panda—2005 N. Locust St., Lawrenceburg, TN 38464: 615-762-5888.

Kuntry Kitchen—2535 S. Locust St., Lawrenceburg, TN 38464; 615-766-0260.

Rick's Barbeque—401 W. Gaines, Lawrenceburg, TN 38464; 615-762-2296.

SPECIAL EVENTS ■ *Lawrenceburg*

May: Lawrenceburg Rodeo—Third weekend in May.

FOR MORE INFORMATION ■ *Lawrenceburg*

David Crockett State Park—Lawrenceburg, TN 38464; 615-762-9408 (office) or 762-9541 (restaurant).

South Central Tennessee Tourism Association—215 Frank St., Lawrenceburg, TN 38464; 615-762-6944.

Lawrence County Chamber of Commerce—1609 N. Locust Ave., Lawrenceburg, TN 38464; 615-762-4911.

ACCOMMODATIONS ■ *Waynesboro*

Sims Motor Lodge—Hwy. 64, Waynesboro, TN 38485; 615-722-3655.

RESTAURANTS ■ *Waynesboro*

Emerald's—Public Sq., Waynesboro, TN 38485; 615-722-5611.

🍃 SHOPPING ▪ *Waynesboro*

Williams & Walker, Something Old Shop—128 High St., Waynesboro, TN 38485; 615-722-7118 or 722-5560.

🍃 FOR MORE INFORMATION ▪ *Waynesboro*

Wayne County Chamber of Commerce—P.O. Box 675, Waynesboro, TN 38485; 615-722-9022.

🍃 ACCOMMODATIONS ▪ *Hohenwald*

Swan View Restaurant & Motel—Rt. 3, Hwy. 412, Hohenwald, TN 38462; 615-796-4745.
Shadow Acres Motel—Rt. 2, Box 179, Hohenwald, TN 38462; 615-796-2201

🍃 ATTRACTIONS ▪ *Hohenwald*

The Lewis County Museum of Natural History—Main St., Hohenwald, TN 38462; 615-796-4084 (Chamber of Commerce); Admission; Wed.–Sat., 10 A.M.–4 P.M.; Sun., 1–4 P.M.
Hohenwald Depot—112 E. Main St., Hohenwald, TN 38462; 615-796-4084.

🍃 RESTAURANTS ▪ *Hohenwald*

Big John's Bar-B-Que—426 Main St., Hohenwald, TN 38462; 615-796-2244.
E.W. James & Sons Deli—Hwy. 412, Hohenwald, TN 38462; 615-796-2480.
Highlander Restaurant—29 E. Linden St., Hohenwald, TN 38462; 615-796-5988.
Swan View Restaurant—Hwy. 412, Hohenwald, TN 38462; 615-796-4745.

🍃 SHOPPING ▪ *Hohenwald*

Helen's Second Impression—35 E. Main St., Hohenwald, TN 38462; 615-796-7718.

Lawson's—100 E. Main St., Hohenwald, TN 38462; 615-796-4380.

Theodocia's Antiques & Gifts—5 E. Main St., Hohenwald, TN 38462; 615-796-1836.

✠ SPECIAL EVENTS ▪ *Hohenwald*

October: Volksmarch, regional arts and crafts festival/High Forest Jamboree and Oktoberfest—Second weekend in October; Contact Hohenwald Chamber of Commerce.

✠ FOR MORE INFORMATION ▪ *Hohenwald*

Tennessee Natchez Trace Corridor Association/Lewis County Chamber of Commerce/The Lewis County Historical Society—112 E. Main St. (Hohenwald Depot), Hohenwald, TN 38462; 615-796-4084.

✠ RESTAURANTS ▪ *Centerville*

Breece's Cafe—111 S. Public Sq., Centerville, TN 37033; 615-729-3481.

Fish Camp Restaurant—406 Hwy. 100, Centerville, TN 37033; 615-729-4401.

Manley's Restaurant—139 N. Central Ave., Centerville, TN 37033; 615-729-2948.

✠ SHOPPING ▪ *Centerville*

Accents & Antiques—222 W. 8th St., Columbia, TN 38401; 615-380-8975.

Nash Antiques—2195 Hwy. 100, Centerville, TN 37033; 615-729-9210.

✠ FOR MORE INFORMATION ▪ *Centerville*

Hickman County Chamber of Commerce—P.O. Box 126 (102 S. Public Sq.), Centerville, TN 37033; 615-729-5774.

✠ ACCOMMODATIONS ▪ *Lyles*

Silver Leaf Country Inn—Rt. 1, Box 122 (Mill Creek Rd.), Lyles, TN 37098; 615-670-3048.

❧ RESTAURANTS ▪ *Lyles*

Silver Leaf 1815 Country Inn—Mill Creek Rd., Lyles, TN 37098; 615-670-3048.

❧ SHOPPING ▪ *Lyles*

Rocking Horse Antiques and Collectibles—Lyles Rd., Lyles, TN 37098; 615-670-3817.

❧ SPECIAL EVENTS ▪ *Lyles*

December: Christmas at Silver Leaf—Lyles, Dec. 3–23, Silver Leaf Country Inn, Rt. 1, Box 122 (Mill Creek Rd.), Lyles, TN 37098; 615-670-3048.

OTHERS

❧ ACCOMMODATIONS ▪ *Duck River*

McEwen Farm Log Cabin Bed & Breakfast—P.O. Box 97, Duck River, TN 38454; 615-583-2378.

❧ ACCOMMODATIONS ▪ *Hampshire*

Ridgetop Bed & Breakfast—P.O. Box 193, Hampshire, TN 38461; 615-285-2777 or 800-377-2770.
Trace Reservation Service—Kay Jones, P.O. Box 193, Hampshire, TN 38461; 615-285-2777 or 800-377-2770.

6 Loop Tour II:
Savannah/Crump/Shiloh/
Pickwick Landing/Iuka

Shiloh National Military Park west of Savannah is where more than 23,000 men died during the battle.

This next loop trip takes you through Savannah, Tennessee, across the Tennessee River to visit **Shiloh National Military Park,** then south to Pickwick Landing and back to the Trace via Iuka, Mississippi. This loop exits the Trace at milepost 370 and returns you at milepost 320. Consult chapter 1 for sites you may miss by leaving the Trace for 50 miles, and compare those to the following text to see which appeals to you more.

Shiloh is a must-see for Civil War buffs. We think visiting the park was one of the most somber experiences we had in our travels.

It's a straight route to Savannah from Waynesboro on Highway 64. Savannah bills itself as the "Catfish Capital of the World." The **Tennessee River Museum** is in Savannah and also houses the **Hardin County Chamber of Commerce.**

Inside the museum there are displays of more than two hundred fossils from the Paleozoic and Cretaceous periods; a large display of Indian arrowheads; one of the finest stone-effigy pipes of a kneeling human ever recovered; a partial reproduction of the USS *Cairo* (the original is in Vicksburg); many artifacts of the Civil War; an especially impressive display of field-artillery projectiles including 132 types of rifle bullets. Some of the bullets are freakishly merged with other bullets and other materials, and one bears the impression of a uniform button.

Among the projectiles exhibited is a canister composed of twenty-seven iron balls. These were fired from cannon, and the balls separated like shotgun pellets when they came out. The display gives us an idea of what it must have been like in the "hornets nest" at Shiloh during the battle.

When charging Confederate troops got within three hundred yards, Yankee batteries began firing double loads of canister. A well-drilled cannon crew could fire a six-gun battery twice per minute. In a fifteen-minute charge, as the Rebels endured, how many iron balls would one battery fire? For computations, a calculator is part of the display. Lift the lid that is marked "Answer" to find the correct number. Imagine running toward cannon firing 9,720 balls at you.

Curator Debbie Frey says, "For every two Confederate soldiers from Savannah, there was one Union soldier. This may have been a Southern state, but not everyone was for the Southern cause."

Grant was in charge of the Union army, and Shiloh, a training ground for raw recruits from the North. It became the second largest "city" in America.

The **Living History Demonstration** takes place each year on the weekend closest to April 6, the anniversary of the battle. Between five hundred and a thousand Confederate re-enactors demonstrate cannon and rifles, play Confederate music, and perform plays for the public. On Sunday a memorial service is held. This is free, except for the regular $2 fee for entrance into the park.

Savannah is the home of the Civil War Headquarters Monument, often referred to as Grant's Monument, where two cannon and a pyramid of cannonballs mark the location of General Grant's headquarters for the Battle of Shiloh. The monument is a traffic island one block west of the museum.

Queen Haley, the subject of the TV miniseries *Queen*, is buried in Savannah. She was the grandmother of Alex Haley, Jr., the author of *Roots* and *Queen*. She married Alex Haley, Sr., ferryman of the Cherry ferry, and worked at the Cherry mansion as a young woman. She and her husband are buried in the hills behind the courthouse. Queen Haley is thought to have died in the early 1930s.

There is one bed and breakfast, **The Ross House,** in Savannah. It was built in 1908 and made into a bed and breakfast in 1990. Many of the antique furnishings had been stored in the attic.

Gen. U. S. Grant commanded the Union forces and Gen. A. S. Johnston commanded the Confederate forces.

Savannah has a number of artisans and antiques shops, but for a shopper's dream, continue west from Savannah over the Tennessee River for 4 miles. There you encounter a heavy concentration of antiques shops and flea markets in the community of Crump.

Peggy Sweats Antiques is open every day except Sunday but you can make an appointment then; this is typical of the hours for the many antiques shops along this strip. The flea markets do most of their business on Friday evenings and weekends.

Just beyond Crump's antiques district, to get to Shiloh National Military Park, turn south on Highway 22 and follow the signs.

It was from Savannah that General Grant went to "work" each day before the Battle of Shiloh. For reasons unknown, Grant did not stay with his 33,000 men at Pittsburg Landing on the other side of the Tennessee River. He took a river steamer back and forth each day and felt so comfortable with the situation that he could sleep cozily in a warm house 9 miles from his troops.

Five miles north of Pittsburg Landing, General Lew Wallace, the author of *Ben-Hur*, commanded 5,000 men on the west bank. Why did Grant leave Wallace vulnerable at Crump's Landing? No answer to this behavior has been given.

Historians have surmised that Grant was off guard, in a slump, as any of us are at times. In Grant's case, the slump became costly.

Twenty miles southwest of Pittsburg Landing in Corinth, Mississippi, Confederate general Albert Sidney Johnston was encamped with 41,000 troops. Johnston had been in Corinth since March 17, 1862, when Grant took command of his troops at Pittsburg Landing.

On April 6 he surprised the Union troops. Reports indicate that the Union army, camping about 2 miles from Shiloh Church, should have been alerted to the Rebels in the woods on the evening of April 5 because hundreds of rabbits and deer ran out of the woods and through the Union lines. Johnston's army was only 2 miles from Grant's.

A small skirmish occurred that evening, and a Confederate hostage was taken for interrogation. General Sherman was given the intelligence that Johnston had moved his 41,000 troops to the area. Sherman concluded that there would be no attack while Grant had gone "home" to Savannah for the night. That evening Grant telegraphed Gen. Henry W. Halleck, stating he had "scarcely the faintest idea of attack being made upon us, but will be prepared should such a thing take place."

Early on the morning of April 6, more birds were stirring than Union soldiers. The sound may have been mistaken for a woodpecker after a tree grub at first, but not for long. Rebels poured from the woods like water through a ruptured levee and gunpowder smoke filled the air like fog.

The Yankees, many caught asleep in their tents, were disorganized and went running toward the river. Other divisions, those farthest away from the ambush, organized and withstood the coming attack. Union soldiers fled through their own standing line, and eventually the Union army yielded and pulled back.

Grant was having breakfast when the cannon's thunder reached his ears and rattled the windows in the house where he was staying. The general and his staff took the river steamer to Crump's Landing to join Lew Wallace. Grant told Wallace to head toward the fighting, but Wallace either took the wrong road or got lost. He arrived at the battlefield that evening after the fighting was over and contended he took the road he was ordered to take.

Grant was at the battle by midmorning, and Gen. D. C. Buell arrived about 1 P.M., but his troops did not get there until the fighting was over. Most of the Union army was atop the bluff over the Tennessee River with too few boats to get them across.

Intelligence came to Grant that the Confederate general Johnston had been killed. It was true: Johnston had been hit in the thigh but, having sent his surgeon back to help the wounded, bled to death because those helping him did not know how to stop the bleeding.

Without Johnston in command, leadership fell to Gen. P. G. T. Beauregard, who was not the man for the job at that time. With victory in his grasp, he ordered the troops to fall back.

That night in pouring rain, Buell's and Wallace's 25,000 fresh troops arrived. By the evening of April 7, the Confederates were retreating back to Corinth.

The Battle of Shiloh was the bloodiest to date: 13,047 Union men lost, wounded, or dead; and 10,699 Confederate losses.

In Hebrew, *Shiloh* means "Place of Peace."

When we walked the grounds of Shiloh among the thousands of graves, we felt a terrible sadness. Although the park is pretty with well-kept lawns, roads, monuments, and woods, the memory of all those who fought pervades everything in sight.

There is a 9.5-mile self-guided tour of the battlefield. Pick up a map and brochure at the visitor center; the drive takes about an hour. If you prefer more detail, rent a cassette tape for a two-hour tour. Another option is a twenty-five-minute movie called *Shiloh—Portrait of a Battle*, which traces events leading up to the battle and gives a description of the fight.

The marker as you enter the cemetery reads, "The muffled drum's sad roll has beat, the soldier's last tattoo, no more on life's parade shall meet that brave and fallen few."

There are rows and rows of graves, many with names, but many with only a number to identify the interred. As you arrive at the

You can't help feeling overwhelmed when walking among the thousands of grave markers at Shiloh.

farthermost edge of the cemetery, you come to a steep slope that goes down to the Tennessee River. The view with your back to the river is a panorama of the memorial.

Every other December, in an even year, a service called **Grand Illumination** is held at Shiloh. "A candle for every wounded, dead, and missing soldier is lit," says curator Debbie Frey. "More than 23,000 are placed throughout the park and concentrated in areas where men were wounded." It begins at dark and lasts until all who wish to drive through the park have done so, often until 11 P.M.

From the park go back to Highway 22 and turn south. At the edge of the park the road forks; bear to the left on 142 for a shortcut to Highway 57 that will take you to Pickwick Dam.

Coming from Shiloh via Highway 57, you will see **Brady's Broken Spoke** in Pickwick Dam on your left. It is open from Labor Day to Easter, Monday through Saturday, from 5 to 10 P.M.; after Easter, seven days a week. The varied menu includes blackened seafood, chicken, steaks, and wonderful desserts; Brady says they specialize in romantic candlelight dinners among a collection of antiques. Also, if you bring your cleaned fish, they will prepare them for you.

Leaving Savannah for Pickwick Dam, the shortest route—12 miles—is Highway 128. You will see **Christopher's Restaurant** and the Toll House Restaurant along this route.

At Pickwick Dam is the Tennessee River Waterway Museum, which features Indian and Civil War artifacts, photographs, drawings, and charts of the Tennessee River. Included is the history of Pickwick Dam. You can also watch boats lock through the dam.

Pickwick Lake provides great opportunities for fishing and other water sports.

This is the place to be for water sports. Pickwick Lake, above the dam, is known for great smallmouth bass fishing. Below the dam, in Kentucky Lake, there are smallmouth, sauger, and plenty of catfish. **Pickwick Landing State Park** offers you a place to stay while you enjoy the outdoors.

Jon's Pier at Pickwick Restaurant, on Highway 57 South, opens at 4 P.M. Jon offers casual dining on baby back ribs, prime rib, seafood, chicken, and steaks at moderate prices. The Harbor of Pickwick Restaurant and Lounge is a little farther down the road. Two doors away is the best barbecue in two states, at the **Rib Cage.** They're open Monday through Saturday from 10 A.M. to 9 P.M., and from 10 A.M. to 8 P.M. on Sunday. We make the Rib Cage a must-stop, even if we aren't hungry. We get the Rib Cage Sampler to go, or at least have a piece of Key lime pie.

Once you cross the state line at the Rib Cage into Mississippi, Highway 57 becomes Highway 25. Stay on Highway 25 for about 4 miles, then turn east for a look at J. P. Coleman State Park and the headwaters of the Tennessee-Tombigbee waterway. The canal forming this waterway was proposed in the last century but was abandoned when railroads became common.

The concept was revived this century, and the canal was finally built. The Tenn-Tom, as it is commonly called, is a much closer water route to the Gulf of Mexico from Tennessee. The voyage to the Ohio River to the Mississippi River and down to the Gulf via New Orleans is avoided, saving time and fuel expense. Now a boat or barge can enter the Tenn-Tom and sail to Mobile, Alabama.

Iuka, Mississippi, is our last destination before returning to the Trace. At the junction of highways 25 and 72, turn east on 72. The modern part of Iuka is on 72, but the downtown area is two blocks north. Iuka is an old yet attractive town.

East Port Inn Bed & Breakfast is at the corner of Pearl and East Port streets. It was built circa 1864.

Iuka has two restaurants: Country Cupboard and Bet's. Country Cupboard specializes in home cooking, and Bet's serves a buffet lunch.

To return to the Trace, take Highway 72 east and you will see Buzzards Roost at milepost 320.3, about 17 miles south of the Tennessee River and Colbert Ferry.

ACCOMMODATIONS ■ *Savannah/Shiloh/Crump*

Bellis Hotel and Restaurant—Rt. 4 (128 Botel Rd.), Savannah, TN 38372; 901-925-4787.

Plantation Inn—1318 Pickwick St. S., Savannah, TN 38372; 901-925-5505.

Ross House Bed & Breakfast—P.O. Box 398 (506 Main St.), Savannah, TN 38372; 901-925-3974 or 800-467-3174.

Savannah Lodge—420 Pickwick Rd., Savannah, TN 38372; 901-925-8586.

Savannah Motel—103 Adams & Main, Savannah, TN 38372; 901-925-3392.

White Elephant Bed & Breakfast Inn—Church St., Savannah, TN 38372; 615-331-5244.

ATTRACTIONS ■ *Savannah/Shiloh/Crump*

Shiloh National Military Park —Rt. 1 , Box 9, Shiloh, TN 38376; 901-689-5696 or 901-689-527; $2 Admission; Daily; Summer, 8 A.M.–6 P.M.; Other seasons, 8 A.M.–5 P.M.

Tennessee River Museum—Savannah, TN 38372: 800-552-FUNN; Admission, $2 (under 16 and over 62 free); Mon.–Fri,. 9 A.M.–5 P.M.; Sat., 10 A.M.–5 P.M.; Sun., 1–5 P.M.

⚜ RESTAURANTS ▪ *Savannah/Shiloh/Crump*

The Back Porch—TN Hwy. 22, Shiloh, TN 38376; 901-689-5701. Daily,
    10 A.M.–10 P.M.
Christopher's Restaurant—1012 Pickwick Rd., Savannah, TN 38372; 901-
    925-9285; Daily, 5 A.M.–10 P.M.
D&D Family Steak House—18970 Hwy. 69 S., Savannah, TN 38372; 901-
    925-6199; Sun.–Thurs., 6 A.M.–9 P.M.; Fri.–Sat., 6 A.M.–10 P.M.

⚜ SHOPPING ▪ *Savannah/Shiloh/Crump*

The BookCase—Main St., Savannah, TN 38372; 901-925-READ.
Henry D. Strickland—1319 Church St., Savannah, TN 38372; 901-
    925-2911.
Peggy Sweat's Antiques—Hwy. 64, Crump, TN 38327; 901-632-1531.
Savannah's Art Gallery—112 Williams St., Savannah, TN 38372; 901-
    925-7529.
Shaw's Antiques—2308 Wayne Rd., Savannah, TN 38372; 901-925-7147.

⚜ SPECIAL EVENTS ▪ *Savannah/Shiloh/Crump*

April: Living History Demonstration—Contact Hardin County Chamber
    of Commerce.
July: Savannah River City Bluegrass Festival—Music and fireworks; Contact
    Hardin County Chamber of Commerce.
December: Grand Illumination—Every other December; Contact Superin-
    tendent, Shiloh National Military Park, Rt. 1, Box 9, Shiloh, TN
    38376; 901-689-5696.

⚜ FOR MORE INFORMATION
▪ *Savannah/Shiloh*

Hardin County Chamber of Commerce—507 Main St., Savannah, TN 38372;
    901-925-2363 or 800-552-FUNN.
Shiloh National Military Park—Rt. 1, Box 9, Shiloh, TN 38376; 901-
    689-5696 or 901-689-5275.

✍ ACCOMMODATIONS ▪ *Pickwick Dam*

Pickwick Landing State Park—Hwy. 57, Pickwick Dam, TN 38365; 901-689-3135.

✍ RESTAURANTS ▪ *Pickwick Dam*

Brady's Broken Spoke—Drawer 304 (Hwy. 57 W. 1 mile west of dam), Pickwick Dam, TN 38365; 901-689-3487.
Catfish Hotel—TN Hwy. 22, Pickwick Dam, TN 38365; 901-689-3327; Tues.–Sat., 11 A.M.–10 P.M.; Sun., 11 A.M.–9 P.M.
Jon's Pier at Pickwick—Hwy. 57 S., Pickwick Dam, TN 38365; 901-689-3575.
The Rib Cage—Hwy. 57 (at state line), Pickwick Dam, TN 38365; 901-689-3637.

✍ SHOPPING ▪ *Pickwick Dam*

The Glass Shade—11220 Hwy. 57, Pickwick Dam, TN 38365; 901-689-5566.
Fay's Odds and Ends—Hwy. 57 W., Pickwick Dam, TN 38365; 901-689-3993.

✍ ACCOMMODATIONS ▪ *Iuka*

East Port Inn Bed & Breakfast—100 S. Pearl, Iuka, MS 38852; 601-423-2511.

✍ RESTAURANTS ▪ *Iuka*

Bet's Family Restaurant—708 E. Quitman, Iuka, MS 38852; 601-423-9006; Mon.–Fri., 5:30 A.M.–2 P.M.
Country Cupboard—709 E. East Port, Iuka, MS 38852; 601-423-2325; Mon.–Fri., 6:30 A.M.–9 P.M.; Sat., 6:30 A.M.–6 P.M.; Sun., 7 A.M.–4 P.M.

✍ FOR MORE INFORMATION ▪ *Iuka*

Iuka Chamber of Commerce—117 East Port St., Iuka, MS 38852; 601-424-0000.

7 *Alabama: Sampling the Shoals*

There are four approaches to Florence from the Natchez Trace Parkway: Highway 13 out of Tennessee, which becomes 17 in Alabama; 157 immediately south of the Tennessee-Alabama line; Highway 20; and Highway 14. Highway 72 south of the Tennessee River takes you to Tuscumbia.

Alabama is named for the Alibamu, a tribe of Creek Indians. The Shoals area of northwest Alabama consists of Florence in Lauderdale County, and Muscle Shoals, Sheffield, and Tuscumbia in Colbert County. With a combined population of around 65,000, this is the largest population center along the Alabama corridor of the Trace. The cities are divided by the Tennessee River. Florence is north of the river, and the other three communities are to the south, just across the Tennessee River Bridge.

The Muscle Shoals area was well known due to the treacherous shoals, which reputedly extended nearly 30 miles before the damming of the Tennessee River in 1916. According to William E. Beard in *Nashville, The Home of the History Makers,* notes made by the leader of the 1780 expedition to settle the area that is now Nashville said the swift shoals "had a dreadful appearance . . . the water made a terrible roaring, which could be heard at some distance . . . the current running in every possible direction." John Donelson, a founder of Nashville and leader of the flatboat flotilla, managed to negotiate the shoals in about three hours without serious mishap.

Dismals Canyon has two of the largest hemlock trees in the South.

During the western expansion by Americans in the early 1800s, contentious Chickasaw, Cherokee, and Creek occupied the area. The territory that is now north Alabama was part of the Illinois country, which was ceded to the United States by England in the 1783 Treaty of Paris.

Colbert County was named for Chickasaw chief George Colbert, who ran the ferry across the Tennessee River on the Old Natchez Trace. The county seat, Tuscumbia, was established around 1817 near the Chickasaw village Occocoposa ("cold water") and incorporated as the town of Cold Water in 1820. In 1822 the name was changed to honor the Indian chief Tash-ka-Ambi ("warrior who kills"); a historic marker in Spring Park on Main Street in Tuscumbia commemorates this event.

Lauderdale County was named after Col. James Lauderdale, a Tennessean who was killed while fighting the British on December 23, 1814, near New Orleans.

The founders of the Cypress Land Company purchased 5,500 acres on the Tennessee River at the lower end of the Muscle Shoals. In 1818 a young Italian engineer named Ferdinand Sannoner was hired to lay out a city and was allowed to name it in honor of his birthplace—Florence, Italy.

During the Civil War several skirmishes took place in this area and General Hood's army camped here in the fall of 1864 before proceeding to the deadly encounter that awaited them at the Battle of Franklin in late November.

In the 1900s the Shoals area was to undergo a transformation as speculators descended on the community. As a result of the National Defense Act of 1916, the world's largest munitions plant and Wilson Dam were constructed here.

Henry Ford and President Franklin Roosevelt came to inspect the site. Ford envisioned a 75-mile strip along the river where people would spend half their time in manufacturing and half the production of their own food. The Shoals area offered the unique combination of unlimited hydroelectric power and a location in the heart of the South's richest mineral deposits. Within a 50-mile radius of Florence, more than forty minerals used in manufacturing are found, including asphalt rock, bauxite, coal, dolomite, red hematite, iron, nitrates, and phosphates.

Nitrates could be used for munitions during times of war and for fertilizer in times of peace. Newspaper headlines from the *Muscle Shoals Bulletin*, June 1933, read: "Greatest Development in the World Begins at Shoals," "Giant Nitrate Plants Here Going into Quick Operation," and "Real Estate Values Going Up Steadily." The articles go on to say that millions were to be spent on a new industrial city here. Remnants of "Ford City" are hidden beneath overgrown lawns that cover sidewalks installed by speculators who were looking for a big boom that never materialized.

Roosevelt planned the development of the entire rich Tennessee Valley on a gigantic scale that would be one of the "greatest achievements in American history." Part of the great development Roosevelt envisioned became the Tennessee Valley Authority in 1933. The legacy of Wilson and Pickwick lakes provides abundant opportunities for outdoor recreation in the area today as well as the hydroelectric power that was foreseen.

Highway 157, in north Florence, leads you past the **1889 Wood Avenue Bed and Breakfast,** which is on the National Register of Historic Places. Owner Albern Greeley greeted us with delicious minted lemonade and homemade pound cake while we settled in at the Queen Anne mansion with its fourteen-foot ceilings and octagonal and square towers. The rooms at the inn all have private baths.

The Rose Room can be used as a four-room suite with a private dining room, where you can sample Mrs. Greeley's wonderful breakfast crêpes, southern-style scrambled eggs with cheese and onions, freshly squeezed orange juice, and a fresh pot of coffee. Reservations are recommended about one month in advance unless you're coming during the fall color season—then you'd better call sooner. The inn is located at 658 North Wood Avenue.

Highway 13 (while in Tennessee), which turns into Highway 17 in Alabama, will also take you to Florence, passing **Taylor's Treasures Antique Shop** just before entering town. This road ends in a somewhat challenging five-points intersection north of the downtown area.

Generally, the preferred route is Highway 20 from the Trace. It takes you past **McFarland Park,** which is operated by the city of Florence on the Tennessee River and which offers campgrounds, boat launches, picnic areas, and a golf course just a few blocks south of downtown Florence.

The road splits as you enter the park. A turn to the right leads you past the park rangers' office and the entrance to the golf course, a small beach, grassy knolls along the river with lots of picnic tables, a covered picnic pavilion, and the campground to the far right. The campground has about forty RV sites that offer electric hookups; a concrete-block bathhouse includes a washer and dryer. All of the campsites are lightly shaded by tall pine trees and close to the water, and there's an abundance of bank fishing. The park also offers an eighteen-hole golf course with clubs and carts for rent. Campground fees are reasonable; there's a fourteen-day limit; first come, first served.

Big Daddy's Barbeque is on the right near the entrance to the park, if lunch is next on your agenda. Children may enjoy a chance to cool off at Funland next door, which is open daily in season. The water slide is half-price from 6 to 10 P.M. There's also a small go-cart track, miniature golf, picnic tables, and a kiddie water slide.

For home-style cooking visit Campbell's Restaurant at 230 East Tennessee.

Begin your sightseeing at the **Indian Mound and Museum,** at South Court Street, just a few blocks east of McFarland Park. The small museum has trade pipes, a good collection of arrowheads, pottery including oil vessels and cooking pots, stone beads, celts, awls, and scrapers.

One display explains that the Great Busk was the new year celebration of the Creek Indians. The eight-day ceremony started in midsummer. Museum hours are 10 A.M.–4 P.M., Tuesday-Saturday, and admission is charged.

The mound across the street was built by Indians of the Mississippian culture about A.D. 1200–1500. Steps lead up to the top of the highest domiciliary mound in the Tennessee Valley, 42 feet high and 180 feet wide at its base. The mound, which once supported a temple dedicated to the sun god, was originally encircled by the river

This forty-two-foot high mound was built by Mississippian Indians A.D. 1200–1500.

The Rosenbaum House in Florence, designed by Frank Lloyd Wright, is open to the public by reservation.

and an earthen wall twelve to fifteen feet high, and there were villages and cultivated fields nearby. In the 1830s the historic Indians of this area were among those forced to leave their homes in the East and move along the Trail of Tears to the area known as the Oklahoma Indian Territory.

Although the Stanley and Mildred **Rosenbaum House,** at 601 Riverview Drive, appears quite modern, it is a National Historic Property because it is the oldest owner-occupied Frank Lloyd Wright house in the United States.

The Rosenbaums were newlyweds in their twenties when they proposed that Mr. Wright, who was seventy-two at the time, build a house for them. Mrs. Rosenbaum laughingly recalls that people would walk through on the weekend and think there were mighty peculiar goings-on. The house is organic in that it is made of natural materials—in this case, plain cypress wood covered with neither paint nor plaster, rough brick made in Athens or Decatur, glass, and concrete. It also adheres to the contours of the two-acre site and is built on a grid of two feet by four feet. This dimension repeats itself throughout the house, from the four-foot concrete grids on the patio to the double two-foot door units.

Mrs. Mildred Rosenbaum conducts tours in her home, the oldest owner-occupied Frank Lloyd Wright house in the United States.

The site for each room was leveled and gravel laid on the ground. In the gravel the builders laid a three-inch-diameter wrought-iron pipe two feet on center, which was later covered with concrete to provide radiant heat. As the brick for the fireplaces went up, steel was laid to form the roof. It was especially difficult for visitors to the site to understand that the multilevel cantilevered roof actually supported itself from the fireplace foundations at the core of the house. The walls, doors, and windows went in last, and every room had access to the outside, so there were many doors and windows.

The original structure was completed in 1940 and was one of twenty-six Usonian houses built in the United States. These homes were intended to be practical works of art that the average American family could afford. When the Rosenbaums first built the house, they had no furniture. They owned a few books, a few records, a piano, and wedding presents, so Frank Lloyd Wright came in and designed all their furniture. New York City's Museum of Modern Art sent photographers to take pictures as soon as they moved in.

Two new wings were completed in 1948 to accommodate the Rosenbaums' growing family. In 1967 they called on Mr. Wright's architectural firm, which sent someone to plan a restoration.

The house celebrated its fiftieth birthday in 1989, and Mrs. Rosenbaum, a widow since 1983, held an open house to celebrate. The challenge of maintaining a structure like this had caused her to consider selling the house; she had even decided that she would live in Europe to compensate herself for not being able to live in the house any longer. But on the day of the open house, she decided that she couldn't give it up, and by the end of the day, more than eight hundred people had filed through the house following a lecture in the auditorium next door. Out of her decision to stay, the Frank Lloyd Wright-Rosenbaum House Foundation was formed and came to the rescue.

As you listen to Mrs. Rosenbaum, it is apparent that more than fifty years ago she began a love affair with this home that has stood the test of time.

If you have any interest in architecture, be sure to visit her, for we believe there is no experience equal to having her explain the construction process and what it was like to raise her family in this gracious home while you sit on a Frank Lloyd Wright chair or sofa. The house is open for tours daily, but reservations are required and admission is charged.

The **W. C. Handy Home and Museum,** on 620 West College Street, is operated by the city of Florence. It's open Tuesday through Saturday, 10 A.M. to 4 P.M., and admission is charged. W. C. Handy is considered the Father of the Blues because he was the first man to write the blues down on paper.

Handy was born here in a log cabin on November 16, 1873. As a young boy, he bought a guitar with hard-earned savings, but his family considered a career in music disreputable. When he brought the instrument home, his mother stood frozen and his father cried, "The devil's plaything! Take it back to where you got it!" He returned the guitar, trading it for a *Webster's Dictionary* as ordered by his minister father, but continued to study music in Florence's black public school with Y. A. Wallace, a graduate of Fisk University. At nineteen, Handy left his home for Birmingham to take the teachers' exam, but after passing the exam, he decided a teacher's pay was too low and went to work at the Birmingham Howard and Harrison Pipeworks for $1.85 a day. He joined a jazz quartet and traveled to the Chicago World's

W. C. Handy, Father of the Blues.

The birthplace of W. C. Handy, now a museum.

W. C. Handy Museum contains his piano, portraits, compositions, recordings, and music memorabilia.

Fair, only to discover the fair had been postponed. Many hard years of performing on the road followed. Although he received the inspiration for one of his biggest hits while he was unemployed and forced to sleep on a cobblestone levee by the riverfront in St. Louis, he would later travel the world as the Father of the Blues.

He eventually composed more than 150 sacred and blues songs, including "Memphis," "Saint Louis Blues," and "Beale Street Blues," and he wrote three books. The piano on which he composed the "Saint Louis Blues" and his trumpet are in the museum, along with many personal papers and a wealth of memorabilia.

Handy endured two bouts of blindness. The second, which became permanent, occurred on October 28, 1943, and was caused by a fall in a New York subway that resulted in a skull fracture. He died on March 28, 1958, at the age of eighty-four.

The **W. C. Handy Music Festival** is held in his honor in early August each year and features toe-tapping celebrations of his musical heritage, a barbecue cookoff, spirituals in his Florence church, and a strutting street parade.

The **Kennedy-Douglas Center for the Arts,** at 217 East Tuscaloosa, is an arts complex consisting of Georgian and Victorian structures and is listed on the National Register of Historic Places. Exhibits change year-round and are free to the public. The center sponsors the Arts Alive juried arts and crafts festival every April in Wilson Park, just across the street. More than one hundred artists and craftspersons exhibit, and entertainment ranging from jazz to bluegrass is offered.

The Renaissance Faire is also held here each fall. Authentic costumes, arts and crafts, and food from the twelfth through the sixteenth centuries are represented. Wilson Park has park benches that invite passersby to stop and enjoy the lovely fountain at the corner of Seminary and Wood; multicolored lights are especially pretty in the evening. Admission and parking are free.

The next point of interest is a few blocks away at 203 Hermitage Drive. The **Pope's Tavern Museum** is one of the oldest structures in Florence. The present structure was built in 1830 by Leroy Pope as a stagecoach stop, tavern, and inn on the military road built by Andrew Jackson from New Orleans to Florence during the War of 1812.

Constructed in 1830, Pope's Tavern served as an inn on the military road built by Andrew Jackson.

Evidence suggests that an earlier structure occupied the same site. The building was later used as a hospital by both Union and Confederate soldiers following a skirmish on the streets of Florence; they were treated by local doctors and nursed by local women. Later, wounded were treated from the battles of Elk River, Franklin, Fort Henry, Fort Donelson, and even larger numbers after the Battle of Shiloh.

In 1874 it was purchased for a residence by Felix Lambeth, whose descendants owned it until 1965, when it was purchased and restored by public donations and city funds. Admission is charged.

Pope's Tavern hosts the annual **Frontier Day Celebration** each June; it features arts and crafts, storytelling, and dulcimer music.

Before you leave downtown Florence, you should consider stopping for a fine dinner at **Dale's,** 1001 Mitchell Boulevard. Dale's offers delicious steaks with special house seasoning, as well as salads, seafood, and chicken selections. Located at the foot of the Florence side of the bridge, it was a little tricky to find the first time but was well worth the effort.

The 350-foot Renaissance Tower houses exhibits by the Tennessee Valley Authority, the Alabama Shoals Aquarium, and the rooftop Renaissance Grill.

Turn east on Union or follow the signs for **Wilson Dam** to visit the **Renaissance Tower.** Admission to the tower is free. On the ground floor are informative and interesting exhibits by the Tennessee Valley Authority.

The second floor houses the four-thousand-square-foot Alabama Shoals Aquarium, recently renovated and revitalized with new fish and exhibits, some designed for children to touch.

The tower, which rises 350 feet from the ground, offers fantastic 40-mile views of the Tennessee River and Wilson and Pickwick lakes as you dine in the **Renaissance Grill,** on the top floor. Their menu includes a variety of delicious specialty sandwiches and salads, steaks, seafood, and pasta.

Several alternative camping sites are found near Wilson Dam. Turn left at the intersection of South Cox Creek Parkway and look for signs on your right to the entrance to Florence's second campground at Veterans Memorial Park. You'll pass tennis courts, playgrounds, ball fields, picnic tables, and a covered picnic pavilion. There's a wheelchair-accessible bathroom by the park. Amenities include a bathhouse and a disc (Frisbee) golf course. This multiple-use park is not a riverfront location.

A right turn at the intersection of South Cox Creek Parkway will take you to Wilson Dam. Here you can observe a barge as it goes through the locks. The change in water level is one hundred feet. The original lock was at one time the tallest in the country. You can walk along the locks for a better view of the river and dam. On the south end of the locks, during low water you can see the only remnants of the Muscle Shoals.

Across the dam you'll find a visitor center with exhibits; a tour of the dam is also offered. You'll learn that there's enough concrete here to pave a two-foot sidewalk completely around the world. Construction was initiated by the U.S. Army in 1918 for use in World War I and was completed in 1925. At its peak, the massive construction project involved more than 18,000 workers. The dam was acquired by the Tennessee Valley Authority in 1933.

The 2,400-acre TVA Wilson Dam/Muscle Shoals reservation offers 10 miles of hiking trails that accent history, energy and environmental awareness, physical fitness, natural history, and photography. Picnickers and campers will be especially interested in the Upper and Lower Rockpile recreation areas below the dam, off Highway 133 (see chapter 20).

For those choosing to visit this site, Highway 133 continues to Tuscumbia.

Several restaurants, motels, and antiques malls in Florence are within 2 miles of the intersection of Cox's Creek Parkway and Florence Boulevard, also known as Highway 72 East. The **Estates Antique Mall** had silver, stained glass, European furniture, and lamps. **Southern Antique Mall** featured collectibles that included an old wagon wheel, a Hoosier kitchen cabinet, Depression glass, and an ice-cream-parlor set. **Bellemeade Antique Mall** offered an Eastlake sofa set, beds, pier mirrors, and antique toys. Several other shops are on your way back to Florence, including Granny's Attic, Victorian Rose Antiques (specializing in dolls, dollhouses, and collectible plates), Antique Mall of Florence, and the Antique Gallery. Most are open Monday through Saturday, 10 A.M.–5 P.M., Sunday, 1–5 P.M.

Highway 72 West takes you to Court Street downtown and eventually to Tuscumbia, across the O'Neal Bridge.

Ivy Green, the family home of Capt. Arthur M. and Kate Adams Keller, was built in 1820 and was the second house erected in Tuscumbia. America's "First Lady of Courage," Helen Adams Keller, was born here on June 27, 1880. The illness that struck Helen at only eighteen months of age left her blind and deaf and her doting parents grief-stricken. Helen's father, an attorney and publisher of the local newspaper, used his extensive contacts to try to find a cure for his daughter, but without success. Helen's mother also refused to admit defeat, and when the child was six her parents took her to see Dr. Alexander Graham Bell.

As a result of this visit, Anne Mansfield Sullivan arrived in Tuscumbia on March 3, 1887, to assume her first teaching assignment. Anne was twenty years old; she stayed with Helen for forty-nine years.

The pump where Helen learned the meaning of the word "water" is just behind the house. Anne had struggled to reveal the

Ivy Green was the home of Helen
Keller when illness left her deaf and
blind at the age of eighteen months.

mystery of language to seven-year-old Helen by spelling the word
W-A-T-E-R into her hand as water flowed over the other hand.
That one word opened up the whole world to her. A year later,
Anne had taught her the manual alphabet, how to read, and how
to write by means of a special wooden groove board using a ruler as
a guide.

When Helen was nine years old, she and Anne went to the
Perkins Institute for further education. There she took voice training
to learn to speak. Helen Keller graduated cum laude in 1904 from
Radcliffe College in Cambridge, Massachusetts.

Later Anne fell in love and married John Macy, who was helping
Helen write her autobiography. The couple lived together a few years,
then separated, but they never divorced. Helen, who lived with them,
had several boyfriends. Eventually she fell in love and made plans to
marry, but her family was so protective of her that she was dissuaded
from doing so. She never married.

Helen worked for the American Federation for the Blind until
she was eighty years old. She raised millions of dollars, started
schools all over the world, and is responsible for the development of
"talking books" for the blind. In later years she was named History's
Most Remarkable Woman. She died June 1, 1968.

The little cottage where Helen and Anne stayed is the spot where

Helen was actually born (her parents had decided to move out there for privacy). In addition to Helen's birthplace and her grandparents' home, Ivy Green has beautiful grounds, with handicapped-accessible concrete paths, garden benches for resting, and a large stage behind the house for an outdoor drama that tells Helen's story.

Ivy Green has beautiful grounds that provide the setting for the outdoor drama *The Miracle Worker.*

There was a fire here in 1972, but all the furniture was removed safely. Eighty-five percent of the furnishings are from the Keller family. Hours for tours of the house and grounds are Monday–Saturday, 8:30 A.M.–4 P.M., Sunday, 1–4 P.M. The outdoor drama is scheduled for evenings in season. Be sure to take insect repellent so you can enjoy the drama production without being attacked by winged hoards in the summertime. Admission is charged.

The **Alabama Music Hall of Fame,** on Highway 72 West, recognizes Alabama musicians who have influenced the course of music history. The story of the Muscle Shoals recording industry is also told. At one time about eight recording studios were active in the Shoals area. During the '60s and '70s, Muscle Shoals was known as the "Hit Recording Capital of the World."

The Alabama Country Music Hall of Fame's executive director, David Johnson, started out as a disc jockey in Muscle Shoals at sixteen and saw the recording industry here blossom firsthand. Visitors will learn about Florence Alabama Music Enterprises (FAME), Quinvy, and other recording companies as well as about the various artists who recorded in Muscle Shoals. (Did you know, for instance, that Percy Sledge was an orderly at Colbert County Hospital when he recorded "When a Man Loves a Woman"?)

The Hall of Fame has such music memorabilia as the band Alabama's tour bus and Elvis Presley's original contract with Sun Records (Elvis was so young his dad had to cosign the contract with him). There are sections devoted to rock-and-roll, country, gospel, soul, and rhythm and blues. We were surprised to see more than five hundred Alabama artists represented, ranging from Hank Williams and Nat King Cole to Bobby Goldsboro and Jim Nabors.

Before you leave be sure to record your own hit record in the recording studio. You can put on a headset and sing along with a favorite song. When the recording is complete, only your voice

Alabama Music Hall of Fame show-cases talented Alabama musicians.

remains on the soundtrack. The gift shop has a collection of hats, mugs, and T-shirts. The Alabama Music Hall of Fame is open daily. Admission is charged.

The hall of fame hosts an annual musical event called Harvest Jam, as well as celebrity golf and fishing tournaments. The band Shenandoah supports Harvest Jam each year and the proceeds are donated to nonprofit organizations in the region.

On your way back to town, come down Main Street and stop at the **Painted Lady Cafe** for lunch or dinner.

The **Holiday Inn,** on Hatch Boulevard, has an outdoor pool, exercise room, and whirlpool, if you decide to spend the night on the south side of the river.

Chuck E. Cheese, next to the Holiday Inn in Sheffield, is a great place to feed the kids and let them run off some energy. The menu includes pizza, salad bar, breadsticks, beverages, and desserts. If you've never been to a Chuck E. Cheese, prepare for an environment perfectly suited for children: sort of an indoor amusement park/arcade/pizza place.

Children are encouraged to run around the restaurant, but sections are geared toward toddlers, grammar-school age, and older children. Some are educational or memory games, others are pure creations of light and noise. The kids are given stickers to wear that identify their families, so they can't wander too far away from Mom and Dad or leave the restaurant unescorted.

There are more than twenty-five games, including a merry-go-round, video games, slides, and ropes to slide down. The kids will receive free tokens for every $2 you spend for food, or you can use quarters to operate the machines. Children play the games and win tickets that can be cashed in for prizes. If games don't keep them busy, the dining room has three stages where mechanical and live characters perform shows. We were amazed at how young we felt watching all the youthful activity and excitement.

Outdoor enthusiasts will be interested in our next stop. Leave Tuscumbia south on Highway 43, go through Russellville for about 10 miles, and look for signs to **Dismals Canyon.** This area is designated a Registered National Landmark. The Dismals Canyon is believed to have been formed by a glacier that long ago created a cave. As the earth shifted over the centuries, the cave collapsed, leaving behind this canyon and unusual flora and fauna apparently brought in with the glacier and deposited when the ice receded at the end of the Ice Age.

Tiny, translucent worms called Dismalites live in the canyon and are visible only at night, due to photochemoluminescence. Believed to be unique to this area, Australia, and China, they grow on moss and at night look like hundreds of soft, blinking greenish lights.

Owners Clint and Beverly Franklin claim their canyon has no mosquitoes, flies, or poison oak and remains a reliable fourteen degrees cooler than the ambient temperature on top of the mountain by the campground, even during the hottest July and August days.

We can tell you that it's a beautiful spot to visit. As you begin the steep decline into the verdant canyon, the feeling of entering another world sweeps over you. It's not hard to visualize Paleolithic Indians using the canyon. You can only imagine how the Choctaw must have

This waterfall is the entrance to
Dismals Canyon, one of the most
exotic locales in the state.

felt as they were held here by troops of Andrew Jackson for almost
three weeks in preparation for embarking on the Trail of Tears.

Notorious outlaws from the nearby Natchez Trace also used the
cave. According to local legend, Aaron Burr used the canyon as a
hideout after killing Alexander Hamilton in their famous duel.

A slender staircase cut from solid stone climbs up sixty feet to
Pulpit Rock and on to Phantom Falls, which rushes loudly over dry
rock (it's only an echo). More than three hundred plant species have
been identified by botanists. A trail guide is available for hikers.
There are 1½ miles of walking trails. You will want to experience this
other world.

Bear Creek float trips are also offered. Canoes are put in at Mill
Creek in the morning and taken out at Rock Quarry for a half-day

run (Class I–IV waters). You have to portage one fall, Lower Factory Falls. If you are willing to risk your own canoe—and your life— they'll take you up to Highway 5 for a run on some Class VI rapids.

In the afternoon you go from Rock Quarry to Military Bridge on what is essentially a float trip (Class I–II waters). There are lots of scenic, secluded beaches and places to swim along the way.

Bear Creek is a TVA dam-control project: the water starts at 6 on Friday afternoon and stops on Sunday at 10 P.M., from Memorial Day to Labor Day. Oftentimes the release continues until October.

A camp store offers candy, gum, soft drinks, marshmallows to roast, cookies, chips, toothpaste, deodorant, shampoo, and so on. There is currently one primitive bunkhouse and several primitive campsites. The two proposed cabins will have two bedrooms, two double bunkbeds in one room and a double bed in the other, fire- places in the living rooms, kitchens, and baths. There are several rock overhangs that allow primitive camping before you descend into the canyon.

The Bear Creek Watershed comprises four lakes: Little Bear, Big Bear, Upper Bear, and Cedar Creek. They all offer fishing, boating, water skiing, and camping. The watershed area also offers excellent

Tishomingo State Park is the first park on the Trace after leaving Alabama offering camping, fishing, and a daily 8-mile canoe float trip down Bear Creek from April to mid-October.

whitewater canoeing. Three of the four lakes are west of the dismals; the fourth lies to the east.

From Bear Creek Development Headquarters on Little Bear Creek, about 12 miles west of Dismals Canyon, it's a short trip back to the Trace via Highway 24 to Red Bay, then 366 to 25, which intersects with the parkway.

If these outdoor activities do not interest you, return to the Natchez Trace Parkway via Highway 72 West from Tuscumbia. On your way you'll pass a sign to the most unusual graveyard we've encountered in our travels: the Coon Dog Graveyard, about 12 miles off Highway 72, created as the final resting place for a beloved coon dog in 1937. Since that time more than one hundred dogs have joined "Troop," and an annual celebration is held in the graveyard each Labor Day. At other times, the remote location is a place of peaceful solitude.

The tiny community of Cherokee contains a bed and breakfast, a restaurant, and an antiques shop. The restaurant is called the **Wooden Nickle** and serves breakfast, a tasty blueplate lunch special, and dinner daily.

The **Easterwood Bed and Breakfast Inn** offers visitors accommodations in four guest rooms, each with private bath and TV. The original house was burned during the Civil War and rebuilt at the turn of the century. Only 3 miles off the Trace, it is an especially good stop for bicyclists. Hosts Nancy and Bill Giles are certain to make guests feel at home in this inn filled with antiques and surrounded by twelve peaceful acres.

ACCOMMODATIONS

Holiday Inn—4900 Hatch Blvd., Sheffield, AL 35660; 205-381-4710 or 800-HOLIDAY.

Easterwood Bed & Breakfast—200 Easterwood St., Cherokee, AL 35616; 205-359-4688; 3 miles east of the Trace via Hwy. 72.

Wood Avenue Inn—658 N. Wood Ave., Florence, AL 35630; 205-766-8441.

ATTRACTIONS

Alabama Music Hall of Fame—Hwy. 72 W., Tuscumbia, AL 35674; 205-381-4417.

Dismals Canyon—Rt. 3, Box 281, Phil Campbell, AL 35581; 205-993-4559 or 800-808-7998.

Indian Mound and Museum—S. Court St., Florence, AL 36730; 205-760-6427.

Ivy Green—300 W. Commons, Tuscumbia, AL 35674; 205-383-4066

Kennedy-Douglas Center—217 E. Tuscaloosa St., Florence, AL 36730; 205-760-6379.

McFarland Park—On Pickwick Lake, turn south off Coffee Dr.; 205-760-6416.

Pope's Tavern—203 Heritage Dr., Florence, AL 35630; 205-760-6439.

Renaissance Tower—One Hightower Pl., Florence, AL 35630; 205-764-5900.

Rosenbaum House—601 Riverview Dr., Florence, AL 35630; 205-764-5274.

W. C. Handy Home and Museum—620 W. College St., Florence, AL 35630; 205-760-6434.

Wilson Lock & Dam—Wilson Dam Hwy.; 205-386-2601.

RESTAURANTS

Big Daddy's Barbeque—305 Coffee Rd., Florence, AL 35630: 205-760-9935.

Campbell's Restaurant—230 E. Tennessee, Florence, AL; 205-764-1213.

Chuck E. Cheese—4700 Hatch Blvd., Sheffield, AL 35660; 205-383-3836.

Dale's—1001 Mitchell Blvd., Florence, AL; 205-766-4961.

Painted Lady Cafe—104 S. Main St., Tuscumbia, AL 35674; 205-389-8256.

Renaissance Grill—P.O. Box 246 (One Hightower Pl.), Florence, AL 35631; 205-718-0092.

Wooden Nickle—Cherokee, AL 35616; 205-359-4225.

SHOPPING

Anderson Bookland—114 N. Court St., Florence, AL 35630; 205-766-1163.

Bellemeade Antique Mall—Hwy. 72 E., Florence, AL 35630; 205-757-1050.

Estate Antique Mall—Hwy. 72, Florence, AL 35630; 205-757-9941.

Taylor's Treasures—Chisholm Hwy at Jacksonburg Rd., Florence, AL 35630; 205-764-7172.

Southern Antique Mall—3801 Florence Blvd., Florence, AL 35630; 205-757-8288.

Red House Books—2105 Woodward Ave., Muscle Shoals, AL 35661; 205-383-3810.

Tuscumbia Treasures—104 W. 6th St., Tuscumbia, AL 35674; 205-381-6880.

❧ SPECIAL EVENTS

Alabama Indian Heritage—Biannual traditional dances, games, arts and crafts in McFarland Park; 205-760-6379.

April: Arts Alive—Last weekend in April; Florence, AL; 205-760-6379.

May: Recall La Grange—Tuscumbia Civil War re-enactment; 205-383-0783.

June: Frontier Day—First weekend in June at Pope's Tavern, 203 Heritage Dr., Florence, AL 35630; 205-760-6439.

June–July: The Miracle Worker—300 W. Commons, Tuscumbia, AL 35674; 205-383-4066; Mid-June through July.

August: W. C. Handy Music Festival—First week in Aug.; 205-766-7642.

October: Renaissance Faire—Fourth weekend in Oct.; 205-764-4661.

❧ FOR MORE INFORMATION

Alabama Mountain Lakes Association—P.O. Box 1075, Mooresville, AL 35649; 205-350-3500 or 800-648-5381.

Chamber of Commerce of the Shoals—104 S. Pine St., Florence, AL 35630; 205-764-4661, FAX 205-766-9017.

Colbert County Tourism & Convention Bureau—P.O. Box 440, Tuscumbia, AL 35674; 205-383-0783 or 800-344-0783, FAX 205-383-2080; Ask for historic tour brochure.

Heritage Preservation—P.O. Box 2836, Florence, AL 35631; Ask for walking tour brochure of Florence.

8 *Tupelo: The Place to Go*

Of the five exits from the Trace into Tupelo, the ones that lead directly downtown are the McCullough Blvd. and Main Street exits.

Legend tells us the ancestors of the Chickasaw Indians migrated from the land of the setting sun in the Far West many years ago. Two brothers, Shataw and Chickasaw, led their people east to the Land of Life. The people carried with them a long pole, which they placed in the ground each night. When the sun rose in the morning, they followed the direction of the leaning pole. When the pole was found upright, they knew they'd reached Naniwaya, "the hill of origins."

At Naniwaya, the brothers parted, forming two distinct tribes with claims to their own territories. Shataw was the first chief of the Choctaw, and Chickasaw was the first chief of the Chickasaw. Although Line Creek, approximately 45 miles south of Tupelo, was the southern boundary of the Chickasaw Nation, the area around present-day Tupelo, known as the Chickasaw Old Fields, was the heart of the Chickasaw Nation. More than two thousand Chickasaw are believed to have lived at the Chickasaw Village site, along the western edge of Tupelo.

In 1541 Hernando de Soto wintered in this area. When his demands became intolerable, the Chickasaw attacked his army, killing fifty men. Although a second attack was later repulsed by de Soto, he soon left the area rather than contend with the fierce warriors of the mighty Chickasaw Nation.

Tupelo is the birthplace of Elvis Presley, the King of Rock-and-Roll.

Chickasaw village near Tupelo shows the layout of an Indian village.

According to Jonathan Daniels in *The Devil's Backbone*, the French attempted to move against the Chickasaw in 1736. The first French contingent was thoroughly overcome along Pontotoc Ridge, and its leader and twenty of his soldiers burned at the stake by the Chickasaw. The second French contingent was met at the Battle of Ackia and sent fleeing to the safety of Mobile.

By the early 1800s, the Chickasaw were negotiating with the U.S. government, utilizing Indian agents as intermediaries to negotiate allowing stands, or inns, to be placed at 20-mile intervals along the Natchez Trace through Chickasaw lands. These agents became powerful men as negotiations involving millions of acres of land passed through them. The increasing pressures of westward settlement led to a series of treaties and by 1832 the Chickasaw had ceded the last of their ancient homeland and were moved west to Oklahoma.

The area around Tupelo was obtained from the Chickasaw by the Treaty of Pontotoc in 1832. The community was originally named Harrisburg in honor of an early settler, Judge W. R. Harris. In 1859 the tracks of the Mobile and Ohio Railroad were laid east of the town in the midst of a grove of tupelo gum trees, and the community moved eastward as well. The inhabitants eventually named their community Tupelo in honor of the trees they'd used to build their homes and businesses. The name Tupelo is thought to be of Indian origin, most likely from *tuh pu luh*, meaning "to scream and make a noise."

The Civil War came to the area because of the importance of the railroad. From his position in North Mississippi, Gen. Nathan Bedford Forrest attempted to penetrate Union defenses and attack Sherman's vulnerable railroad supply line from Nashville to Chattanooga. The Battle of Brice's Crossroads, to the west of Tupelo, was the first engagement in the Confederates' attempt to damage this supply line. Alerted to the enemy's position, Sherman sent Gen. Samuel D. Sturgis to hold Forrest, who planned to attack at Brice's Crossroads.

In spite of torrential rains that slowed the arrival of many of their troops, the Union cavalry reached the site before the Confederates arrived. Forrest engaged Union troops a mile east of the crossroads and pressed them back to the crossroads by midafternoon. Sturgis began to withdraw but encountered trouble when they tried to cross the swollen Hatchie River. Many of the retreating Union soldiers panicked, abandoning artillery and supplies in a chaotic run for Memphis. More than 1,500 Federal troops were captured by the Confederates.

The Battle of Tupelo took place one month later. On July 14 and 15, 1864, Forrest led 9,460 Confederate forces to attack 14,000 Union troops. The village of Harrisburg, destroyed during the battle, was never rebuilt. Opinions differ as to the outcome of this battle: Some consider it a Northern victory, although the Union troops withdrew from the field of battle and were pursued by the Confederate forces. The one-acre battlefield site is on West Main Street.

In 1887 the Memphis and Birmingham Railroad crossed the Mobile and Ohio tracks in Tupelo, and the town found itself with two railroads—and with abundant opportunities for growth. Before the turn of the century, Tupelo boasted a population of more than 1,500, including five doctors, twelve lawyers, and a number of wealthy cotton merchants.

Cotton was grown in the thousands of acres of boggy bottomlands that had been reclaimed through an ambitious drainage program undertaken by the citizenry. In order to cut expenses, the founding fathers did not object to pushing wheelbarrows themselves. As the water receded, so did the tupelo tree, which thrives under boggy conditions. Today you can see a few fine specimens in the nature trail along Cypress Swamp, about 140 miles south of Tupelo on the Natchez Trace Parkway. (Be sure you protect yourself with insect repellent before you venture into the beautiful and strange world of the Cypress Swamp. You can relax and enjoy the dramatically filtered light through the towering trees much better if you're not dashing to escape the persistent mosquitoes!)

On April 5, 1936, a devastating tornado tore into Tupelo. In less than one minute, 201 people were killed and 1,000 injured. In addition to the human toll, property damage was extensive, and many of the antebellum structures that survived the Civil War were destroyed.

Within six months, though, this community of cooperative spirit had rebuilt many churches, schools, and homes.

Today Tupelo is a growing community of 31,000 people, who enthusiastically proclaim it to be one of America's best places to live. We hope you'll find it a pleasant stop on your trip down the Trace.

The **Natchez Trace Parkway Visitors Center**, on the parkway at mile marker 266, is a good source of information about the Trace and the surrounding community. In addition to housing the park's administrative offices, you'll find an interpretive center, a reference library, and a good selection of books on the Trace, Mississippi flora and fauna, and Indian and Civil War history.

Cyclists will find the most convenient accommodations at the **Trace Inn** (motel and restaurant) on Mississippi Highway 6, also known as Main Street, adjacent to the parkway at milepost 260.1. The inn is across the street from Ballard Park and the Tupelo Museum. An unmarked gravel road behind the museum will lead bikers back to the Trace with an absolute minimum of traffic. The nearest bike shop is Bicycle Shop and Racquets, Inc., at 1143 West Main.

Accommodations in Tupelo range from the **Mockingbird Inn Bed and Breakfast** to campgrounds and such national chains as **Ramada Inn** and **Holiday Inn.**

If you are interested in camping, 4 miles north of the intersection of East Main Street and Veterans Boulevard, you'll find the 850-acre **Elvis Presley Lake and Campground.** The 350-acre lake is the centerpiece of this clean, well-maintained, and underutilized facility operated by the city of Tupelo. Picnicking, hiking, skiing, fishing, and overnight camping are available.

On the eastern side of Tupelo, about 6 miles south of the East Main Street intersection off Mississippi Route 6, you'll find the **Tombigbee State Park** and more opportunities for boat launching, canoe rental, paddleboat rental, picnicking, hiking, tennis, and overnight camping in campsites or vacation cabins. The hardwood trees surrounding the lake provide a lovely setting for this Civilian Conservation Corps-constructed park, the oldest in the Mississippi Park System.

The Tombigbee State Park east of Tupelo has hiking trails, paddle boats, fishing, and campgrounds. It was constructed by the Civilian Conservation Corps.

We had the pleasure of staying at the delightful **Mockingbird Inn,** on Gloster Avenue near downtown Tupelo. Jim and Sandy Gilmer put a lot of time and research into choosing the site for their bed and breakfast as well as developing their own style of innkeeping. All of their rooms have private baths, queen-size beds, cable TV, and phones, but we particularly enjoyed the L-shaped double Jacuzzi tub in the Athens Room. The attractive 1925 inn and cool fruit drinks on the sunporch welcomed us, and a tasty breakfast of fresh fruit and baked French toast sent us on our way the next morning; but it is the Gilmers' love of Tupelo—and their southern hospitality—that make the Mockingbird really special.

The Mockingbird offers a romance package for honeymooners or the romantic couple, a special treat that includes a rose on your pillow, lighted candles in your room, and a basket filled with mementos.

If you decide to stay at the Mockingbird, you'll be able to leave your car parked and enjoy a lively evening at **Jefferson Place,** one

Mockingbird Inn provides delightful
accommodations for travelers.

block down the street, featuring sandwiches, seafood, beef, and an
accommodating bartender.

Other dinner choices are only a short drive north on Gloster,
where fresh seafood and steaks await you at **Woody's.** We took our
search for the perfect plate of fried catfish to the **Front Porch,** west
of town on Cliff Gookin Boulevard, and found a top contender
amid the flying cornbread, a feat performed by your waiter. Our only
complaint was the inability to clean our plates, but a doggie bag kept
us from turning surly.

If you're looking for an entertaining breakfast, you may want to
check out the menu—and the microphones—at the **Coffee Pot and
Orleans Deli,** in the alley on Spring Street. The owner hosts a local
radio show live from the premises. If you arrive later in the day, the
deli features Cajun-American foods. **Doe's,** on North Spring Street,
serves tamales, gumbo, seafood, and steaks for dinner, from 4 P.M. to
midnight, except Sundays. **Harvey's,** on South Gloster, has several
delicious salad selections in addition to the usual sandwich menu.
A word of caution: Many of the locally owned restaurants are closed
on Sundays.

One notable exception is **Vanelli's,** on North Gloster, known for its pizza and pasta buffet; salads, sandwiches, and chicken are featured as well. Casual diners with a taste for barbecue will probably want to try the **Rib Cage,** downtown on Troy Street, which specializes in ribs but is also known for taterque—a baked potato with barbecue chicken on top. The other exception, the **Stables Restaurant,** in the alley on Spring Street, specializes in plate lunches.

For a burger, fries, milkshake, and a touch of local color on a budget, check out **Johnnie's Drive-In,** on East Main, on your way to **Elvis Presley's birthplace.**

Even if you don't consider yourself an Elvis fan, you'll probably find yourself heading east on Main Street to Elvis Presley Drive. These humble beginnings offer a glimpse into the life Elvis lived before the glitz and the sequined costumes heralded the King of Rock-and-Roll. Born Elvis Aaron Presley on January 8, 1935, in a tiny two-room house built by his father, he was the survivor of twin boys born to Gladys and Vernon Presley. Times must have been hard in the Presley household, for the little shotgun-style house was repossessed three years later. Elvis, like many of us, grew up with the

Portrait of a young Elvis with his parents, Gladys and Vernon Presley.

Elvis Presley's birthplace.

The Elvis Presley Memorial Chapel was built solely by donations from loyal fans.

effects of the Great Depression surrounding him. The youngster who was to become a legend continued to live in Tupelo until he was thirteen. He attended Lawhon School, where the future teen idol won second place singing in a talent show. He made A's in music at Milam Junior High School, which he attended until his family moved to Memphis. Although he would sing before audiences all over the world, he bought his first guitar at **Tupelo Hardware,** on East Main Street. He must have roamed the streets of Tupelo dreaming of the success he'd have someday, of living in a fine home no one could ever take away. A special collection of memorabilia, including items he gave to his longtime friend, Mrs. McComb, is housed at the **Elvis Presley Museum** next door. Two years after his death in 1977, the Elvis Presley Memorial Chapel was built with funds donated from his fans and friends around the world. It is open to the public as he had requested.

While you're downtown, visit the **Mississippi Museum of Art at Tupelo,** in the old bank building on Main Street. For antiques shoppers, the **Downtown Antique Mall,** at 624 West Main, has an assortment of Victorian, primitives, and pottery that should be interesting. Just next door you'll find **George Watson Antiques,** and four blocks to the east vintage clothing and jewelry are featured at the **Main Attraction.**

A turn off Main to Madison will lead bibliophiles to the **Cottage Bookshop,** which offers a fine assortment of rare, out-of-print books conveniently arranged to invite a thorough assessment in your areas of interest. We found an out-of-print treasure for a friend here that we'd sought for at least two years. Civil War enthusiasts will be very pleased with the history section.

At the western end of Main Street, the **Tupelo City Museum,** in Ballard Park, features a hodgepodge of exhibits ranging from Indians to astronauts, the Civil War to World War II. There is a train station with a caboose, a furnished log dogtrot cabin, a schoolhouse, and fire engines, all displayed in converted dairy barns.

Mrs. Jimmie Cole will tell you all about the museum, 8 A.M.– 4 P.M. Tuesday through Friday, 1–5 P.M. on Saturday and Sunday. Inside you'll find Elvis photos and Apollo spacesuits, mammoth teeth estimated to be 40,000–50,000 years old, a left-handed ammonite 170 million years old, a T-Rex tooth, a replica of a telegraph station, and a model of the Battle of Tupelo. You'll also see a pair of size 98 overalls worn by the heaviest human—Robert Earl Hughes—when he only weighed 700 pounds. He topped out at 1,069 pounds. Catch a peek at a 1926 touring car, physiotherapy and Swedish massage equipment, reconstructed radio station WELO, and a representation of Roosevelt's visit in 1934.

Some handsome Chickasaw artifacts include arrowheads, bird points, pots, and fishhooks. A timeline explains that from 15000 to 6000 B.C. big-game hunters thrived. During the Archaic period (6000–2000 B.C.) hunting for smaller animals predominated, because mammoths and other larger game had died out. The Gulf Formational period (2000–100 B.C.) saw the use of pottery for the first time. During this period the first mounds were being built and simple agricultural practices appeared. During the Woodland period (100 B.C.–A.D. 1100) mounds became more common. Conical in shape, they were often used for burials. Agriculture became more developed; pottery use was widespread. Mounds were flat-topped, and societies became centrally located in permanent villages during the Mississippian period (1100–1540). The Historic period extended from 1540 to 1834, when the forced removal of the Indians to Oklahoma took place.

When you come out of the parking lot if you turn right you'll return to the Trace very quickly. There's a small section of the road that's still gravel.

ACCOMMODATIONS

The Mockingbird Bed & Breakfast—305 N. Gloster, Tupelo, MS 38801; 601-841-0286, FAX 601-840-4158.

All American Coliseum Motel—767 E. Main, Tupelo, MS 38801; 601-844-5610; For reservations, call collect.

Comfort Inn—1190 N. Gloster, Tupelo, MS 38801; 601-842-5100 or 800-221-2222.

Days Inn—1015 N. Gloster, Tupelo, MS 38801; 601-842-0088 or 800-329-7466.

Econo Lodge—1500 McCullough Blvd., Tupelo, MS 38801; 601-844-1904 or 800-424-4777.

Economy Inn—708 N. Gloster, Tupelo, MS 38801; 601-842-1213.

Executive Inn—1011 N. Gloster, Tupelo, MS 38801; 601-841-2222 or 800-533-3220.

Holiday Inn Express—923 N. Gloster, Tupelo, MS 38801; 601-842-8811 or 800-465-4329.

Ramada Inn—854 N. Gloster, Tupelo, MS 38801; 601-844-4111 or 800-228-2828.

Tombigbee State Park—Rt. 2, Box 336-E, Tupelo, MS 38801; 601-842-7669.

Town House Motel—927 S. Gloster, Tupelo, MS 38801; 601-842-5411 or 800-414-2066.

Trace Inn—3400 W. Main, Tupelo, MS 38801; 601-842-5555.

Elvis Presley Lake and Campground—Rt. 4, Box 387E, Tupelo, MS 38801; 601-841-1304; 2.5 miles northeast of Hwy. 78 and Veterans Blvd.; Camping, swimming, fishing, skiing, hiking, and picnicking; 350-acre lake amid 850 acres of wooded playgrounds.

ATTRACTIONS

Elvis Presley Birthplace and Museum—306 Elvis Presley Blvd., Tupelo, MS 38801; 601-841-1245; Birthplace, $1 adult, 50¢ under 12; Museum, $4 adults, $2 under 12; Mon.–Sat., 9 A.M.–5:30 P.M. (May–Sept.); 9 A.M.–5 P.M. (Oct.–April); Sun., 1–5 p.m. (year-round).

Pvt. John M. Allen National Fish Hatchery—111 E. Elizabeth St., Tupelo, MS 38801; 601-842-1341; Millions of fish are hatched here each year for stocking Mississippi's reservoirs; Contact Tupelo Convention and Visitors Bureau for appointment to Victorian home on the property, former residence of hatchery manager; Free tour.

Mississippi Museum of Art at Tupelo—211 W. Main, Tupelo, MS 38801; 601-844-ARTS; Free; Tues.–Sat., 10 A.M.–5 P.M.; Sun., 1–5 P.M.

Natchez Trace Parkway Headquarters Visitors Center—Rt. 1, NT-143, Tupelo, MS 38801; 601-842-1572; At mile marker 266 (5 miles north of Tupelo); No admission; Closed Christmas Day; Books, maps, information, brochures, and questions answered; Not to be missed!

The Tupelo Museum—Hwy. 6 W. at James L. Ballard Park, Tupelo, MS 38801; 601-841-6438; Tues.–Fri., 8 A.M.–4 P.M.; Sat.–Sun., 1–5 P.M.; $1 adults, under 12 50¢, under 3 free; Artifacts from Indians to astronauts; Interesting and worthwhile.

❧ RESTAURANTS

Cafe Bravo—854 N. Gloster; 601-844-5371; Mon.–Sat., 6 A.M.–10 P.M.;
 Sun., 6 A.M.- P.M.

Coffee Pot & Orleans Deli—208 Spring St.; 601-842-9191; Mon.–Fri.,
 8 A.M.–6 P.M.

Doe's—202 N. Spring St.; 601-842-2182; Mon.–Sat., 4–12 P.M.

The Front Porch—2827 Cliff Gookin Blvd.; 601-842-1591; Mon.–Sat.,
 4–11:30 P.M.

Harvey's—424 S. Gloster; 601-842-7663; Mon.-Sat., 11 A.M.-2 P.M.;
 Mon.–Thurs., 5–9:30 P.M.; Fri.–Sat., 5–10 P.M.

Jefferson Place—823 Jefferson; 601-844-8696; Mon.–Sat., 11 A.M.–12 P.M.

Johnnie's Drive-In—908 E. Main; 601-842-6748; Mon.–Thurs., 5:30 A.M.–
 8 P.M.; Fri.–Sat., 5:30 A.M.–9 P.M.

Pancho's Mexican—201 N. Gloster; 601-844-7523; Mon.–Thurs.,
 11 A.M.–10 P.M.; Fri.–Sat., 11 A.M.–12 P.M.; Sun., 11 A.M.–9 P.M.

The Rib Cage—206 Troy; 601-840-5400; Mon.-Sat., 10 A.M.- 12 P.M.

Russell's Beef House—3400 W. Main; 601-680-8673; Mon.–Fri., 11 A.M.–
 2 P.M.; Sun.–Thurs., 4:30–9:30 P.M.; Fri.–Sat., 4:40–10:30 P.M.

Stables Restaurant—206 N. Spring (Alley); 601-791-0440; Mon.–Wed.,
 7:30 A.M.—8:30 P.M.; Thurs.–Fri., 7:30 A.M.–12 P.M.; Sat.,
 10 A.M.–12 P.M.; Sun., 10 A.M.–2 P.M.

Vinelli's—12 S. Gloster; 601-844-4410; Mon.–Thurs., 11 A.M.—10 P.M.;
 Fri.–Sat., 11 A.M.–12 P.M.; Sun., 4–9 P.M.; Carryout available.

Woody's—619 N. Gloster; 601-840-0460; Mon.–Sat., 5–10 P.M.

❧ SHOPPING

The Cottage Bookshop—214 N. Madison, Tupelo, MS 38801; 601-844-1553;
 Rare books.

Downtown Antique Mall—624 W. Main, Tupelo, MS 38801; Mon.–Sat.,
 10 A.M.–5 P.M.

George Watson Antiques—628 W. Main, Tupelo, MS 38801; 601-841-9411
 or 844-8744; Mon.–Sat., 10 A.M.–5 P.M.

The Mall at Barnes Crossing—P.O. Box 106 (1001 Barnes Crossing Rd.),
 Tupelo, MS 38801; 601-844-6255; Mon.–Sat., 10 A.M.–9 P.M.; Sun.,
 12:30–6 p.M.; 700,000 square feet of shopping! Handicapped accessible, wheelchairs available.

Main Attraction—214 W. Main, Tupelo, MS 38801; 601-842-9617;
 Mon.–Fri., 11 A.M.–5 P.M.; Sat., 11 A.M.–4 P.M.

Nostalgia Alley Antiques—1604½ W. Main, Tupelo, MS 38801; 601-842-5547; By appointment.

Red Door Antique Mall & Collectible Emporium—1001 Coley Rd., Tupelo, MS 38801; 601-840-6777; Mon.–Sat., 9:30 A.M.–5:30 P.M.; Sun., 1:30–5:30 P.M.

Tupelo Hardware—P.O. Box 1040 (Front & Main), Tupelo, MS 38801; 601-842-4637; Mon.–Fri., 7 A.M.–5:30 P.M.; Sat., 7 A.M.–noon.

❧ SPECIAL EVENTS

Gigantic Flea Market—Spring; Hundreds of vendors; Contact Tupelo Convention and Visitors Bureau for dates.

Sportsman's Bonanza—Fall outdoor recreation show; Contact Tupelo Convention and Visitors Bureau for dates.

Tupelo Knife and Gun—Fall collectors show; Contact Tupelo Convention and Visitors Bureau for dates.

June: Oleput—First weekend in June; A two-day Mardi Gras-style celebration with music, street dancing, fireworks, parade, carnivals, 5K run/walk, and children's activities; $5 per person per day or $10 for entire family, children under 12 free; Contact Tupelo Convention and Visitors Bureau for dates.

December: Christmas Celebrations—Contact Tupelo Convention and Visitors Bureau for dates.

❧ FOR MORE INFORMATION

Tupelo Convention and Visitors Bureau—P.O. Drawer 47, Tupelo, MS 38802-0047; 601-841-6521 or 800-533-0611.

9 Loop Tour III:
New Albany/Pontotoc/Houston

Old Trace Site—One of several preserved sections of the Old Trace.

One of our favorite loop tours is the New Albany/Pontotoc/Houston tour out of Tupelo. An alternative route would include Baldwyn in order to visit the national battlefield site at Brice's Crossroads. If you're taking a Civil War tour, visit the site; the three flags of the Confederacy fly here. If not, save yourself for other Civil War sites, because the battlefield has one interpretive marker, which we include in the chapter dedicated to Natchez Trace Parkway markers, but no museum or interpretive site on the scale of what you'll see at major battlefields like Shiloh or Vicksburg.

Leave Tupelo on Highway 78 West. You'll pass markers showing where the Old Natchez Trace passed through Pontotoc County, a county particularly rich in Indian history. Pontotoc is derived from *Paka-Takali*, an Indian phrase meaning "land of the hanging grapes." You'll travel about 20 miles to New Albany through what was once the heart of the Chickasaw lands.

It is believed that de Soto camped in this area during the winter of 1540–41. On Christmas Day 1540, the first Christian marriage in America took place between Juan Ortiz and a captive Seminole princess, Sa-Owana.

According to Jonathan Daniels' *The Devil's Backbone*, the Chickasaw at first accepted de Soto's arrival. He demanded two hundred women as carriers and treated them so roughly that some died and others ran away. Rather than attack directly, the infuriated Chickasaw waited until night, eventually driving the Spaniard westward to the Mississippi River.

About two hundred years later, in 1713, the Chickasaw successfully repelled an attack known as the Battle of Ogoula Tchetoka, intended to destroy their nation led by the Frenchman Pierre D'Artaguette. In fact, the French army retreated, soundly defeated in March 1736. D'Artaguette and twenty of his men were burned at the stake by the ferocious Chickasaw. The men who were to have been his reinforcements, under the command of Bienville, arrived from Natchez in May 1736 and were also defeated, at the Battle of Ackia, and retreated to Mobile.

These battles may have been decisive points in the relations of the Chickasaw with Europeans, leaving them distrustful of the Spanish and French and more amenable to dealings with the British. John McIntosh, a British agent, established the community of Tockshish around 1770. By 1801 Tockshish, or McIntoshville, was Mississippi's second post office and a relay station between Nashville and Natchez.

The Chickasaw eventually signed treaties ceding more than six million acres of their lands to the U.S. government by 1832.

In the 1830s legendary frontiersman Davy Crockett had a horse corral near the present location of the Trace State Park. His business thrived until he departed for Texas to assist his friend Sam Houston. He was later killed at the Battle of the Alamo on March 6, 1836.

The area again saw invading armies during the Civil War when Union troops came through repeatedly between 1862 and 1864. The battles of Tupelo, Mud Creek, and Brice's Crossroads all took place in this vicinity.

NEW ALBANY

We were told by Jim Dickerson, owner of the Picket Fence Antique Mall, that New Albany was torched as punishment by Grierson's Raiders in June 1863 after the citizens established lines to repel the Union forces. That's why so very few antebellum homes in the area survived. The town was originally named after an Indian who lived on the Tallahatchie River and was laid out and surveyed in the 1840s by a Mr. Camp, who renamed the town "new" Albany.

Lunch choices include the Village Cafe and Java Shop, Jimbo's for sandwiches and steaks, Bryant's Fish and Steak House, and West Side Barbeque. Don't worry—we found the natives these days to be quite friendly, unlike in the days of the fierce Chickasaw warriors.

Two antiques malls await those of you interested in seeking memorabilia of times gone by: **The Picket Fence Antique Mall,** 103 West Bankhead, is open Tuesday through Saturday from 9:30 to 5:30 and Sundays from 2 to 5 P.M. (Tell Jim we said hello, and be sure to save your local history questions for him—he's a wealth of information.)

To enter Pontotoc, continue on Highway 15 South until you reach the intersection with Highway 6 to enter Pontotoc. As you travel down Highway 15, you will pass the site of the Ingomar Mounds on your right, about 5 miles out of New Albany. Some historians believe de Soto made his second winter encampment here, because evidence of Spanish contact was found when the mounds were excavated by the Smithsonian in 1885. As you enter Pontotoc, you'll pass the Pontotoc City Cemetery. The land was donated by the Chickasaw in 1852 because "many Chickasaws and their white friends were buried there." Among the gravesites is that of William Colbert.

PONTOTOC

Pontotoc is a small community located about 5 miles northwest of the original Pontotoc settlement. It can also be reached from Tupelo via Highway 6.

You'll find several reasons to be glad you stopped in Pontotoc, including the delightful **General Store Deli and Fountain,** located at 17 South Main Street: from its tin ceilings, complete with three antique fans run by a single motor and a system of pulleys overhead, to the lovely soda-fountain bar rescued from a site in California. Owners Gerry and Sandy Gilbreath have done a wonderful restoration.

Jane Bard served us the creamiest milkshake ever to pass between our lips one hot summer day. The menu also includes salads like the orange walnut salad with chunks of chicken breast and sweet-and-sour dressing, potatoes (plain or loaded), specialty sandwiches (or create your own from the deli selections available), ice cream (cones, floats, shakes, and sundaes), and a personal favorite, fresh lemonade.

There are two antiques malls definitely worth visiting. Mitchell and Anita Thomas's **Main Street Antique Mall,** 102 South Main, specializes in Victorian and Empire furniture but also offers cut glass and collectibles as well as primitive American pieces. You may be lucky enough to visit when an auction is planned.

Mason Jar Antique Mall is just up the street on Liberty Street off North Main. They're open Tuesday through Saturday from 10 A.M. to 5 P.M. and stay open until 8 P.M. on Thursday nights. They offer varied collectibles and antiques.

There are several small shops in town that you may want to visit, but if there's a reluctant male in the car who needs some new walking shoes for exploring all the sites you've yet to visit, you may want to stop by the Progressive Shoe Store on West Marion Street. Much larger than it looks, the Fauvers' shoe store also sends shoes to customers, including the occasional celebrity, all over the South. The guys can pull up to the front door and run in—no need to venture into a mall here!

One way to leave Pontotoc and return to the Trace is to continue on Highway 6 to Tupelo. This route will take you past the marker for the Federal Land Office, which handled the sale of Chickasaw lands ceded in the Treaty of Pontotoc Creek.

Trace State Park, 10 miles east of Pontotoc, offers six air-conditioned cabins; twenty-five RV sites with picnic tables, grills, electric and water hookups, and bathhouse nearby; twenty shaded tent camping sites, fishing, and water sports in the six-hundred-acre lake, and hiking more than 25 miles of trails. We strongly suggest you make reservations for accommodations, as this is a very popular park.

Fishing boats are available for rent and there are ramps and docks. One hiking trail has been dedicated to the memory of a local young outdoorsman, thirteen-year-old Jason Stewart, who was helping construct the trail. He was killed in a horseback-riding accident at his home. Be alert when walking the trail system—sections are also utilized by equestrians (stables available) and ATVs. An eighteen-hole golf course at the Pontotoc Country Club is available for cabin and campground guests of the park.

An alternate route will take you through the site of Old Pontotoc. Exit Pontotoc on Highway 15 and look for the junction with Highway 342, just before you reach Lochinvar. Old Pontotoc was built in 1842 by Robert Gordan, using Scottish craftsmen and slave labor. A freestanding spiral staircase vaulting from the first floor to the cupola is an outstanding feature.

A sudden summer storm clouds the Trace.

The story is told that Captain Gordan befriended a wounded Union general. In gratitude, the general gave Gordan his saber and a letter requesting the reader to extend courtesy to Gordan for his kindness. When raiders came through the area pillaging and burning, Gordan's wife appeared with the saber and the letter. Not only was the house spared, a Union guard was posted there to keep it from being burned.

You will encounter several markers as you travel along Highway 342, which runs parallel to and south of Highway 6 back to the Trace. The first is Allen's Tavern, a seat of government for the Chickasaw villages. James Allen, the proprietor, married the daughter of William Colbert. Andrew Jackson is believed to have stayed with them in his journeys over the nearby Trace.

The marker describing the Chickasaw defeat of D'Artaguette's forces in 1736 is next. A marker commemorates the nearby site of the Chickasaw council house, where the Chickasaw ceded six million acres of their homeland to the U.S. government in 1832.

The final marker before entering the Trace is at Bullen's School, begun in 1799 to educate the Chickasaw. The site of the school was thought to be at the present-day Black Zion Cemetery.

You may chose to return to Highway 15 South from Highway 342 to visit Houston. Or if you elect to bypass New Albany and Pontotoc and want to go to Houston from the Trace, take the eastern turn onto Highway 8, just south of milepost 230.

Houston was named for Sam Houston, as requested by a man named Pinson, who donated eighty acres for the town in 1836. We didn't find any antiques malls or thrift stores here. On Highway 15 north of town, Moore's Restaurant served a good ribeye and salad.

Owl Creek Indian Mound is just off the Natchez Trace Parkway on the way to Davis Lake.

Harmon Hall Bed and Breakfast offers reasonable overnight accommodations. Your hosts, Lynn and Hazel Harmon, prefer reservations in order to give you a bedroom with private bath and color TV. You'll be offered your choice of sausage or ham, eggs or hotcakes, juice, and coffee.

To return to the Trace from Houston, go east on Highway 8 and travel 4 miles to reenter the parkway near milepost 230.

Davis Lake is 4 miles west of mile marker 243.1. Owl Creek Indian Mounds is on your right, 2.8 miles from the parkway; there is no interpretative marker, but there is a big mound. When you come to a crossroads, bear to your left to Davis Lake, part of the Tombigbee National Forest Recreation Area. The area closes at dark except for campers.

Davis is a small lake with several earthen piers that jut out for easy bank fishing. It also has wooden fishing piers and a boat ramp for anglers wanting to catch bass, bream, crappie, or catfish, and it has sheltered picnic tables, bathrooms, bathhouse, and fees on a honor system. Overflow camping is on the right as you enter.

Davis Lake is part of the Tombigbee National Forest Recreation Area and offers fishing and camping.

It's very shady in summer. One family is requested per campsite, with a maximum of seven people. It has twenty-five developed camp-sites and RV pads with grills. Primitive camping is offered up the hill. Although it's 4 miles off the trace via a narrow road, the road does not look heavily traveled and is probably safe for bicyclists.

Witch Dance, at mile marker 233.2, offers horseback riders the Tombigbee Horse Trail, which is a joint venture of the U.S. Forest Service and the National Park Service. Loop A is 9 miles, and Loop B is 6 miles. Camping is available for trail riders only. There are a water fountain and several picnic tables, but restrooms were closed when we visited.

Bynum Mounds at mile marker 232.4 is handicapped accessible. The path is asphalt but uneven in places. There are two mounds—one about ten feet tall, the other about fourteen feet—and three house foundations. Take the narrow asphalt path to inspect the mounds and the house sites.

❧ ACCOMMODATIONS

Harmon Hall Bed and Breakfast—435 N. Jackson St., Houston, MS; 601-456-2131.

❧ ATTRACTIONS

Trace State Park—Rt. 1, Box 254, Belden, MS 38826; 601-489-2958.

❧ RESTAURANTS

The General Store Deli and Fountain—17 S. Main, Pontotoc, MS 38863; 601-489-8831.

Terry's Village Restaurant—258 Turnpike Rd., Pontotoc, MS 38863; 601-489-7049.

❧ SHOPPING

Main Street Antique Mall & Auction House—102 S. Main, Pontotoc, MS 38863; 601-489-7585.

The Mason Jar Antique Mall—Court Sq., 34 Liberty, Pontotoc, MS 38863; 601-844-6866.

The Picket Fence Antique Mall—103 W. Bankhead, New Albany, MS 38652; 601-534-7610.

❧ FOR MORE INFORMATION

Pontotoc Chamber of Commerce—81 S. Main, Pontotoc, MS 38863; 601-489-5042.

Union County Development Association—City Hall, New Albany, MS 38652; 601-534-4354.

10 Starkville: Stop along the Road Less Traveled

Starkville is 30 miles off the Natchez Trace via Highway 82. Originally known as Boardtown, the town was founded in 1831 but was renamed to honor Gen. John Stark, a Revolutionary War hero, and incorporated as Starkville in 1837. Once known as the "Dairy Center of the South," this community of 18,000 is home to Mississippi's largest university, Mississippi State. With an enrollment of nearly 14,000 students, the university generates a lot of enthusiasm in Starkville, especially on football weekends.

Mississippi State University sporting weekends draw visitors to Starkville.

Campers and fishermen will notice the sign for Oktibbeha County Lake Park, 13.5 miles off the Trace as you travel toward Starkville on Highway 82. A northern turn will take you to fishing docks, a sandy beach area for swimming, camping for both RVs and tents, and picnicking. The park appeared to be underutilized at the time of our visit during the summer. We did notice a large population of purple martins taking advantage of the gourds placed about for them. Boat rentals are available.

Most of the accommodations available are situated along two main corridors. Highway 82 offers the **University Motel** and the **Regal Inn,** in addition to the historic **Statehouse Hotel.**

We turned right on Jackson Street to visit with Glen Potts at the beautifully renovated Statehouse Hotel, which is on the National Register of Historic Places. Located at the corner of Jackson and Main streets, the hotel was built in 1925, originally called the Hotel Chester, and later renamed the Stark Hotel in honor of General Stark. The latest renovation took place in 1985.

The Ivey Suite has a sitting room with a TV and wet bar, bedroom with king-size four-poster bed, and an armoire concealing a second TV. Room rates begin at $50; suites complete with sitting room start at $68 (one of the best buys we saw on our trip).

Fine dining is available at the hotel in Antoine's Restaurant. The lunch menu includes chef salad, spinach salad, sandwiches, grilled chicken, stuffed crab, blackened chicken, and bananas Foster for dessert. The dinner menu is nicely endowed with seafood, surf and turf, poultry, pasta dishes, sandwiches, oysters on the half-shell, and Crab Rangoon. The Library Lounge, next door to Antoine's, looks dark and cozy with loveseats and comfortable chairs. They also offer room service.

The downtown location means you'll have to park on Main. There's no parking on Jackson, but the slight inconvenience is more than balanced by the comforts you'll find inside. There is a small loading and unloading area designated in front of the hotel on Jackson.

The **Starkville Visitors and Convention Council** is located on East Main Street, in case you'd like to stop by for information now that you're in town.

The next stop for hungry travelers might well be the **Starkville Cafe.** Just around the corner from the Statehouse Hotel on Main, the cafe is open Monday through Friday from 5 A.M. to 3 P.M. and Saturdays from 5 A.M. to 2 P.M. For less than $4 you'll be offered your choice of savory meat and vegetables, cornbread or hot rolls, and iced tea or coffee. The menu varies from day to day, but samples include chicken and dumplings or meatloaf with green beans and new potatoes.

The college crowd tends to choose **Rick's,** between Jackson and Montgomery near Highway 82.

While you're still downtown you may want to visit the **Artists and Crafters Gallery,** near Main and Washington. They offer T-shirts, ceramics, towel racks, teddy bears, stained glass, and a few antiques and collectibles downstairs, including quilts, lamps, needlepoint, old hats, and some furniture.

Before you leave the downtown area, stop by the **Oktibbeha County Heritage Museum**, located in a restored railroad depot at the corner of Fellowship and Russell streets. Open Tuesday, Wednesday, and Thursday afternoons, the museum has a collection of local artifacts that may interest you.

You'll find the **Best Western, Holiday Inn,** and **University Inn** along Highway 12 from Ackerman, which can be reached by turning right on Jackson. Also located along Highway 12 West is the **C. C. Clark Coca-Cola Museum,** which features more than 2,300 items. Admission is free. A turn in an easterly direction on Highway 12 will lead you past portions of the Mississippi State campus.

You'll be able to find more than football to interest you at Mississippi State if you care to tour. There are several museums you can visit, including the **Cobb Institute of Archaeology Museum** (American Indian artifacts), the **Dunn-Seiler Museum** (paleontology, mineralogy, and geology), the **Entomological Museum** (featuring more than 700,000 insect specimens); and special group tours of the **McKay Enology Laboratory** (grapes and wine) and the **Herzer Dairy Research Center** may be arranged.

The **Templeton Music Museum and Archives,** on Blackjack Road, houses a collection of ragtime phonographic instruments, a

Gramophones at Templeton
Music Museum.

player piano and organ, roller organettes, music boxes, sheet music, and recordings. No admission is charged. Most university museums are open on academic schedules, so call to arrange tours.

Check out lunch and dinner choices at the **Cotton District Grill** while you're in the university area. Other lunch sites include the nearby **Bulldog Deli** and **Little Dooey's Barbeque,** at the corner of Fellowship and University, for the young at heart.

Sports enthusiasts will find golf accommodations for the public at the eighteen-hole Mississippi State University Lakeside Golf Course, east of downtown on Highway 82.

One of the more interesting choices for accommodations is 2 miles south of downtown Starkville, the **Carpenter Place Bed and Breakfast,** on Highway 25 South. You need to watch carefully for the sign on the left side of the road, just across from a big red-brick apartment building. Drive up a long pea-gravel drive, through a grove of pecan trees, and across a small wooden bridge to reach Oktibbeha County's oldest home.

The present owners are Lucy and Roy Carpenter. Descendants of the original owners, they completed restoration of the 1835 white frame structure in 1992. The landscaping is very attractive, thanks to their efforts, and even includes a rose garden. Bed and breakfast accommodations in this home, listed on the National Register of Historic Places, consist of two bedrooms with private baths in the main house, and the carriage house, which is available for a family. One guest bedroom has a double bed as well as a single. The other has a double bed, and a Victorian claw-footed tub in the bath.

The carriage house suite has two bedrooms (a double bed and twins), private bath, living room, and a refreshment center with a small refrigerator and microwave. In the main house, you'll see the evidence of a shotgun blast in the corner of the present-day dining room. During the Civil War, a Union soldier was shot as he tried to break in the side door.

Guests are invited to walk the 140 acres and fish in the pond. A southern farm breakfast is served.

The John W. Starr Memorial Forest and Noxubee National Wildlife Refuge offer outdoor recreational opportunities for visitors, ranging from hiking and fishing to overnight camping and birdwatching. You can reach them both by traveling Highway 25 South from Starkville. The forest lies approximately 3 miles south of town and offers overnight camping; while the wildlife refuge is about 8 miles south and is of special interest for birdwatchers.

If you continue on Highway 25 South, you will reach the Tombigbee National Forest and more outdoor opportunities for fun. You will have the choice of turning west on Highway 15, to rejoin the Trace, or continuing on 25 to Louisville and intersecting with Highway 19, to lead you back to the Trace near Kosciusko.

ᔕ ACCOMMODATIONS

Carpenter Place Bed & Breakfast—1280 Hwy. 25 S., Starkville, MS 39759; 601-323-4669 or 323-3322.

The Cedars Bed & Breakfast—Rt. 1, Box 362, Oktoc Rd., Starkville, MS 39759; 601-324-7569

Statehouse Hotel—Corner of Jackson & Main streets, P.O. Box 2002, Starkville, MS 39759; 601-323-2000 or 800-722-1903, FAX 601-323-4948.

Best Western—119 Hwy. 12 W., Starkville, MS 39759; 601-324-5555 or 800-528-1234.

Holiday Inn—P.O. Box 751, Starkville, MS 39759; 601-323-6161 or 800-HOLIDAY.

Regal Inn—Hwy. 82 E., Starkville, MS 39759; 601-323-8251.

University Inn—P.O. Box 905, Starkville, MS 39759; 601-323-9550 or 800-475-UNIV.

University Motel—Hwy. 12 W., Starkville, MS 39759; 601-323-1421.

ATTRACTIONS

A. B. McKay Food & Enology Lab—MSU, Starkville, MS 39759; 601-325-2440; Tours by appointment; Research with grape and wine quality.

C. C. Clark Coca-Cola Museum—Hwy. 12 W., Starkville, MS 39759; 601-323-4150; Free by appointment; More than 2,300 Coca-Cola memorabilia items on display.

Cobb Institute of Archeology Museum—MSU, Starkville, MS 39759; 601-325-3826; Free; Artifacts from Holy Land, Near East, and North American Indians.

Dunn–Seiler Museum—MSU, Starkville, MS 39759; 601-325-3915; Free; Mon.–Fri., 8 A.M.–5 P.M.; Special tours by appointment; Paleozoic, Mesozoic, and Cenozoic paleontology, mineralogy, and geology.

Frederick Herman Herzer Dairy—MSU, Starkville, MS 39759; 601-325-2440; Tours for groups by appointment; Milk, cheese, and ice cream processing; Sales store, 601-325-2338.

Greensboro Historic District—601-323-3322; Free; Thirty Victorian homes.

Mississippi Entomological Museum—MSU, Starkville, MS 39759; 601-325-2085; Free; Relevant literature, displays, and exhibits of more than 700,000 insects.

Mississippi State Univ. Art Gallery—Starkville, MS 39759; 601-325-6900; Free; Monthly exhibits.

Oktibbeha County Heritage Museum—GM&O Railroad Depot, Starkville, MS 39759; 601-0211; Free; Local artifacts.

Rose Garden—MSU, Starkville, MS 39759; 601-325-3138; Free; Driving tour; Peak season, May–June.

Templeton Music Museum—MSU, Starkville, MS 39759; 601-325-8301;
   Free, by appointment; A tribute to ragtime music and phonographic inventions.

✼ RESTAURANTS

Allgood's Burgers—323-1323
Bulldog Deli—324-3354; 702 University Dr.; 10:30 A.M.–10 P.M.,
   Mon.–Sun.
Blue Goose—324-2603; 1500 Russell St.; Mon.–Fri., 10:30 A.M.–9 P.M.;
   Sat.–Sun., 11:30 A.M.–2:30 P.M., 5:30–9 P.M.
China Inn—323-6922; 608 Hwy. 12 E.; Mon.–Sun., 11 A.M.–10 P.M.
CJ's Pizza—323-8897; 600 Hwy. 12 E.; Mon.–Sun., 11 A.M.–10 P.M.
Cotton District Grill—323-6062; 106 Maxwell St.; Mon.–Sat.,
   11 A.M.–10 P.M.
Harvey's Restaurant—327-1639; 406 Hwy. 12 E.; Mon.–Thurs.,
   11 A.M.–9 P.M.; Fri.–Sat., 11 A.M.–9:30 P.M.
Jack Salmon's Fish House—323-6110; 105 Hwy. 82 W.; Mon.–Thurs.,
   10 A.M.–10 P.M.; Fri.–Sat., 10 A.M.–midnight.
Little Dooey's Barbeque—323-6094; 100 Fellowship St.; Mon.–Sat.,
   11 A.M.–9 P.M.
Petty's Carryout Bar-B-Q—323-8901; 103 Hwy. 12 W.; Mon.–Sun.,
   10 A.M.–10 P.M.
Starkville Cafe—323-1665; 211 University Dr.; Mon.–Fri., 5 A.M.–3 P.M.;
   Sat., 5 A.M.–2 P.M.

✼ SHOPPING

Artists and Crafters Gallery—102 Main St.
Crafts and More—436 Hwy. 12 W.
College Park—100 Russell St.
Downtown Starkville—Main St.
La Galerie—Russell St.
Starkville Crossing—Hwy. 12 W.
Southdale Shopping Center—Hwy. 12
State Shopping Center—Hwy. 12 W.
University Square Shopping Center—Hwy. 12
Village Shopping Center—Hwy. 12 W.
82 Plaza Shopping Center—Hwy. 82

✒ SPECIAL EVENTS

Community Theater—Year-round
MSU Lyceum Series—Year-round
MSU Music Makers Concert—Year-round
January: Frostbite Half Marathon
January–May: MSU Baseball Season
April: Super Bulldog Weekend
August: Street Rod Car Show
September: Boardtown Jubilee
September–October: Black Hills Festival
September–November: MSU Football Season
October–November: Oktoc County Store
November–December: Union Crafts Fair
November–March: MSU Basketball Season

✒ FOR MORE INFORMATION

Starkville Area Chamber of Commerce—P.O. Box 2720, Starkville, MS 39759; 601-323-5783.
Starkville Visitors and Convention Council—P.O. Box 2720, Starkville, MS 39759; 601-323-3322.

II Jeff Busby and French Camp: Two for the Road

Thomas Jefferson Busby was the congressman who during the 1930s got the Natchez Trace surveyed and later designated part of the National Park System. Because of his contribution we have the Jeff Busby site on the Trace, named in his honor.

Facilities at Jeff Busby include the only service station and convenience store on the parkway. The store has public restrooms, phone, snacks, and cold drinks. In addition you'll also find a free first come,

Little Mountain Overlook above Jeff Busby campgrounds and the only gas station on the Natchez Trace.

173

first served campground, comfort station, ranger residence, overlook, picnic tables, and hiking trail. The campground is closed 10 P.M. to 6 A.M. except for campers. Nestled among tall pine trees, here is a clean, shady campground with paved campsites but no shower or electric hookups.

Markers show where the hiking trail starts. The overlook at the top has an extensive vista and a covered pavilion with clean restrooms and a water fountain. Naturalists and historians will find interpretive information on the great eastern hardwood forests and such extinct species as the Carolina parakeet and ivory-billed woodpecker. There's also a display concerning Native Americans' use of the forest and its inhabitants.

FRENCH CAMP

At mile marker 180.8 you can pull into a parking lot and walk across a bridge to see the restored house that was built by Col. James Drane in 1846. This is one of the entrances to French Camp.

A view from the parkway of the wooden walkway leading to the Drane house.

French Camp Bed and Breakfast is operated by French Camp Academy.

In 1812 a stand built and operated by Louis LeFleur came to be called French Camp because of his nationality. LeFleur figures prominently in the history of Mississippi. A school was established here in 1822, and French Camp Academy is in operation today.

Much of French Camp is wheelchair accessible due to extraordinarily long wooden walkways. They lead in one direction to a complex of log buildings that includes a student-run cafe and a gift shop and behind the house, in another direction, to the **French Camp Bed and Breakfast.** There's also a private residence with a glass-enclosed room in which is displayed a stagecoach that belonged to Louis LeFleur's son, Greenwood LeFlore. LeFlore became a prominent politician having a town and county named after him. The Council House Cafe is open 8:30 A.M.–2 P.M., Monday–Friday, and the gift shop from 9 A.M.–5 P.M., Monday–Saturday. Seasonal sorghum-making demonstrations are also held.

The French Camp Bed and Breakfast, operated by Ed and Sallie Williford, was unique in our experience. The two-story log house is situated in the middle of a beautiful green pasture ringed by hardwood trees and operated primarily as part of the mission of French Camp rather than for profit.

If you're traveling in a group, we strongly recommend that you stay in the separate cabin, because the rooms in the main log house do not currently have individual thermostatic controls for central heat and air. Comfort zones can vary widely from upstairs to downstairs. A country-style breakfast is served and includes delicious French Camp bread made by the students.

French Camp Academy has 1,200 acres and a resident student population of 160. The students are often from troubled or broken homes. French Camp faculty make a point of privately interviewing potential students and asking them whether attending school there is something they want to do or if it is being imposed on them. They require that all students be willing participants in the French Camp experience.

There are approximately one hundred day students from the surrounding communities who are not particularly needy or at risk. They come to experience French Camp Academy's excellent academic program.

Rainwater Observatory at French Camp has the second-largest telescope in Mississippi. There are about twenty-two telescopes set up in a nearby field. Interested visitors can contact Jim Hill, who voluntarily assists amateur astronomers.

For groups larger than the bed and breakfast can handle, group camping and a field for overflow campers can be arranged. Other activities, including fishing and hunting, are available by special arrangement.

Because French Camp Academy depends heavily on donations to support its mission, staff members are always delighted to discuss their program with interested visitors.

ཡ ACCOMMODATIONS

French Camp Academy Bed and Breakfast—French Camp, MS 39745; 601-547-6835.

Jeff Busby Campground—At mile marker 193.1; Primitive camping on a first come, first served basis.

12 Kosciusko: "Treasure of the Trace"

At mile marker 160, just a hop, skip, and jump off the Trace, is one of our favorite towns.

Kosciusko, a community of about 10,000, calls itself the "Treasure of the Trace," and after spending a little time here we think you'll agree. Its name is noteworthy, and so is the town. We found a wonderful bed and breakfast called the **Redbud Inn,** unusual restaurant choices, a marble tribute to love, and gift and antiques shops worth browsing.

Your visit should begin with a stop by the **Museum/Information Center,** on the parkway at mile marker 160. We were impressed with the center, even more so when we learned that it was built with donations and is staffed seven days a week with volunteers who are very fond of their town and its history and are happy to discuss it with you.

The center keeps records of its visitors. At the end of 1993, it had 382,048 guests from all fifty states, the District of Columbia, and eighty-four countries.

There you'll learn that this community actually began as a stop at a watering hole. Redbud Springs was located near what is now the court square and was reputed to have the purest drinking water in Mississippi.

With the Treaty of Dancing Rabbit Creek in the 1830s, Attala County was formed and a site selected for its county seat. The task of choosing the name for the county and the county seat fell to the

Kosciusko Museum and Information Center details the life of Tadeusz Kosciuszko.

Statue of Kosciuszko, a Polish engineer who served the United States during the Revolutionary War.

The stately courthouse is surrounded by restaurants, shops, and an antiques mall.

area's representative to the legislature in Jackson, Sam Dodd. He chose Attala as the name of the new county as tribute to a popular novel's fictional Indian princess and Kosciusko to honor Tadeusz Kosciuszko, a Polish engineer who offered his services to George Washington during our nation's struggle for independence. Kosciusko had been much admired by one of Dodd's ancestors. (He apparently altered the spelling slightly.) Although many sites in Mississippi were sites of Civil War battles, Kosciusko never heard a shot fired and has a long tradition of preserving its peaceful environs.

Kosciusko was the home of three young women who founded Delta Gamma sorority in 1873 while they were students in Oxford at the University of Mississippi: Eva Webb (who later married Sam Dodd), Anna Boyd, and Mary Comfort.

Leaving the Museum/Information Center, continue into town on Huntington after you cross the Highway 35 bypass. **Gaf's Restaurant,** one of the most popular dining choices, is a short distance down the bypass. They offer breakfast, lunch, and dinner, Monday–Saturday, and breakfast and a tasty lunch buffet until 2:30 P.M. on Sunday. The **Best Western** and **Days Inn** are both on the bypass as well.

Stop by the **Chamber of Commerce,** at 301 East Jefferson on the corner of Huntington Street, to pick up a driving tour brochure to direct you to more than two dozen historic homes and other points of interest.

If you continue northwest on Huntington, the 1897 courthouse will be toward your left. The surrounding streets are named for presidents Washington, Jackson, Madison, and Jefferson.

Park on the square and you'll find two more restaurants that might interest you. **The Cafe on the Square,** on Jefferson Street, is next door to **Peeler House Antiques and Gifts.** The menu generally includes salads, sandwiches, frozen yogurt, hot sandwiches, soups, bakery goods, and fresh pie, depending on the season. Be sure to do a little exploring at Peeler House before you leave. We found antique jewelry, glassware, and some fine European antiques, but being avid gardeners we were especially pleased to find the Through the Garden Gate section at the rear of the store. After two years of searching for

The Queen Anne style Redbud Inn gets its name from Redbud Springs, the watering hole for travelers of the Trace.

wind chimes with just the right deep, mellow tones, we found them at the Peeler House.

At the corner of West Washington, the **Cornerstone Cafe** plays '50s and '60s music while serving sandwiches like the Dobie Gillis (Cajun roast beef, hickory-smoked turkey, honey-baked ham, and fresh sliced corned beef with Monterey Jack, cheddar, and Swiss cheese, lettuce, and tomato on toasted wheat, white, or French bread) and the I Love Lucy stuffed baked potato (mushrooms, bacon, red onions, melted Swiss cheese, sour cream, black olives, and alfalfa sprouts).

If you really want a treat, go have lunch with Maggie Garrett at the **Redbud Inn,** at 121 North Wells just off the square. We stayed at the Redbud and thoroughly enjoyed our accommodations, but Maggie's cooking is something special for travelers who just can't take another fast-food meal. We made arrangements for dinner the night we stayed, and she served some of the best baked chicken we've ever tasted (it had a light crumb topping and was incredibly moist), broccoli with a delicious artichoke sauce, and desserts you'll have to figure out how to save room for! If you can't stay the night in the 1884 Queen Anne-style inn, try to arrange at least to have lunch.

The Hammond-Routt House is a museum and bed and breakfast located on the original Natchez Trace.

The Hammond-Routt House, at 109 South Natchez, offers an unusual choice for bed and breakfast accommodations. Located on the original Natchez Trace, the 1837 structure, which has been restored, is adjacent to the site of the spring that provided water for Natchez Trace travelers, including Andrew Jackson and his volunteer army.

While some rooms are of museum quality (complete with plexiglass "gates" to prevent entry but to allow full viewing), there are two rooms available for overnight stays, usually for one family (there is only one bath). One room has a queen-size four-poster bed. The other is a two-room suite. A kitchen is also available.

The owner does not live on the premises, but his office is next door. A Continental breakfast is provided, and guided tours are available by appointment only.

We'd be remiss if we didn't tell you about one more choice for lunch or dinner. The **Rib Alley Restaurant,** on South Natchez Street, isn't upscale by any means, but a sign tells you to make yourself at home while you sample a great buffet. The Rotary Club was meeting and eating when we arrived, but we found plenty of barbecue chicken and vegetables on the steam table for $5.35 including tax. The menu includes barbecue, steaks, salads, and sandwiches; items on the buffet vary from day to day. One tip: It seemed cooler in the back room.

At the corner of East Washington and North Huntington, you'll find **Back Pew Gifts and Antiques,** in the old Presbyterian church that now houses the Kosciusko-Attala Historical Society. The items for sale have been donated to the society and include copper and silver trays, glassware, jewelry, and homemade candies and breads.

Kosciusko is the birthplace of TV personality Oprah Winfrey. She lived here with her grandmother until she was six years old, and stories are told locally about her ability to recite Bible verses by the age of three. Tendencies to deliver impromptu sermons at an early age were met with teasing by her peers but may have heralded the talk show career that was to follow. The community has named

Kosciusko is Oprah Winfrey's hometown. She learned to recite Bible verses at this church.

a road for her, but there are no tourist sites associated with
her birthplace.

Before you leave Kosciusko stop by to see the marble tribute to
love in the cemetery between Natchez and Huntington. A bereaved
husband named Kelly sent photos of his beloved late wife, Laura, to
a sculptor in France. The statue was erected in the family burial plot,
where it could be viewed from an upstairs window of his home on
East Jefferson Street. The story is told that its perfect likeness to
Mrs. Kelly in her wedding gown so "refreshed his grief that he could
hardly bear to look at it."

This cemetery is the site of an annual tradition, held each
Memorial Day, when the burial flags of Kosciusko war veterans line
the cemetery in an Aisle of Honor.

Other events of note include the Central Mississippi Fair,
in August, and the **Natchez Trace Festival,** held the last Saturday
in April. This celebration includes an arts and crafts show, food,
and special events for children and adults, including competitive
running/walking events. RV campers can park at the fairgrounds
for $7 a night.

Camping for hikers and bicyclists only is available near the
Natchez Trace Parkway Maintenance Center, just south of the
Museum/Information Center exit. Follow the signs to the maintenance center and look for the entrance to the small, shady primitive
camping area on your right before you pass through the gates to the
maintenance center.

ACCOMMODATIONS

Redbud Inn and Antiques—121 N. Wells, Kosciusko, MS 39090; 601-
   289-5086.
Hammond-Routt House—109 N. Natchez, Kosciusko, MS 39090; 601-
   289-4131 or 800-870-8037 in MS.
Best Western—Parkway Inn, Hwy. 35 Bypass, Kosciusko, MS 39090; 601-
   289-6252.
Campbell's Motel—Hwy. 12, Kosciusko, MS 39090; 601-289-4151.
Days Inn—Hwy. 35 Bypass, Kosciusko, MS 39090; 601-289-2271.

❧ ATTRACTIONS

Museum/Information Center—Natchez Trace Pkwy. & Hwy. 35, Kosciusko,
    MS 39090; 601-289-2981; 9 A.M.–5 P.M.; year-round.

❧ RESTAURANTS

The Cafe on the Square—117 W. Jefferson St., Kosciusko, MS 39090; 601-
    289-5888; Mon.–Sat., 9 A.M.–3 P.M.
Cornerstone Cafe—140 W. Washington, Kosciusko, MS 39090; 601-
    289-8255, FAX 289-8256; Mon.–Thurs., 10 A.M.–5:30 P.M.; Fri.–Sat.,
    10 A.M.–10 P.M.
Gaf's Restaurant—Hwy. 35 Bypass, Kosciusko, MS 39090; 601-289-9990;
    Mon.–Thurs., 6 A.M.–9 P.M.; Fri.–Sat., 6 A.M.–10 P.M.; Sun.,
    6 A.M.–2:30 P.M.
Peking Restaurant—NW Corner of Downtown Sq., Kosciusko, MS 39090;
    601-289-9558; Sun.–Sat., 11 A.M.–2 P.M.; Sun.–Sat., 4:40–9 P.M.
Redbud Inn—121 N. Wells, Kosciusko, MS 39090; 601-289-5086; Lunch,
    11:30 A.M.–1:30 P.M., Mon.–Fri.; Dinner, Sat., 6–9 P.M.
Rib Alley—110 S. Natchez St., Kosciusko, MS 39090; 601-289-9800;
    Mon.–Fri., 11 A.M.–2 P.M.; Tues.–Fri., 5–9 P.M.

❧ SHOPPING

Back Pew Gifts & Antiques—Corner of E. Washington and N. Huntington,
    Kosciusko, MS 39090; 601-289-5165; Tues.–Sat., 1–4 P.M.
The Peeler House Antiques & Gifts—117 W. Jefferson St., Kosciusko, MS
    39090; 601-289-5165; Mon.–Sat., 9 A.M.–5 P.M.

❧ SPECIAL EVENTS

April: Natchez Trace Festival—Juried arts and crafts show, booths, 5K-walk,
    5K/10K-run, and 1-mile fun run; Registration fee; Held last Saturday
    in April; Contact Chamber of Commerce.

❧ FOR MORE INFORMATION

Kosciusko-Attala Chamber of Commerce—P.O. Box 696 (310 E. Jefferson St.),
    Kosciusko, MS 39090; 601-289-2981.

13 Canton: Flea Markets and More

If you like flea markets, you'll love the quaint community of Canton, about 5 miles west of the Trace on Highway 43.

A town of fewer than 15,000, Canton swells to more than double that size for one day each spring and fall when it hosts the juried **Canton Flea Market Arts and Crafts Show,** on the second Thursday of each May and October. Residents we talked to say they think the fall show is better, but neither is to be missed!

Shoppers arrive by the busloads each May and October for the Canton Flea Market.

Busloads of shoppers begin arriving from out of town and even out of state early Thursday morning in preparation for Canton-style "shop till you drop." Enterprising youngsters offer themselves for hire to help carry all your newfound treasures, and find them you will.

Outstanding artists and craftsmen from twenty to thirty different states display their works on the grounds and surrounding streets of the 1858 Greek Revival Madison County Courthouse. Antiques are usually offered at the Catholic Parish Center, across from City Hall, and yard sales spring up along the streets leading to the courthouse square.

Parking is allowed throughout the city as available, and a special parking area is designated south of downtown on Highway 51, with shuttle service to and from the square. It seems especially fitting that this celebration of arts, crafts, and antiquities should take place in a community that is so supportive of these resources.

Canton survived two Union invasions during the Civil War, the yellow fever epidemic of 1870, the loss of its timber-milling industry during the 1920s and 1930s, and the racial strife of the 1960s to become the friendly, lively community it is today. Family names have changed little here through the years, but the community makes every effort to welcome visitors. Shopkeepers may know most of their customers by first names, but they have a friendly greeting for newcomers as well. The residents are rightfully proud of their appreciation and preservation of their heritage.

The Canton Historic Square District was placed on the National Register of Historic Places in 1982 and is considered one of the best in the state of Mississippi. Today there are benches that invite you to linger on the square as many Cantonites have through the years.

Folks here still talk about some of the community's characters. Many years ago, Lot Cheek used to shuffle around the square when he was in Canton after one of his many trips to the jungles of Brazil or the streets of Bombay. He shuffled because his sister once shot him; not much is known about why. Gossips claim he quoted Shakespeare the whole time the doctor was tending his wound.

The Canton Flea Market centers around the courthouse square.

Burton Clark appointed himself town crier and carried a mega-phone around the square shouting all the news, including ballgame scores and special sales.

On tension-filled election days during Reconstruction, a group of officials dispersed an angry crowd that threatened to become a mob—by climbing up in the twenty-foot-diameter dome of the courthouse and pelting the crowd with rocks fired from slingshots.

The courthouse, which is the center of town, is Greek Revival in style and originally cost $26,428. The cornerstone was laid in 1855

by the members of the local Masonic Order, and to this day the
building is one of seven unaltered courthouses remaining in the state.
The courthouse square becomes the center of the two large flea markets each year.

Most of the structures on the square are post-Civil War buildings. One was spared Gen. William Tecumseh Sherman's torch only
because it proved useful for housing wounded soldiers during Union
invasions. In fact, a Union dispatch during 1863, when the army
invaded Canton to destroy the Dixie ordnance works and tear up the
railroad, claimed that "not a dollar's worth of public property was
left in Canton."

During the invasion by his troops, Sherman refused to stay in any
of the homes in the area, fearing treachery by their Rebel owners. He
chose instead to camp beneath a spreading oak tree on East Peace
Street (known locally for many years as the Sherman Oak). The tree
was across the street from the Shackleford House, at 326 East Peace,
which was used as a hospital for wounded soldiers.

When Sherman's soldiers took Canton, they also took all the
livestock they could find. Mrs. Amanda Cage, who lived at 313 East
Peace, needed her missing cow for milk for her baby and proceeded
to Union headquarters to ask for its return. The kindly commanding
officer returned her cow, advising her to keep it close—which she
did, in her bedroom on the east side of the house for the five days
and nights the Union army remained bivouacked.

Many of the antebellum homes along Center and Peace streets
have their share of tragedies, eccentricities, and reputed ghosts in residence. One story told about the Wohner-Rucker House, at 239 East
Center Street, concerns the betrayal of the master of the house. As
Captain Rucker lay dying, a friend who was caring for him (his family had been sent away to avoid exposure to the deadly disease) had
him sign over his house and possessions. When the new widow
returned and learned of her plight, she marshaled the resources to
stand among her neighbors, who refused to bid at the subsequent
estate auction, and repurchased her home piece by piece.

The Mosby House, at 261 East Center Street, is purported to
have an ephemeral resident who appears only to someone in danger

of dying. You would expect such a creature to be gloomy and foreboding, but the ghost has been described as a "cute little twinkly fellow dressed in gray"!

One family member had so much affinity for this house that although she had married and moved down the street, she still came to pick "her" camellias. Although the new owners noticed this, she nevertheless continued to claim ownership of the camellias, because her father had originally planted them. Persisting in the belief that the house was hers, in her later years she would occasionally appear if illness threatened her and stretch out on the floor so she could come back to her own home to die. In spite of her visits, she died elsewhere, and the family suspects that she may have had so many near-fatal illnesses in order to see who was visiting "her" house.

The Presbyterian church on East Fulton Street was like a second home to a young minister's daughter who became widely known with the publication of her best-selling book *A Man Called Peter.* While she lived in Canton, she was known as Catherine Wood; today she is loved and remembered by readers everywhere as Catherine Marshall, the author of *Christy.*

If history is of special interest, stop by the Old Log Cabin, on East Fulton Street. It is the home of the Madison County Historical Society. The nearby old jail was restored by the society after being put on the National Register of Historic Places.

The arts in Canton are nurtured at the **Allison Wells School of Arts and Crafts.** The school is the rebirth of the Allison Wells Resort and the Allison Art Colony, which was established in 1879 and burned in 1963. The new school is located in the renovated Trolio Hotel on the downtown square and features a variety of intensive weeklong workshops for adults in fine and traditional arts, fiber, metal, clay, writing, wood, glass, watercolor, papermaking, weaving, basketry, blacksmithing, clogging and buck dancing, wood carving, quilting, silversmithing, nontraditional bookbinding, and ribbon and Brazilian dimensional embroidery. Accommodations are offered with the workshops for a reasonable rate and include single or double rooms with private or shared baths and meals. Most sessions begin with Sunday registration and dinner and end on Saturday after breakfast. Rates for tuition begin at $185; room and board with shared facilities begin at $185 for the week.

Many courses are offered through Elderhostel, a nonprofit educational organization, and senior citizens who register through Elderhostel receive a discount. The **Colony Gallery** features for sale the work of local and national artists and craftsmen, as well as some of the Allison's Wells instructors.

Other gift shops on the square include **Sulm's** and the **Market Gallery.** At Sulm's we bought a copy of a locally produced cookbook containing only recipes with five ingredients, which we've really enjoyed. The Market Gallery had great T-shirts, posters, and dinnerware tucked among framed prints and an interesting variety of other gift ideas.

Accommodations for travelers in Canton include the **Comfort Inn** and **Days Inn.** The closest camping facilities are offered by **Ratliff Ferry Campground,** a half-mile east of the Natchez Trace Parkway (exit after mile marker 124 when heading south on the parkway) on the Pearl River. It has thirty-five sites, LP gas, thirty- and fifty-amp electric hookups, a sewage system, showers, three boat ramps, and good bank fishing year-round.

Camping facilities are also available at **Holmes County State Park,** 4 miles south of nearby Durant. The park features two fishing lakes, tent camping, twelve cabin units, twenty-eight camping pads, and a skating rink. Both campgrounds accept reservations.

Other events of interest include the Hot Air Balloon Fest and the Red, White, and Blue Talent Show and Barbecue, during the Fourth of July weekend.

If all this shopping and sightseeing has you tired and hungry, stop by **Fontaine's Restaurant** on the square. The decor is tasteful and appropriate for the square. Other restaurants include **Blue's Fish House,** Hardee's, McDonald's, Penn's-to-Go, **Penn's Fish House,** Pizza Hut, Subway, and Wendy's.

⮞ ACCOMMODATIONS

Comfort Inn—199 Frontage Rd., Canton, MS; 1-601-859-2643.
Days Inn—123 Sidney Runnels Ave., Canton, MS; 1-601-859-0760.

Ratliff Ferry Campgrounds—1275 Ratliff Ferry Rd., Canton, MS 39046;
   601-859-1810; 12 miles east of Canton on the Pearl River; Full-
   service RV sites, tent camping, restaurant, three boat ramps; Open
   year-round.

ATTRACTIONS

Holmes County State Park—Rt. 1, Box 153, Durant, MS 39063, 1-601-
   653-3351.
Ratliff Ferry Campground—1275 Ratliff Ferry Rd., Canton, MS 39046; 601-
   859-181; Fishing and camping on the Pearl River, with access to Ross
   Barnett Reservoir.
Coal Bluff Park—3 miles north of Hwy. 25 for camping, canoeing, fishing,
   picnicking, swimming, and nature trail; 601-654-7726.
Leake County Water Park—8 miles north of Hwy. 25 for camping, canoeing,
   fishing, picnicking, swimming, and nature trail; 601-654-7355.
Allison Wells School of Arts and Crafts—P.O. Box 950 (234 E. Fulton St.),
   Canton, MS 39046; 601-859-5826 or 800-489-2787, FAX 601-
   859-5819.

RESTAURANTS

Blue's Fish House—601-859-7487
Fontaine's Restaurant—601-859-7182
Penn's Fish House—601-859-1315

SHOPPING

The Cameo Shop—601-859-1991
Colony Gallery—601-859-5826
The Market Gallery—601-859-8055
Primitives—601-859-4887
Sulm's—601-859-7851

SPECIAL EVENTS

Contact Canton Convention and Visitors Bureau for dates and particulars
   of the following events:
Elmo James Hickory Street Festival—Blues and jazz musician Elmo James
   is celebrated.

May: Flea markets—May and October.

July: Mississippi Hot Air Balloon Races—Independence Day celebration of balloons, fireworks, parade, entertainment, and much more.

October: Flea markets

❧ FOR MORE INFORMATION

Canton Chamber of Commerce—P.O. Box 74 (226 E. Peace St.), Canton, MS 39046-0074; 601-859-5816; ask for the walking tour guide that lists antebellum homes and points of interest.

Canton Convention and Visitors Bureau—P.O. Box 53, Canton, MS 39046; 601-859-1307 or 859-3369.

Canton Flea Market—P.O. Box 382, Canton, MS 39046; 601-859-8055.

14 *Madison: Hometown, Mississippi*

Located 10 miles north of Jackson, Madison is small but prosperous. To get there from the Trace, turn west off the parkway on Highway 463. You'll pass by a little airport and the Strawberry Patch Park (so named because Madison was the "Strawberry Capital of the World"), on the northern side of the road as you're coming in. The park has a little lake and a playground.

Madison averages one new family per day, as well as one new building permit per day. The community boasts the highest per capita income and the highest standard of living in the state. The population in 1990 was 7,471 and is expected to double by the year 2000.

Come into Madison down Main Street to Depot Antiques, an antiquer's delight. Located within walking distance are many antiques shops, a cafe for lunch, and a bookstore.

Ann-Tiques features country and European; Talk of the Town has European; and **Alene's Antiques and Collectibles** is in a restored dining car. Across the street from Depot Antiques, the **Inside Story** has antiques and gifts. At the corner of Herron and Main streets is **Pickenpaugh Pottery.**

Take Highway 463 west of Madison toward Annandale to see a magnificent structure, Chapel of the Cross, erected in 1852 for the Johnston family by builders of Annandale. This church is an outstanding example of nineteenth-century Gothic revival architecture. The nearby Johnston home was used as headquarters by General Sherman.

❧ ACCOMMODATIONS

Kirkhaven B & B—187 Dogwood Ln., Madison, MS 39110; 601-
982-7381 or 856-8163.

❧ RESTAURANTS

The Strawberry Cafe—Main St., Madison, MS 39110; 601-856-3822;
Mon.–Sat., 11 A.M.–9 P.M.

❧ SHOPPING

Alene's Antiques & Collectibles—Madison Depot, Main St., Madison, MS
39110; 601-853-1023.
Ann-Tiques—118 Depot St., Madison, MS 39110; 601-853-4939.
Antique Alley—Madison Depot, Main St., Madison, MS 39110; 601-
853-1349.
Gretchen's Bookstore—180 Main St., Madison, MS 39110; 601-853-3932.
The Inside Story—Main St., Madison, MS 39110; 601-856-3229.
Madison Antiques Market—Post Oak Rd. at Main, Madison, MS 39110; 601-
856-8036.
Pickenpaugh Pottery—P.O. Box 314, Madison, MS 39110; 601-856-4985.

❧ FOR MORE INFORMATION

Madison Chamber of Commerce—601-856-7060.

15 Jackson: From Chimneyville to the "Bold New City"

The temporary terminus north of Jackson requires you to get on I-55, then turn west on I-20 to get back on the Trace. But don't be in a hurry; there is far too much you might miss.

Today's Jackson, a thriving community of 260,000 friendly folks, offers visitors a variety of activities ranging from museums to water slides, international ballet competitions and blues to fishing and camping at **LeFleur's Bluff State Park** and to the elegant **Millsaps Buie House** bed and breakfast.

Jackson Skyline—A modern southern city arose from the ashes of "Chimneyville" after Jackson was burned during the Civil War.

The history of the city began in 1789 with the establishment of a trading post on Choctaw land by a Canadian, Louis LeFleur. LeFleur's Bluff, as it came to be called, was selected in 1820 as the central site for a new seat of Mississippi government after the land was acquired as part of a treaty negotiated with the Choctaw by Andrew Jackson and Thomas Hinds. LeFleur's Bluff, renamed Jackson in honor of Andrew Jackson, had the dual virtues of navigable waters and proximity to the Natchez Trace. The city grew and prospered until it became the target for General Grant in his quest to control Vicksburg and the Mississippi River during the Civil War.

Most of the antebellum structures of Jackson were destroyed by fires that raged through the city, causing it to be referred to as "Chimneyville." Grant chose to neutralize the city by burning it rather than leave indispensable troops behind as occupational forces. We've all heard the phrase "war is hell." That was General Sherman's sentiment as he watched the people leave the burning city.

After the war Jackson revived, and today it is one of the most progressive metropolitan areas of the South. We were surprised and delighted by Jackson, known as the "bold new city," and we hope you will be too!

Just before you get to Jackson traveling south on the Trace, you will come to a couple of exits for Ross Barnett Reservoir. The view from the reservoir overlook on the Trace is lovely. Turn east on U.S. 471 to go across the lake. On the eastern side is a campground and marina. Look in the Mississippi Outdoor section of this book for names and numbers of campgrounds. There are also two marinas on the west side of the dam, just south of the reservoir overlook.

Within the downtown area you'll find restaurants, hotels, and motels to fit your budget and tastes. If you arrive during business hours, a good place to go for complete information on what's available is the **MetroJackson Convention and Visitors Bureau,** on 921 North President Street. We found spots we especially enjoyed and are happy to share them with you. Some are institutions, likely to survive the shifting sands of time; others are more entrepreneurial but well worth the search if you take the time.

The Ross Barnett Reservoir on the Pearl River is the source of Jackson's water supply.

Millsaps Buie House is a deluxe bed and breakfast in the heart of downtown Jackson.

First on our list, because we feel you really must find suitable accommodations before you can set out for proper adventuring, is the **Millsaps Buie House.** If it fits into your agenda, don't miss it. The house was beautifully and lovingly restored not once but twice. As it was nearing completion, it was burned by a young runaway, and the work had to be undertaken again.

With its nice combination of privacy and intimacy, the house has the feel of a small luxury hotel. We spent the night in a lovely room with a gorgeous half-tester ("tee-ster") bed, a color TV hidden in an armoire, and period occasional chairs. We think you'll agree, the result is akin to being given the keys to a lovely museum. Museums, however, usually have signs warning you not to touch, but not so here. You are even invited to play the antique piano in the parlor.

The folks at the Millsaps Buie House have a wonderful knack for making visitors feel right at home from the first welcoming smile. In fact, we decided Nancy Fleming, our hostess, needs to have some sort of designation as a living local landmark. She and her traveling buddy, Mary Current, have visited Mississippi's highways and haunts many a weekend and will happily regale you with tales if you too have an adventurous spirit. Nancy claims to be the butler referred to by John Grisham in *The Chamber* (she'll show you the page).

If reading is a special interest, you'll want to ask about Jackson's first lady of literature, Eudora Welty, who lives just a few blocks away. Just down the street you'll find the **Eudora Welty Library,** which has a Mississippi writers room that proudly displays memorabilia associated with more than 1,500 Mississippi authors, including Welty, William Faulkner, Tennessee Williams, Shelby Foote, and Ellen Gilchrist. An adjoining audiovisual room offers viewing screens and a variety of videotapes by and about various authors as well.

(A conversation between William Faulkner and Clark Gable: Faulkner was working as a screenwriter in Hollywood, and the two were dove-hunting together. Gable asked Faulkner, "Who do you think is a good writer, Mr. Faulkner?" The latter replied, "Thomas Mann, Willa Cather, John Dos Passos, Ernest Hemingway, and myself." Gable: "Oh, Mr. Faulkner, do you write?" Faulkner: "Yes, and what do you do, Mr. Gable?")

Regarding his Nobel Prize, Faulkner is reported to have said, "I fear that some of my fellow Mississippians will never forgive that $30,000 that durn foreign country gave me just for sitting on my ass and writing stuff that makes my own state ashamed to own me."

For those of you desiring slightly less luxurious accommodations, there's an ample assortment of national motel chains nearby.

Now that you're settled in your room, how about something to eat? Assuming you're more adventurous than room service at this point, Jackson has quite a menu from which to choose. You already know what to expect from fast-food chains, so we'll clue you in on our experiences with local establishments, although we'll give you a more complete listing under Restaurants at the end of this chapter.

For the upscale diner, **Nick's,** on Lakeland Drive, takes dinner reservations. Also for the upscale diner willing to drive a bit is **Shapley's,** on Centre Street in Ridgeland, open for dinner only. **Amerigo,** on Old Canton Road in Ridgeland, offers fine dining, including Italian and American, for lunch and dinner.

For the moderate budget, the **Iron Horse Grill,** on Pearl Street, is a good choice if you like southwestern fare. Still of interest to the moderate diner looking for a lively crowd and good food is **Hal and Mal's,** in an old converted warehouse on Commerce Street, featuring a varied menu for lunch and dinner along with live bands and dancing.

Hal and Mal's menu includes Papa's Oyster Stew (in season), seafood gumbo, stuffed jalapeños, all kinds of salads, po' boys, burgers from heaven, red beans and rice, quiche, sweet potato pecan pie, bread pudding with whiskey sauce, apple pie à la mode, and Kentucky Derby pie.

Hal told us they have a scholarship program that offers an internship to student chefs from local Hinds Community College. The night we visited, the chef-in-residence's specials were grilled shrimp with a jalapeño cream sauce, red snapper, and curried corn with tasso soup.

One of the few spots open for dinner on Sundays is the local institution known as **Crechale's,** on Highway 80 West. So many local folks had fond memories of special events occurring in a certain booth while dining at Crechale's that a howl was heard throughout Jackson when they tried to redecorate. We hate to think what would happen if they tried to change the menu!

Speaking of local institutions, for breakfast, lunch (featuring Greek salads), and dinner, including fresh seafood, visit the **Mayflower Restaurant** on Capitol Street (which has probably remained unchanged for the past twenty years, so turn your attention to the fresh raw oysters and seafood salad, not the decor).

Don't let the Millsaps College crowd keep **CS's,** at the corner of West Street and Adelle Street, to themselves. We heard about Inez Burgers, a staple at CS's, from a nurse we met in Tupelo; she swore they were responsible for giving her the energy to get through nursing school. CS's also offers plate lunches.

If good home-style cooking sets your mouth to watering, **Perry's Soul Food Kitchen,** on Highway 51 North in Ridgeland, has a buffet that can't be beat. Marie Perry says, "When you can't go to Mama's, come see us!" on Highway 51 North in Ridgeland. One of the best barbecue spots in Jackson: **Gridley's,** on Old Square Road. They're open on Sundays, and they serve breakfast on Saturdays only.

Mississippi Crafts Center is at the
temporary terminus of the Trace
north of Jackson. It offers a wide
variety of crafts.

Wood carving is one of the crafts displayed at the Mississippi Crafts Center.

Mississippi Crafts Center has a variety of offerings, including
some really nice pottery, rocking chairs, and baskets. It's at the temporary end of the Trace, on the north side of Jackson.

We think you'll find Jackson especially rich in opportunities
for kids of all ages. While we ventured to the **Mississippi Museum
of Art,** at the corner of Lamar and Pascagoula, especially to see a
traveling Degas exhibit, we were mesmerized by a video camera in
the children's Impressions Gallery; it translated our movements into
vibrant colors that flowed across a larger-than-life screen. Several
other activities were equally appealing, including a plasma globe
containing neon and argon arcs that follow your hand as you move
it across the surface.

If you want to rest a bit before heading next door to the **Russell
C. Davis Planetarium,** the museum has a well-stocked gift shop and

a cafe that offers lunch selections like chicken-salad sandwiches and hot dogs that span the generations.

Judging by the excited whispers of twenty or so well-mannered five- and six-year-olds, the transition from earthbound child to awestruck space explorer is rapidly made. The planetarium is home to the Ronald E. McNair Space Theater, named for one of the astronauts, a Mississippi native, who perished during the ill-fated *Challenger* flight in January 1986. He was the cinematographer for the orbital scenes in the film shown in the theater. The planetarium has laser shows throughout the week. Call the planetarium at 601-960-1550 for a current schedule.

Every four years the USA International Ballet Competition takes place in Jackson. The Jackson location alternates with Varna, Bulgaria; Helsinki, Finland; Moscow; and Paris as the competition's host city, and awards include cash and gold, silver, and bronze medals. The next competition in Jackson will be in 1998 at the City Auditorium.

Also of interest for the whole family is the **Jim Buck Ross Mississippi Agriculture and Forestry/National Agricultural Aviation Museum,** on Lakeland Drive. There are a variety of inside and outside activities and enough room for young legs to stretch a bit. You can visit a muscadine vineyard; herb and rose gardens; re-creations of an 1860s farmstead with farmhouse and outbuildings; and Smalltown, Mississippi, a town of the 1920s complete with gas station, church, schoolhouse, jail, and general store. Artifacts from Indian arrowheads to airplanes used for crop-dusting are on display in the museum.

Jim Buck Ross Museum has a forestry auditorium, merry-go round for the kids, Ethnic Heritage Center, Chimneyville Crafts Center, the Fitzgerald collection, two emu, a church, an infirmary, and a children's barnyard. The Fortenberry-Hartman Farm represents a typical family farm in operation from 1860 to 1960; a cotton gin and buildings were moved here from Jefferson Davis County. A good spot for children to explore and expend some energy, the farm is located north on I-55 at County Line Road.

The Arts and Crafts Pavilion houses an information desk for the Jackson Visitors Center along with a fine collection of crafts by the

The Jim Buck Ross Mississippi Agriculture and Forestry/National Agricultural Aviation Museum is a family oriented attraction.

Craftsmen's Guild of Mississippi for sale. You can walk a short forest-study trail, stop by the refreshment stand, or have a picnic before you leave the park to travel just next door to visit the **Dizzy Dean Museum.** Or take in a ballgame at the Smith-Wills Stadium, home of the AA Houston Astros farm club, the Jackson Generals.

Just across the street is the entrance to **LeFleur's Bluff State Park.** Day-use facilities are available for fishing, paddleboats, canoes, swimming (pool), golfing, tennis, picnic facilities, and hiking on a series of short nature trails. Anglers must have a Mississippi fishing license, which may be purchased from the park office.

Mayes Lake is stocked with crappie, catfish, bass, and bream. Although you can rent a fishing boat if you wish, there's good access for bank fishing, and some is wheelchair accessible. We recommend that you bring your own tackle and bait, because the camp store had a very spartan supply: crickets, worms, a few hooks, and some cane poles.

The nine-hole golf course and driving range has golf carts, clubs, and pull carts available for rent. The park also offers a bathhouse and camp store, sites for thirty RVs, and tents equipped with water and electricity. A limited number of these sites are available with advance reservations; the remainder are first come, first served. We visited in mid-June, and several lakeside sites were open. We found the campground nice and shady and the facilities clean and well kept.

If you continue on Lakeland, it turns into Highway 25. Follow it until you intersect with Spillway Road, at the southern end of Ross Barnett Reservoir, to experience some cool summertime fun at **Rapids on the Reservoir.** For the young and young at heart there are twin typhoon slides to pump you up and cool you down! The Whip offers 215 feet of wet and winding fun; the Rip Tide slides you more directly to the big splash. A wave pool and a host of amusement-park rides keep you entertained until it's time to picnic. The Tadpool provides supervised fun and safety for the wee ones. If your family has divided interests, the park offers a day camp from 7 A.M. to 6 P.M. for children six to twelve years of age. It's complete with drinks, snack, hot lunch, and activities that include swimming, swimming lessons, water and amusement rides, volleyball, softball, and arts and crafts; in the meantime, the adults can sample Jackson's dining, shopping, and cultural amenities. Contact the water park for more information and a schedule of concert appearances, as well.

Nearby, water lovers will find **Waterland, USA** another of Jackson's summer hot spots for cooling off in the pools and water slides.

The Discover Zoo section of the **Jackson Zoo,** at 2918 West Capitol Street, gives children a chance to burrow through a prairie dog exhibit or walk like turtles in kid-size turtle shells, so be sure to bring your cameras to catch your kids monkeying around. The zoo staff is quite proud of the attention given to the natural environments they have created for the animals in their care; they are also justifiably proud of their emphasis on children's programs that allow them to educate through entertainment.

The Smith Robertson Museum and Cultural Center, at 528 Bloom Street, is home to the Smithsonian Institution's Field to Farm exhibit, as well as powerful exhibits and artifacts that tell the story of the struggles and achievements of Mississippi's African-Americans.

The site, located in the heart of the black community known as the Farish Street Historic District, was that of Jackson's first public

The Oaks House is one of the few pre-Civil War structures remaining in Jackson.

The Manship House contains fine examples of wood graining and many furnishings from the family's collection.

school for African-American children and is named for Smith Robertson, who was born a slave in Fayette, Alabama, in 1840. After moving to Jackson in 1874, he earned his livelihood as a barber and served as an alderman from 1893 to 1899. At his urging the school was established. Special activities are held here during Black History Month each year.

Early on, his area was the center of black business and culture not only for Jackson but also for much of the rest of the state. Rural blacks came to the area to transact business, and Farish Street bustled with activity from morning to night as people sold their goods, stopped to visit with friends and family, or entertained the crowd. In its heyday the Crystal Palace Night Club, on Farish Street, welcomed entertainers like Duke Ellington and Louis Armstrong. During the '50s and '60s, civil rights organizers, including Martin Luther King, Jr., and Medgar Evers, held meetings in the area. Today the fact that the African-American community in Mississippi claims more government officials than in any other state is due in no small part to all who sacrificed personal safety for civil rights.

Downtown, several other historic sites are open for tours, including Jackson's oldest house, the **Oaks House Museum.** General Sherman occupied this unpretentious house during the siege of Jackson, in June 1863. A picket fence is shaded by the oak trees that give this home its name. Visiting hours are Tuesday through Saturday, 10 A.M.–3 P.M.

The Gothic Revival **Manship House,** on the other hand, was occupied by the mayor of Jackson, who was forced to surrender the city to General Sherman. Charles Henry Manship was trained as an ornamental painter, and examples of his wood graining survive and have been restored. (Pay close attention to the graining done over the wallpaper in the dining room.) Manship House dons its summer dress—white cotton slipcovers—to protect its furnishings from insects. There is a considerable amount of furniture from the family's collection. Tours are available Tuesday through Saturday.

The **Old Capitol,** built in the 1830s while the dirt streets of Jackson were traveled by fewer than one thousand residents, also survived the Civil War. These walls have seen many dramas unfold, including the passage of the first law in America giving property rights to women (1839) and Jefferson Davis's final address to the legislature (1884). It also served as the state capitol from 1839 to 1903.

Beautiful twin stairways spiral to the third floor of this Greek Revival building, which was restored to its former grandeur in 1961. It now contains the **State Historical Museum** beneath its 120-foot-high rotunda, columns, and elaborate moldings. The museum shares Mississippi's story, her defeats, and her glories.

Restored from 1959 to 1961 as the State Historical Museum, a division of the Mississippi Department of Archives and History, it is wheelchair accessible via a ramp to the left. Open doors lead to each of the display areas, which include one devoted to Hernando de Soto, the first white man to explore the Mississippi River. Native American effigy pipes, vessels, arrowheads, and pottery are also on display.

The Civil War resolved two major questions left unanswered by the Constitution: Could states secede, thereby breaking up the Republic? and Could slavery continue in a society dedicated to individual freedom?

The Civil War room offers a variety of interesting exhibits, including one that explains that Mississippi women fought their own war to maintain plantations and farms, to provide food, clothing, and housing for their families, and to supervise slave labor. They provided supplies for soldiers at the front, served as nurses to the wounded, and acted as blockade runners. Threatened pillaging by Union deserters and possible slave uprisings were constant concerns. Of the more than 78,000 men who marched off to war, 28,000 were killed and thousands more maimed. People struggled to rebuild their personal lives while public buildings, roads, and railroads had to be rebuilt by a newly emerging political order in this land of defeated former Confederates and black freedmen.

There is also a Jefferson Davis room, which depicts events from his life, including his marriage to the belle of Natchez and his imprisonment in solitary confinement after the war.

The Old Capitol has become the State Historical Museum and is wheelchair accessible.

The 120-foot high rotunda in the Old Capitol looks down upon exhibits that illustrate Mississippi's story.

A primary election system established in Mississippi in 1902 brought to power politicians who championed the white working class. The supporters of James K. Vardaman and Theodore Bilbo adopted red neckties as their badge, playing up to the "redneck" voters—those rural workers whose necks became sunburned from working in the fields.

Another powerful exhibit highlights the struggle for equal rights, including activist Medgar Evers' march in Jackson in 1964.

Across the railroad tracks you'll find the Mississippi Museum of Natural Science, which includes more than a quarter-million specimens of the plants and animals that inhabit Mississippi's waters, skies, woods, and fields, all exhibited in dioramas and aquaria.

Just a few blocks away, on East Capitol Street, you can tour the Mississippi **Governor's Mansion** Tuesday through Friday between 9:30 and 11 A.M. Although designated a National Historic Landmark, this is the official residence of the governor, and the staff asks that groups of five or more please notify them in advance of the time they wish to tour the mansion. Tours begin at the West Street entrance. This residence was briefly occupied by General Sherman as he hosted a dinner here after the fall of Vicksburg, but today it is the scene of happier events for Mississippians.

The Governor's Mansion is a national historic landmark. Tours are available Tuesday through Friday.

The **New Mississippi State Capitol,** built in 1903 for approximately $1.9 million, was restored from 1979 to 1982 for approximately $19 million. Stained-glass skylights jewel this splendid structure, modeled after the plan of the National Capitol in Washington, DC. The rotunda is exquisite, and there's a statue in front dedicated to the women of Mississippi: mothers, daughters, sisters, and wives. Weekday tours are available. It is open on weekends, and you can use a self-guided tour.

You have to see this building to appreciate how beautiful its ornate beaux arts architecture really is. The stained-glass domes are breathtaking, and the life-size statues that grace the lobby are truly magnificent.

Jackson offers many opportunities for shoppers ranging from antiques to crafts, artwork to the latest fashions. Contact **MetroJackson Convention and Visitors Bureau** for a complete listing. We have a special fondness for old books, so we were especially pleased to find Cottage Antiques, on North State Street, along with several other antiques shops. For a mixture of antiques and decorative arts, we enjoyed locating the **Interiors Market** (yes, there is also one in Atlanta, and you have probably seen them mentioned in *Architectural Digest*), on 659 Duling Avenue, by going north on State Street until we intersected Duling. There are thirty antiques booths and decorative arts shops containing an interior decorator's treasure trove: furniture, lamps, pieces of sculpture, carpets, mirrors, garden accents, and wrought iron. Owners Linda Shelton and Kathy Guyton have items ranging in price from $2 to $34,000.

The Interiors Market also contains a restaurant called Market Bites, which daily serves pasta dishes, sandwiches, a chicken-and-artichoke salad, a salad plate, turtle brownies, and cookies.

Ridgeland, north of Jackson, offers the Antique Mall of the South and several other similar shopping opportunities.

To return to the Trace, take I-55 or I-220 to I-20 West and watch for the sign for the exit to the parkway. If you stay on I-20, it will take you to Vicksburg, which is the focus of the next chapter.

The new Mississippi State Capitol is a breathtaking example of beaux arts architecture.

❧ ACCOMMODATIONS

There are many motel chains in Jackson. Contact the MetroJackson Convention and Visitors Bureau for a brochure.

Millsaps Buie House—628 N. State St., Jackson, MS 39202; 601-352-0221.

❧ ATTRACTIONS

Dizzy Dean Museum—1202 Lakeland Dr., Jackson, MS 39216; 601-904-2404; $1; April–Sept.; Tues.–Sat., 12–6 P.M.; Sun., 1–5 P.M.

Eudora Welty Library—300 N. State St., Jackson, MS 39201; 601-968-5811.

Governor's Mansion—300 E. Capitol St., Jackson, MS 39202; 601-359-3175; Free; Tues.–Fri., 9:30–11 A.M.

Jackson Zoo—2918 W. Capitol St., Jackson, MS 39209; 601-352-2580; Nominal charge; June–Aug., daily, 9 A.M.–6 P.M.; Sept.–May, 9 A.M.–5 P.M.

Jim Buck Ross Mississippi Agriculture & Forestry/National Agricultural Aviation Museum—1150 Lakeland Dr., Jackson, MS 39216; 800-844-TOUR; $3 adults, $1 children, $2.75 seniors; Mon.–Sat., 9 A.M.–5 P.M.; Sun., 1–5 P.M.

LeFleur's Bluff State Park—2140 Riverside Dr., Jackson, MS 39202; 800-467-2757.

Manship House—420 E. Fortification St., Jackson, MS 39202; 601-961-4724; Tues.–Fri., 9 A.M.–4 P.M.; Sat., 1–4 P.M.

Mississippi Museum of Art—210 Pascagoula St., Jackson, MS 39201; 601-960-1515; Tues.–Sat., 10 A.M.–5 P.M.; Sun., 12–5 P.M.

Mississippi Museum of Natural Science—111 N. Jefferson St., Jackson, MS 39202; 601-354-7303; Free; Mon.–Fri., 8 A.M.–5 P.M.; Sat., 9:30 A.M.–4:30 P.M.

New State Capitol—400 High St., Jackson, MS 39202; Free; Mon.–Fri., 8 A.M.–5 P.M.

The Oaks—823 N. Jefferson St., Jackson, MS 39202; 601-353-9339; Tues.–Sat., 10 A.M.–4 P.M.; Sun., 12–4 P.M.

Rapids on the Reservoir—24 Spillway Rd., Jackson, MS 39242; 601-992-0500.

Smith Robertson Museum & Cultural Center—528 Bloom St., Jackson, MS 39207; 601-960-1457; $1 adults, 50¢ children; Mon.–Fri., 9 A.M.–5 P.M.; Sat., 9 A.M.–12 P.M.; Sun., 2–5 P.M.

Russell C. Davis Planetarium—210 E. Pascagoula St., Jackson, MS 39201; 601-960-1550.
State Historical Museum (Old Capitol Bldg.)—P.O. Box 571, Jackson, MS 39205; 601-359-6920; Donations; Mon.–Fri., 8 A.M.–5 P.M.; Sat., 9:30 A.M.–4:40 P.M.; Sun., 12:30–4:30 P.M.
Waterland USA—700 Hwy. 51 N., Jackson, MS 39202; 601-957-1323.

✌ RESTAURANTS

Amerigo—6592 Canton Rd., Ridgeland, MS 39157; 601-977-0563; Mon.-Thurs., 11 A.M.–10 P.M.; Fri.–Sat., 11 A.M.–10:30 P.M.
Cafe Creole—5852 Ridgewood Rd., Jackson, MS 39211; 601-956-4563; Sun.–Thurs., 11 A.M.–10 P.M.; Fri.–Sat., 11 A.M.–11 P.M.
Crechale's—3107 Hwy 80 W., Jackson, MS 39206; 601-355-1840; Sun.–Thurs., 4–11 P.M.; Fri.–Sat., 4–11:30 P.M.
CS's—1359 1/2 N. West St. Jackson, MS 39202; 601-969-9482; Mon.–Sat., 11 A.M.–11 P.M.
Dennery's—330 Greymont Ave., Jackson, MS 39202; 601-354-2527; Mon.–Fri., 11 A.M.–10 P.M.; Sat,. 5–10 P.M.
Gridley's Fine BBQ—1428 Old Jackson Sq. Rd., Jackson, MS 39211; 601-362-8600; Sun.–Thurs., 11 A.M.–9:30 P.M.; Fri.–Sat., 10:30 A.M.–10:30 P.M.
Hal & Mal's—200 S. Commerce St., Jackson, MS 39201; 601-948-0888; Mon.–Thurs., 11 A.M.–11 P.M.; Fri.–Sat., 11 A.M.–1 A.M.
Iron Horse Grill—320 W. Pearl St., Jackson, MS 39201; 601-355-8419; Daily 11 A.M.–11 P.M.
Mayflower Cafe—123 W. Capitol St., Jackson, MS 39201; Mon.–Sun., 7:30–12:30 A.M.
Nick's—1501 Lakeland Dr., Jackson, MS 39216; 601-981-8017; Mon.–Thurs., 11 A.M.–11 P.M.; Fri.–Sat., 11 A.M.–11:30 P.M.
Perry's Soul Food Kitchen—820 Hwy 51, Ridgeland, MS; 601-856-9595.
Shapley's—863 Centre St., Ridgeland, MS 39157; 601-957-3753; Mon.–Thurs., 5–9 P.M.; Sat., 5–10 P.M.

✌ SHOPPING

Chimneyville Crafts Gallery—1150 Lakeland Dr., Jackson, MS 39216; 601-981-2499.

The Craftsmen's Guild of Mississippi/Mississippi Crafts Center—P.O. Box 69, Ridgeland, MS 39158; 601-856-7546.

Interiors Market—659 Duling Ave., Jackson, MS 39205; 601-981-6020; Mon.–Sat., 10 A.M.–5:30 P.M.

❧ SPECIAL EVENTS

October. Craftsmen's Guild Pioneer and Indian Festival—P.O. Box 69, Ridgeland, MS 39158; 601-856-7546; Fourth Sat. in Oct. at mile marker 102.4; Crafts sales and demonstrations, historical demonstrations and exhibits, food, square dance, African-American gospel, Choctaw stickball game, and bluegrass-gospel sing.

❧ FOR MORE INFORMATION

MetroJackson Convention and Visitors Bureau—P.O. Box 1450 (921 N. President St.), Jackson, MS 39202; 601-960-1891 or 800-354-7695, FAX 601-960-1827.

16 Vicksburg: The South's Friendliest River Town

Three reasons to visit Vicksburg come to mind immediately: history, hospitality, and home-style cooking.

There are three ways to enter modern Vicksburg: approximately 25 miles southwest of Jackson via I-20, 18 miles west of the Natchez Trace Parkway via Highway 27, and 28 miles northwest of Port Gibson via U.S. Route 61.

One day just isn't enough time to properly visit all that Vicksburg offers, so plan for at least a three-day visit. We'll begin our recommendations with accommodations and trust you'll take our advice and let yourself be seduced by this spirited city.

The Mississippi River drains more than 1,250,000 square miles or nearly 41% of the continental United States.

The lovely parterre gardens at the Corners Mansion Bed and Breadfast look toward the Yazoo and Mississippi rivers.

Accommodations tend to be located along two main corridors, the battlefield area and Washington Street. You'll find several local motels and national chains near the battlefield, including Holiday Inn, Hampton Inn, and Scottish Inn. To reach this area, take Exit 4B from I-20. The **Vicksburg Convention and Visitors Bureau** is just across the street from the entrance to the **National Military Park**. To reach the Washington Street area, take Exit 1A from I-20 just before you cross the Mississippi River Bridge.

We enthusiastically suggest you experience some of Vicksburg's finest antiquities on a more intimate level by staying at some of the city's many fine bed and breakfasts. We must warn you, however, that this can be a life-changing decision. Just ask Bettye and Cliff Whitney of the **Corners** (one of the best bed and breakfasts we've encountered and very deserving of their AAA four-diamond rating!).

The Whitneys were on their way to the District of Columbia from Dallas, took a wrong turn, wound up in Vicksburg, and stayed at **Cedar Grove,** at the corner of Klein and Oak streets. The next morning they took a stroll down Oak Street, fell in love with the Corners, and bought the 1872 Greek Revival and Victorian mansion.

It was built as a wedding present for Susan Klein and her husband, Isaac Bohnam, by Susan's father, John Klein, the owner of Cedar Grove. Susan ultimately returned to live at Cedar Grove, taking all her possessions with her, after the death of her husband.

That meant that the Whitneys were faced with the formidable task of locating period furnishings for eleven rooms. They have managed to accumulate an impressive collection, ranging from elegant half-tester and tester ("tee-ster") beds, which are typical of the fine furnishings found in the homes of wealthy southerners, to a fine example of an Eastlake bedroom set. A large double parlor is graced by a beautiful grand piano, Italian marble mantels, and Victorian settees. The ceiling medallions were constructed of horsehair, molasses, and plaster on the site by traveling craftsmen from New Orleans. At about the time the house was being built, electricity was being introduced. This unproven utility caused concern, and people were uncertain of its future, so many light fixtures were designed to offer illumination by both gas and electricity.

The front facade of the Corners boasts a sixty-eight-foot-long gallery that looks toward the sun setting over the Yazoo and Mississippi rivers to the west and accented with columns sporting hand-carved clubs, spades, diamonds, and hearts celebrating the city's colorful riverboat days.

The Whitneys rediscovered the mansion's unusual formal parterre gardens and original brickwork beneath years of accumulated soil. The wrought-iron fence enclosing the gardens was made in Philadelphia and shipped down the Ohio and Mississippi rivers to Vicksburg. We chose to stay in a guest room in the converted servants' quarters overlooking the lovely informal gardens at the rear of the property. The scent of jasmine drifted across the porch to the rocking chairs where we sipped fresh lemonade. A pine four-poster bed, fireplace, and Jacuzzi awaited us inside. The Whitneys had even thoughtfully provided fresh flowers from Cliff's garden and candles by the tub. Now, that's my idea of resting at the end of a long day of sightseeing! We hope you'll find the Corners as charming as we did.

At Cedar Grove, across the street, visitors can choose to stay in the main house or in one of eight bed and breakfast accommodations in

Cedar Grove Mansion features eighteen guest rooms with private baths.

the carriage house. The house was built around 1840 by John Klein, who began his career as a jeweler and clockmaker and invested his profits in lumber. His lumber business prospered, and next he invested in railroads before becoming president of Mississippi Valley Bank. The Italian marble mantels, gasoliers, and pier mirrors were brought to Vicksburg from Europe by John and his wife, Elizabeth. There's a hole in the front door, courtesy of a cannonball fired from a Union gunboat (the ball is still lodged in the wall of the ladies' parlor).

The mansion probably survived the war because Elizabeth was a cousin of General Sherman's, who ordered his troops to spare the house. History enthusiasts can reserve the Grant Room and sleep in the king-size canopy bed, which was made by New Orleans furniture-maker Prudent Mallard and is believed to have been used by General Grant when he occupied the house after the siege. In the Music Room you'll find a rare Centennial Edition piano valued at more than $1 million. The Library Suite contains many of John Klein's books and has a circular stair that descends to the bedroom below. The Master Suite has Italian marble fireplaces in both the sitting room and the bedroom, a Jacuzzi, and a private balcony. Many locals venture to Cedar Grove at cocktail hour to enjoy the piano bar from 6 to 9 P.M. Delicious meals are also served for guests and the public in the Garden Room Restaurant, where the specialty is New Orleans cuisine.

As you continue into downtown Vicksburg via Washington Street, you can turn right onto First East Street to visit **Anchuca,** the first bed and breakfast in Vicksburg. Owner May Burns has made a science of southern hospitality, welcoming road-weary travelers from the world over to visit Anchuca. Built in 1830 on land purchased from the city's founder, the Reverend Newit Vick, the house originally consisted of four rooms. After it was bought by Victor Wilson, a massive construction project doubled the size of the original structure and added the new entrance with the Greek Revival columns that greet visitors today. According to May, Jefferson Davis once addressed the citizens of Vicksburg from the second-story balcony. Although the house is graced with an extensive collection of period antiques, we must admit that one of our favorite features on a warm Mississippi evening was the swimming pool. Set amid attractive landscaping, the four corners of the pool are graced with garden statues

Anchuca invites guests to enjoy a refreshing swim in the pool or a soak in the hot tub.

spouting cool, clear water. After we'd cooled off in the pool, a poolside cabana offered an inviting hot tub whose bubbling jets did wonders for tired muscles. What a prelude to a good night's sleep in a four-poster canopy bed!

The next morning we had breakfast with May and her mother, Baby Doll, at a beautiful Sheraton table. Tennessee Williams met May's mother when they were youngsters and later used her name for one of his characters.

We told them about our delightful dinner at the Delta Point Restaurant, and they told us about the Drifters concert they'd attended at the **Ameristar Casino** the night before. We had all had a great time, it seemed. May took us on a tour of the house and pointed out several unusual pieces in her collection, which included an "apostle style" tester bed, so named for the groupings on the posters, and a pair of fainting couches unlike any others we've seen. One room contained a massive Waterford chandelier; there are several outstanding chandeliers throughout the house as well as ornate mirrors and oriental rugs.

The Balfour House, built in 1835, was the home of Emma Balfour. It was also where guests at a Christmas Eve ball received word that seven Yankee gunboats and ninety-nine troop-laden transports were heading for Vicksburg. The news was brought by Major Falls, who was stationed at a telegraph shack just across the river. According to his written account, he ventured across the swollen river after midnight on a cold and rainy night. Carrying a small red lantern to identify himself to the Confederate batteries on the opposite shore, he feared its light would be extinguished and they would open fire on him. He reported to Gen. Martin Luther Smith, who was at the ball; General Smith declared the ball to be at an end and ordered all noncombatants to leave the city.

Three days later there was a large battle at Chickasaw Bayou, about 3 miles above Vicksburg, which the outnumbered Southerners won. Grant eventually crossed the Mississippi at Bruinsburg, attacking Vicksburg from land after Admiral Farragut had failed in the attack from the river. Vicksburg would fall seven months later, on July 4.

The three-story Duff Green Mansion has been beautifully restored and has seven generous guest rooms with private baths and a large ballroom for private parties and receptions.

Open for public tours and offering bed and breakfast accommodations with private baths on the top floor, the three-story Balfour house features a lovely diamond parquet entry-hall floor of hickory and walnut. The unusual elliptical staircase on the back side of the house enabled the family and staff to move freely in the personal living areas without being visible to guests in the front parlors and dining room. An additional bed and breakfast suite has an outside entrance and features a sitting room furnished in wicker.

Our final recommendation for bed and breakfast accommodations has a most unusual history. The **Duff Green Mansion,** just down the street from Anchuca, figures prominently in Vicksburg history. Built in 1856, the mansion was the site of many social events in prewar Vicksburg. Duff and Mary Lake Green once entertained visitors in the exquisite pale peach ballroom, now lovingly restored by Alicia and Harry Sharp. Former Florida residents, the Sharps searched throughout the South for a house suitable for a bed and breakfast in a pleasant community that offered a family oriented environment before rescuing the mansion from abandonment in 1985.

Harry found the mansion while on a business trip. The couple conferred and decided to take on the monumental task of restoring the grand old home. The wrought-iron balconies had been melted down during the war, but research led Harry to discover the original molds and have them recast—the kind of attention to detail indicative of the approach the Sharps have taken to the mansion. Like Cedar Grove, this house has a souvenir cannonball—it's lodged in the ceiling of an upstairs room.

The Duff Green Mansion was used as a Confederate hospital during the siege of Vicksburg, which may be the only reason it was not destroyed. Tales from former inhabitants include hearing what sounded like people walking across the second floor when no one was actually there. Speculation centers on ghostly soldiers searching for amputated limbs, but no earthly or unearthly sounds disturbed our sleep in a tastefully decorated first-floor room that was large enough to qualify as a suite by most standards.

In contrast, during the siege the former owner, Mary Lake Green, was forced to inhabit a cave dug into the hillside on the western side of the house site. She gave birth to a son, named Siege Green, while in hiding. It is typical that these privileged, wealthy Southerners were possessed of grit and determination when faced with the prospect of Grant's thousands amassed in a semicircle 15 miles around the city to the east and Union gunboats shelling ferociously from the river to the west. They literally dug in and held on while the rest of the Confederacy looked on, unable to come to the aid of the proud city. Legend tells us rats were a delicacy for the starving populace by the time General Pemberton surrendered.

There's no need for today's visitors to go hungry at Duff Green—menu selections for breakfast range from French toast to eggs, grits, fresh fruit, and a variety of breakfast meats. Guests are thoughtfully served morning coffee in their rooms before joining the other guests for breakfast in the dining room. The fifteen-foot-high entry also offers an evening bar (we had mint juleps before heading out for a swim), and what a pool they have! Beneath a full moon in August, we found the delicate perfume of the gardenia hedge that borders the pool to be breathtaking.

Campers will find the interstate offers access to a forty-acre rural campground, **Askew's Landing Campground,** 15 miles east of Vicksburg just off I-20, in case you want to camp between Vicksburg and Jackson, enjoy a nature trail, or fish the seventeen-acre lake stocked with bass, bream, crappie, and catfish. No license is required, and they'll even loan you a cane pole.

The campground is a short distance from the site of Askew's Ferry, which carried passengers and supplies across the Big Black River beginning in 1843. Four miles from the **Champion Hill Battleground Museum,** the campground can be reached by leaving I-20 at Exit 19 and heading north. Almost immediately you'll see a road on the left that parallels the interstate, Askew's Ferry Road. The campground is 2.5 miles down the road on the right. There are other campgrounds closer to Vicksburg, if you prefer to head on into town.

Several excellent campgrounds are located in or near Vicksburg.

Battlefield Campground offers a prime location adjacent to the **Vicksburg National Military Park.** Take Exit 4B and turn right on Frontage Road. Battlefield's facilities include a swimming pool, playground, laundry, hot showers, concrete pads with all hookups, and tent camping. **River City RV Park** offers similar amenities at a site closer to Ameristar Casino and the Mississippi River. Take Exit 1B from Interstate 20 and proceed south on U.S. 61 approximately 1 mile to 211 Miller Street.

Once you've decided where you'll stay in Vicksburg, you may find yourself interested in some home-style cooking. If so, tops on our list is **Walnut Hills Restaurant,** on Adams Street (one block off Clay Street). They have smoking and nonsmoking areas and a full-service bar and accept checks, credit cards, and cash. They reliably serve meals every day like your grandma made on Sundays. This was the first time I ever recall having English peas that had been snapped and stewed in their hulls, and they were absolutely delicious. As a matter of fact, all the vegetables tasted garden fresh.

Mack, the owner's brother, invited us back for their famous round-table luncheon, where diners select from fried catfish, fried chicken, buttered potatoes, green beans, sweet potatoes, okra, fried corn, coleslaw, greens, and rice and gravy. Cornbread and biscuits are

The Old Southern Tearoom is in the former Vicksburg Hotel.

served, and if you have room, the desserts are great too. Handicapped facilities are available.

Another good choice for a lunch buffet with traditional meat and three vegetables or tasty Lebanese specialty items, as well as a dinner menu with seafood and steaks, is **Eddie Monsour's,** on Mission Street (if you're headed west, take a left off Clay after passing the entrance to the military park on your right).

A nearby luncheon or tea choice for antiques shoppers would be **Harrison House Antiques and Tea Room,** on Harrison Street (also take a left off Clay after you pass Mission Street). Reservations are suggested.

If you're downtown, the **Old Southern Tearoom,** in the Vicksburg Hotel (now converted to apartments), is worth trying. They accept personal checks and have smoking and nonsmoking areas. Their menu includes plate lunches, sandwiches, and salads. Vernon liked the fried chicken and sweet potato casserole. Music is '30s and '40s and befits the stylized decor.

Now let's venture down to the other end of Washington Street near the Mississippi River Bridge to visit one of our favorite dinner choices. **Delta Point Restaurant** offers a very nice sunset view of the Ameristar Casino and the Mississippi River in the distance, attentive and impeccable service, and fine dining accompanied by the soft strains of classical jazz piano. We enjoyed the seafood gumbo and assorted sourdough rolls. The spinach salad, however, prepared tableside by Dorothy Hollands (who really seemed to enjoy sautéing bacon and fresh mushrooms, adding brown sugar, mustard, and vinegar topped with a brandy flambé just before inverting the whole savory concoction over a fresh bowl of spinach leaves to lightly steam it!) gave a whole new dimension to salad preparation that we'll not soon forget. Vern pronounced the blackened Delmonico delicious, as were the potato au gratin (which was actually layers of white potatoes followed by layers of sweet potatoes and cheese, repeated, and baked), julienne carrots, and a side dish of okra sauce (it may sound odd if you haven't tried it, but it was delightful) as a steak condiment. Try to save room for the *crème brûlée* tart served with fresh blackberries, whipped cream, fresh raspberry sauce, and shaved chocolate—it was absolutely wonderful. Delta Point Restaurant was among the three most memorable dinners of our research for this book.

The **Top of the River** next door served tasty catfish, French fries, coleslaw like our mamas make, and jalapeno cornbread on tin plates. Cold beer served in Mason jars dampened the jalapeno fires to a nice smolder. Get the small order of fried dill-pickle chips unless you have about six people to share them! Broiled dinners are available if you can maintain enough self-control to turn down the great fried catfish.

If barbecue at its best whets your appetite, you're in luck: **Goldie's** is just across the street. It's been featured in *Southern Living* and plans to live up to the accolades it's received by serving you the best pit pork, beef, chicken, sausage, and ribs to be found in these parts. Side orders range from barbecue beans to combination salads. Mesquite-grilled chicken breast with a green salad presents a lighter option.

One last choice, as you head back down Washington Street toward downtown Vicksburg: Watch carefully on the right side of the road for **Solly's,** at 1921 Vicksburg. It's a tiny place, nothing fancy, but those tamales are the first thing many former residents coming home to visit Vicksburg want to taste again. When they say hot tamales, they do mean hot! They come wrapped in newspaper when you get them at Solly's, but in case it's a taste you start to crave, they'll ship them to you frozen. Other selections include hamburgers, cheeseburgers, and hot dogs (all with onion, mustard, pickles, and Solly's famous chili) for the fainthearted.

The New Orleans Cafe has Louisiana cuisine, including crawfish dishes and po' boy sandwiches. Try their honey-blackened shrimp.

Now that you've satisfied your hunger, let's entice you with some of the many activities Vicksburg has to offer.

The Grey and Blue Naval Museum has lots of books for sale. There are models of forty-six Civil War vessels in cases lining the walls, twenty-eight Union and eighteen Confederate. The museum offers a multitude of videos you can watch about the Civil War on topics from Antietam to Vicksburg. Model ships and kits are for sale, as are issues of *Blue and Grey* magazine and prints of the USS *Cairo*.

Yesterday's Photo is just around the corner, if you'd like to see yourself in a Civil War uniform or a riverboat queen's finery to commemorate your visit to Vicksburg.

The **Corner Drugstore,** although a functioning drugstore, has an interesting rifle and gun collection on display along with artifacts related to the pharmacy trade and an extensive crock collection.

Biedenharn Candy Company Museum contains the history and story of the first bottled Coca-Cola by a candy merchant named Joseph Biedenharn in 1894. The syrup was first formulated in Atlanta in 1886 by pharmacist J. S. Pemberton. Asa Griggs Candler became the sole owner of Coca-Cola in 1888.

In the summer of 1894, Joseph A. Biedenharn had the idea that was to shape the American soft-drink industry when he bottled a popular fountain beverage and shipped it into rural areas outside Vicksburg. His idea stemmed from the lack of deodorant in those days. To keep his store's atmosphere "fresh," he devised a way to get the soft drink to the field hands.

The self-guided tour culminates in an old-fashioned soda fountain, where you can purchase a cool Coke float if you've worked up a thirst.

The **Collection** has gifts ranging from china, crystal, and silver to jogging suits. **B and E Antiques** next door has furniture, stained glass, even a baby buggy from the turn of the century.

The **Doll Museum** offers bisque and glazed porcelain, Madame Alexander, 1920s, 1930s, and 1940s composition dolls; a Shirley Temple exhibit; foreign dolls, including 1870s French dolls by Emile Jumeau valued in the tens of thousands of dollars and German dolls by Simon Halbig with paperweight eyes and French bodies; large show dolls from the 1890s that were designed for window displays to catch the eyes of passing shoppers; and a few dolls for sale in the front of the museum.

The **Courthouse Museum** has a gift shop that accepts cash and out-of-town checks. The museum has period furniture, tools, Indian exhibits, art objects, Civil War artifacts, and lots more. One display tells the story of the minié ball pregnancy. During the Battle of Raymond, Mississippi, in 1863, a minié ball reportedly passed through the reproductive organs of a young Rebel soldier and immediately penetrated a young lady who was unfortunately standing on the porch of her nearby home. Eleven years later, a story by Dr. Legrand G. Capers of Vicksburg appeared in the *American Medical Weekly*. Capers claimed that he tended the wounds of the woman, who became pregnant from the fertile minié ball, that he delivered the baby, and introduced her to the soldier, and that the two were eventually married and had two more children (by the more conventional method).

You'll also have to see Grant's chair, which was used by the general during the occupation of Vicksburg, in 1863. It probably came from the Lum house on South Washington Street, where Grant lived briefly with his family (the Lums were allowed to inhabit the attic). When Sherman left Vicksburg, he left orders that the house be protected, but it was nevertheless destroyed by Union occupation forces.

There are several issues of the *Daily Citizen* that were printed on wallpaper during the siege when newsprint ran out.

You'll also read about a hunt—24 miles north of Vicksburg on plantations near Onward, Mississippi, in 1902—by President Theodore Roosevelt that resulted in America's favorite toy, the teddy bear.

Roosevelt had failed to bag a bear, and someone tied one in a cane break for him to kill. Roosevelt, a sportsman, refused to shoot it, and the resulting publicity led a man in New York to have his wife sew and stuff bears they named Teddy bears. More than a million were sold the first year, and its success led Morris Mitchum to found the Ideal Toy Company.

One room honors President and Mrs. Jefferson Davis. Davis's family was captured in southern Georgia in May 1865 as they made their way with a Confederate escort to the West, where an army was waiting with plans to continue the war for Southern independence. Mrs. Davis and the children were sent to Savannah and kept under house arrest after the president was jailed at Fortress Monroe, Virginia, in shackles and chains. He was kept under surveillance twenty-four hours a day with a light burning at all times. Any communication with the outside world was forbidden, and his guards were not allowed to speak to him. He was eventually released under $100,000 bond signed by ten Northern men who were not his personal friends. He was never brought to trial, although he had wanted one in order to vindicate himself.

Because the government had taught him at West Point that secession was legal, Davis felt that he had put into practice what he had been taught. When he died in 1889, many former slaves attended his funeral and marched in the procession. Others sent Mrs. Davis the following telegram: "We, the old servants and tenants of our beloved master, Honorable Jefferson Davis, have cause to mingle our tears over his death, who was always so kind and thoughtful of our peace and happiness. We extend to you our humble sympathy."

Although he was a slave owner, he treated his slaves kindly and provided good housing, clothing, and food as well as free time to earn personal money. None was ever sold, and families were always kept together.

Davis's wife, Varina Hall, was born into an aristocratic family at Meringo Plantation, across the river from Natchez. She was well educated, tall, and dark. She was the belle of Natchez when at eighteen she married Jefferson Davis, who was twice her age. After his death, Mrs. Davis declined a lucrative offer for their last home, Beauvoir, on the Mississippi Gulf Coast, selling it for a much smaller amount to the United Confederate Veterans so that it could serve as a home for old Confederate veterans and their wives and eventually become a memorial to her husband. She lived from 1891 to 1906 in New York City, where she was an author and wrote for a New York newspaper.

The **Toys and Soldiers Museum,** on the corner of Cherry and Grove, is just across from the Old Courthouse Museum. A gift shop in the front offers toy soldiers and Civil War artifacts. Displays include carousel and circus characters, Mickey Mouse, Superman, and Tarzan figures, toy trains, cowboys, Indians, knights, and more than 32,000 toy soldiers of every size, description, and nationality.

The **U.S. Army Corps of Engineers Waterways Experiment Station** is off I-20 on Halls Ferry Road. Follow the signs indicating a left turn if you're headed south and travel 1.2 miles. Tours normally last one and a half hours and are conducted twice daily on weekdays, unless arrangements are made for special tours. Studies are ongoing for problem areas, including estuaries, coastal areas, and geotechnical areas. On weekends a self-guided tour lets you visit three sites. One of the more dramatic tour demonstrations involves problems with construction instability on sandy Mississippi soils with potential flooding problems. Coastal engineering exhibits include large-scale mock-ups of various harbors in the United States that have requested studies by the corps for problems they are encountering, impact of proposed construction, and so on.

The downtown mall, on Washington Street, has a variety of shops. The curb breaks make both sides of the street wheelchair accessible.

The **Cinnamon Tree** has all kinds of gift ideas, ranging from cookbooks and candles to baskets and button jewelry. All the pottery in the shop is made in Mississippi.

Yesterday's Treasures antiques mall, with its collections of glassware, furniture, old books, and Civil War artifacts, is next to the park that overlooks Harrah's Casino.

The **Sassafras Shop** has china, baskets, preserves, and cookbooks. Upstairs you'll find the **Attic Gallery,** which features photographs, watercolors, sculpture, whimsical compositions by Elaine Goodman, Floyd Shaman's unusual sculptures, and Hugh Wilkinson's whimsical "found object" sculptures. Artist Earl Simmons is also represented.

The **Flea Market** is a great place to prowl through scads of furniture and collectibles. We found an oak mirror and an art nouveau bronze statue.

You can find a little of everything from wood carvings, fishing supplies, and kerosene lamps to rolling pins and pickle jars at **Wilson's,** on the corner.

The **Vicksburg National Military Park** offers an excellent opportunity to achieve greater understanding of the complexities of one of our nation's greatest tragedies, the Civil War. The park should not be missed because of Vicksburg's strategic importance as the last port on the Mississippi to fall to the Union. At the time of the war,

Visitors to the Vicksburg National
Military Park can take the 16-mile driving tour on their own, with a cassette
rental, or accompanied by a tour guide.

Vicksburg was Mississippi's largest city and the cultural center
between Memphis and New Orleans. There are excellent interpretive
facilities here. A documentary film produced by the park service will
familiarize you with the siege of Vicksburg, which lasted six weeks
and ended July 4, 1863, when John C. Pemberton, under a flag of
truce, surrendered Rebel forces to General Grant.

If you'd like to learn more about the history of the area, there is
a gift shop here with a good selection of pertinent books, including
the diary of Emma Balfour, *Vicksburg—A City Under Siege*, and *My Cave
Life in Vicksburg*, by Mary Webster Loughbrough. Civil War buffs will
appreciate the excellent collection of books on the subject.

The park, which closes at sunset, includes a 15-mile bicycle trek
and hiking trails through the park's 1,800 acres.

The tour we took with Betty England was so fascinating we
thought you'd enjoy portions of it. The following excerpts are
gleaned from her wealth of knowledge about Vicksburg. A history
graduate and lifelong student of history, she has a wonderful
ability to bring the past to life before your eyes, letting you appreciate Vicksburg in a way that only familiarity with its colorful
past can bring.

First let's set the stage and introduce you to the principal players
in this drama: U. S. Grant, John C. Pemberton, and Jefferson Davis.

At the time of the war, Vicksburg had a population of about 4,500. Grant's army was 77,000 soldiers, and Pemberton's was 19,000.

In 1861 Grant was seen by a friend sitting under a tree in Ironton, Missouri, drawing on a map of the United States with a red pencil. His friend asked what he was doing, and he replied he was planning how to move south and win the war, because that was the only way to do it. His friend laughed—at the time no one imagined Grant would play an important role because of his past. Grant's drinking had caused problems in Washington State in 1851, and those problems had led to his resignation. After realizing his affinity for military life, he was reinstated and vowed never again to drink when he was planning or executing military maneuvers. Although he kept his vow, the newspapers of the day kept alive his reputation for problems with alcohol.

On October 10, 1862, he was named commander of the army of Tennessee and started for Vicksburg five days later. It took seven attempts, but he got there.

Pemberton, born in Philadelphia, had always believed in states' rights. He married a woman from Virginia, was a close friend of Jefferson Davis, and felt he had to offer his services to the South. When he did, his parents refused to speak to him again. They had the sad distinction of having one son a Confederate general and the other two Union colonels. They removed his name from the family Bible as if he had never been born. The state of Pennsylvania confiscated his land and his money. After the war, he lived in an unhappy situation for most of his life. Many in the South never forgave him for surrendering Vicksburg, and the North felt betrayed by his service to the South. He was eventually allowed to return to his Pennsylvania home a few years before his death. He and his wife both died there and are buried on his farm.

Jefferson Davis, the president of the Confederacy, was born in Kentucky but moved to Mississippi at the age of three. He and his brother farmed south of Vicksburg at Davis Bend. He made his first political speech at the courthouse here. He was a hero of the Mexican War, had been secretary of war under Franklin Pierce, but was treated quite badly after the Civil War ended.

He was placed in solitary confinement without being charged for two and a half years, even the young men who brought him his food were not allowed to speak to him. Going blind from the paint that had been used in his cell, he was shackled for portions of his confinement. Horace Greeley, the famous Colorado newspaperman, started a campaign to have Davis freed, saying it was wrong for one man to be held responsible for an entire war or for that man to be held without charges. The campaign was taken up by northern senators who had served with him when he was a senator from Mississippi before the war. His supporters arranged and paid his bail, and he was eventually released from prison.

Davis sent John Pemberton to beef up the line at Vicksburg and get ready for what they felt was inevitable.

There were thirty-four states in the United States when the war broke out; twenty-eight states had troops fighting in Vicksburg. When the area became a park in 1899, the states sent men back to locate the areas that had been most important to their states and to their regiments, and monuments were placed on those spots.

Today only Tennessee and Kentucky do not have monuments here. There are 1,348 monuments on the battlefield. To stop and read each one would take you a week, so let's hit some highlights.

The arch that leads into the park was built at the entrance to the city of Vicksburg in 1920 with money left over from the last joint reunion ever held of Confederate and Union veterans. This meeting was held in Vicksburg in 1917, and we are told that 10,000 veterans came together on a Sunday afternoon. Everybody was delighted to become reacquainted and it was a wonderful day. The veterans camped in tents on the battlefield.

By Monday they were remembering the war, and by Tuesday they were fighting it all over again. They came to blows, hitting each other with their walking sticks, and the editor of the Vicksburg paper dubbed it the "Walking Stick War."

The slanted black markers (you'll see them every fifty to one hundred yards) designate sharpshooters, who lay in wait for those Confederates off to the west to stand up. General Pemberton had 178 cannon, and General Grant had 220, but presently only 150 are

Gen. U. S. Grant brought 77,000 men to the battlefield outside Vicksburg. Vicksburg was surrendered by Confederate general Pemberton after a six-week siege.

found in the park. The Federal Park Service divides the total cannon available for display among all the military parks according to the number of visitors per year. Here one cannon stands for a battery, although the battery would have consisted of two to twenty-two cannon. Most of the time a battery had four. All the cannon here are authentic.

Albert D. J. Cashier was a private in the Ninety-fifth Illinois. He cared for the horses when he wasn't fighting, but in battle he was called "the fiercest fighter of them all," because he could out fight anyone in his regiment. His regiment was reputed to be a tough one, referred to as "the fierce." After fighting all through the war, he was drawing a pension from the state of Illinois in 1915 when he was involved in a traffic accident. He refused to let the doctor remove his trousers to inspect his badly mangled legs until the doctor promised to keep his secret—he was a woman.

Born Jenny Hodgers in Ireland, she became engaged to a young man named Albert D. J. Cashier, who was killed in an Irish rebellion. Deciding to live Cashier's life for him, Hodgers assumed his name and identity, stowed away on a ship to the United States, went to Illinois, and enlisted in his name, obtaining American citizenship upon enlistment. This was not without precedent: there were 220 women who fought in this war dressed as men, and five kept their secret until they died. In Jenny's case, the story got out, and petitions were circulated by people who felt the name of Albert D. J. Cashier should be removed from the Illinois monument. The men of the Ninety-fifth called a meeting in Chicago; no one mentioned Albert Cashier or Jenny by name, but a statement was issued saying that if one name was ever removed from the roster of the Ninety-fifth at Vicksburg, then every name in the Ninety-fifth would come down at the same time. That ended the controversy.

Illinois has the most monuments, because nearly half of General Grant's army was from that state, with seventy-nine regiments. The Illinois Peace Memorial is modeled after the Pantheon in Rome and topped by a dome with a hole in the center that allows sunlight in but keeps rain out. A marble trough inside the dome collects any rain that enters. There is no word of war anywhere on this monument— every quotation is about peace. Lincoln's words on the outside proclaim "malice toward none, charity toward all." History is in the center writing in the book of time, North on her right hand, South on her left. Forty-seven steps lead to the memorial, commemorating the forty-seven days of siege. Inside are the names of 36,325 men from Illinois who fought at Vicksburg.

The peach-colored monument is that of Missouri, the only state unfortunate enough to have troops fighting on both sides at Vicksburg. During one battle, a Confederate boy in the Missouri Twenty-second realized that he had been fighting his brother's regiment that afternoon. That night he wanted to get a letter home to his mother, but there was no mail going in and out of Vicksburg. He approached his sentries asking them to talk to the Union sentries and see whether the two brothers could meet between the lines to exchange the letter. They did meet (this true story was dramatized in the miniseries *North and South*), and when they returned to camp telling what they had done, other Missourians wanted to meet. A group of them showed up the next night, more the next night, and eventually it led to what is called "the trysting place" midway between the two lines. Sentries on both sides kept watch so the officers wouldn't discover them. An uncle and nephew and a father and son found each other in the next few nights.

The Missouri monument, forty-two feet tall, is the only one on the battlefield dedicated to both sides. Missouri had forty-two regiments here; fifteen were Confederate, the remainder Union, and they fought each other on the site of the monument.

At Grant's Circle you'll see the Massachusetts monument. The base is a sixteen-ton boulder brought by train from Massachusetts Bay, where the pilgrims landed. It was the first monument erected in 1902 and required twenty oxen pulling an oxcart to deliver it to the battlefield site.

At the site of the dual Ohio monuments, the nearest Confederate fort was four hundred yards from the Union trenches, which were zigzagging to the hill in Grant's quest for Vicksburg. The fight at the Third Louisiana redoubt was one of the few nighttime battles. Fierce fighting lasted twenty-six hours. When the Union pulled back to the hill behind, they enlisted the services of thirty-one coal miners to dig a tunnel beneath the nearby Confederate fort. Although the Confederates knew a tunnel was being dug, the shafts they dug never hit the tunnel. Frustrated but resourceful, the Confederates used Mason jars to eavesdrop on conversations on the other side of the wall and knew in advance that the first attack was coming on June 25.

The Shirley House was the home of Union sympathizers Judge and Mrs. Shirley of New England. Today the house is in a poor state of repair, so visitors are not allowed inside. Judge Shirley was from New Hampshire; Mrs. Shirley had been Adeline Quincy of Massachusetts. Her grandfather was John Hancock, one of the signers of the Declaration of Independence. They had lived in Mississippi about ten years. Their daughter, Alice, who was sixteen years old, was in college at Clinton, between Vicksburg and Jackson (Mississippi was the first state to allow women to attend college and the first state to have a female college graduate). Judge Shirley, knowing that Grant was on the way to Vicksburg, went to get his daughter and got caught on the other side of the battle lines. Mrs. Shirley was in the house with several servants when the Union troops arrived. She sent a servant out on the balcony with a white sheet to let the Union know she was on their side. They came in and took her house but treated her well. Mrs. Shirley, however, had nowhere to go—everyone in Vicksburg sympathized with the Confederates, and she had been vocal about her beliefs, so she stayed right where she was, hiding in a chimney corner, while her two maids sat in the other chimney corner for three days as the battle raged all around them. She eventually had a cave dug behind her house by former slaves, and she stayed in that for the remainder of the siege.

The people of Vicksburg were also living in caves dug by former slaves, who were paid $35 for a one-room cave and $50 for a two-room cave. One held 250 people. The caves were horrible, dark, dirty, and dank, but they saved lives during the siege. Only nine civilians were killed and twenty-two wounded.

Notice the graves of Judge and Mrs. Shirley, behind the house. You'll also see the grave of a Confederate soldier near the rain barrel. In a siege you are unable to tend to the dead on any sort of organized daily basis, so the dead at Vicksburg were buried where they fell in hastily dug, oftentimes shallow, graves.

Bodies began to surface all over Vicksburg after the battle, and the U.S. government purchased land overlooking the Mississippi River and brought in the bodies of 13,000 Union soldiers who died within a 60-mile radius of Vicksburg. Of course, the Confederates had lost their American citizenship and could not be buried in a national cemetery. The only place in Vicksburg left for them was a mass grave in the pauper section of the city cemetery. More than 6,500 Confederates were buried there.

The Wisconsin monument is 220½ feet tall; the names of 9,075 men from Wisconsin are on the balustrade. A six-foot-tall bronze eagle on the top is not the familiar national symbol but instead the likeness of Old Abe, an eagle who rode into battle on a six-foot red, white, and blue perch built by the men of the Eighth Wisconsin. By the time the war ended, Old Abe was a hero. The people of Wisconsin made him a citizen of the state, cleaned out a room in the basement of the capitol, and moved him in—and the first thing he did was build a nest, lay an egg, and prove that she was not a he at all. During World War II, the 101st Airborne was looking for a symbol of bravery, and they decided on Old Abe, calling themselves the Screaming Eagles in her honor.

With 77,000 men, Grant could have one-third in the trenches, one-third digging new trenches, and the other third in the shelter of the trees in the ravines, resting from the rigors of battle.

The first attack Grant made brought 35,000 men to the top of Graveyard Road, and a thousand died there in the ravines. At the time of the battle, the hills did not have grass on them, nor were there any trees left. This was a corn-growing area, so Vicksburg's defenders left the stalks to try to impede the Union forces and cut down the trees so there was nothing to hide behind during an advance. When Pemberton had the trees cut in anticipation of Grant's arrival, he specified that the trees be dropped with their limbs pointing toward the enemy's anticipated line of approach from the ravine. Points were put on the limbs, and telegraph wire was woven through the branches to create a deadly abatis ("ab-a-tee").

For the next attack, three days later, Grant announced he wanted no one on the low ground, but when that attack failed, the Union forces began digging a series of zigzag trenches up the deadly slopes. General Sherman, not at all happy with the idea of sending his men down the denuded Graveyard Road, knew the Confederates would be watching everything they did. The night before the attack, he had a little wooden house on the battlefield torn down and the planks stacked up. The next morning he asked for 150 volunteers for a suicide mission to strap their rifles on their

backs, carry one plank apiece, and run down Graveyard Road ahead
of the main body of troops to throw their planks across the deep
ditch that surrounded the Confederate fort. Sherman told his men
that it was a forlorn hope but it was the only hope he could see of
getting into Vicksburg that day, so the volunteers called themselves
the Forlorn Hope. When they reached the ditch, the Confederates
stood up and mowed them down. The road was so clogged with
their bodies that the troops behind could not get through, and the
attack ground to a halt. Of the 150 men, 78 lived to receive the
Congressional Medal of Honor. Four other medals were given on
that same day at the same spot in the road—making it the place
where the most Congressional Medals of Honor have ever been
given, 82, on May 22, 1863.

The people of Vicksburg and General Pemberton had anxiously
awaited the arrival of Gen. Joseph E. Johnson. Nearly all the Confederates' ammunition had been expended on June 19 and 22. Throughout the South, everybody knew how desperate conditions were in
Vicksburg. Others tried to send needed items, but Grant had drawn a
tight ring around Vicksburg. Of the hundred different couriers trans-
porting a million percussion caps, only two men penetrated Grant's
lines. One of them cut down a tree on the Louisiana side of the Mississippi and let the current carry him to Vicksburg.

The Confederate forces formed an 8.5-mile semicircle around
Vicksburg. They were enclosed by a 12-mile semicircle of Grant's
troops and a ring 15 miles in diameter to the east, commanded by
General Sherman, which reportedly a kitten couldn't penetrate.
Union gunboats patrolled the river. Nothing came through—no
food, no water, no mail, no supplies of any kind. Johnson had failed
to arrive with reinforcements, and the people were eating any sort of
animal they could catch.

Pemberton realized that he was going to have to surrender. He
sent Gen. John Bowen to call on Grant, because Bowen and Grant
had been next-door neighbors and best friends back in St. Louis.
Grant recognized Bowen riding up and informed him by a note that
as long as they were enemies, they could not meet, but as soon as
Vicksburg fell he looked forward to renewing a friendship that was

very dear to him. Bowen told Pemberton it was time for him to go talk to Grant himself.

Pemberton rode his horse to Grant and asked his old friend what terms he would give him, to which Grant replied "unconditional surrender." Pemberton was extremely disappointed, having deliberately planned to surrender on July 4 in the hope that he would get better terms by allowing Grant to send word to Lincoln that Vicksburg had fallen on that day.

Pemberton lost his temper and proclaimed angrily that much more blood would flow before Grant took Vicksburg, and it would all be Union blood. He was turning to mount his horse when one of Grant's generals approached him and suggested that the two generals visit for a while beneath a nearby tree and let their staffs attempt to work out some terms. Union soldiers later cut this tree down and distributed pieces as souvenirs. Descendants of Grant and Pemberton replanted a tree on the site some years later. Grant wrote in his memoirs that he treated Pemberton as a friend because they were friends and that they didn't discuss Vicksburg. They talked about their wives and their children for about twenty minutes. Then they returned to their respective lines and corresponded all through the night. Grant was magnanimous, allowing Confederate officers to keep their sidearms and horses and Confederate soldiers to march out of their trenches with their bands playing and their flags flying. They stacked their weapons before the Northern troops entered Vicksburg, and Grant addressed his troops, saying there would be no jubilation at the surrender of the Confederates who had fought so bravely. The only cheer that the Northern soldiers gave was for the brave defenders of Vicksburg as the Confederate flag came down at the courthouse.

When the Union troops saw the plight of the starving people, they opened up their knapsacks and gave away all their food; then Grant opened the warehouses and let the people of Vicksburg claim anything that would be of use to them. He said he did this because he believed they would fight less fiercely for the remainder of the war and make better citizens when it was over if they were treated with dignity.

Bowen unfortunately died of dysentery only a few days later, at the age of thirty-three. He and his old friend Grant were able to visit with each other after surrender. Dysentery was a big killer—two men died of the disease for every one who died of wounds. The biggest killer to Northerners coming south was malaria; the biggest killers of Southerners going north were mumps and whooping cough.

Vicksburg was occupied for thirteen years after the surrender. Grant returned to Vicksburg in 1880 and was asked what he'd like to see; "only his men," he replied. He went out to the cemetery and stayed for two and a half hours, walking from grave to grave. He went back to the courthouse and spoke to the people of Vicksburg, telling them he had tried as president to get bills through that would have made Reconstruction less difficult but Congress made it impossible.

In 1885, when he learned that he was dying of cancer, he told his wife to make sure that if any Union generals were appointed by the president to be his pallbearers, an equal number of Confederate generals would be asked also. There were two of each at his funeral.

Pemberton, who did not receive another posting after Vicksburg and resigned his commission thinking this was due to the outcome at Vicksburg, said he would fight as a private. Jefferson Davis believed this was unfair treatment and made him a lieutenant colonel, but no one sought his services in this role either until Robert E. Lee asked for him to join his staff in Richmond. Lee always continued to address Pemberton as "general" and made a point of including him in staff meetings and soliciting his counsel.

Admiral Farragut had come up the Mississippi in 1862 with plans to build a canal to divert the Mississippi River. Grant came down from Illinois and tried unsuccessfully to cut a canal from the Louisiana side. His men were in wool uniforms, unused to either the humidity or the Mississippi mosquitoes, and the spring rains started early. The rising water destroyed the digging they had done. In 1876, a mile up from where the two men had been digging, the river cut through on its own overnight. The people in Vicksburg heard water running about two o'clock on an April morning. By 6:30 the next evening, the water had cut completely through and there was no water left in Vicksburg's riverbed. Grant was president of the United States at the time, but no comments by him are on record. Vicks-

The USS *Cairo* sank to the bottom of the Yazoo River on December 12, 1862, after a Confederate mine was electrically detonated.

burg's economy suffered with the loss of river access. In 1902, the corps of engineers dammed the Yazoo River and diverted it into the old Mississippi River bed. Visitors to the park may also see the remains of the USS *Cairo*, which was part of the Anaconda Plan, attributed to Gen. Winfield Scott, that culminated in the surrender of Vicksburg on July 4, 1863. This was the grand Union strategy for winning the Civil War that proposed blockading the Confederacy's southern coast and controlling commerce on the Mississippi River.

The *Cairo* is the only ironclad left of the seventy-eight that were built during this war. It sank in deep mud at the bottom of the Yazoo River on December 12, 1862, the first victim of the electrically detonated mine.

The mine had been placed in the Yazoo River by Zedekiah McDaniel and Francis M. Ewing of the Confederate navy. The mine consisted of a five-gallon glass demijohn filled with black powder, with a flood-float and wires attached to a galvanic cell on shore. Volunteers detonated the mine from their hiding place on shore.

Damage from the blast can be seen on the port bow. The *Cairo* went down in twelve minutes. Of the 175 officers and enlisted men

A Hydro-Jet Boat Tour offers an intimate perspective of the Yazoo and Mississippi rivers.

aboard there were no fatalities. This Union vessel had thirteen cannon onboard, and when it was brought up, twelve were still loaded. The *Cairo* surfaced thanks to the efforts of Edwin Bears, Warren Graybau, and Don Jacks on December 12, 1964, 102 years after it sank. All the personal possessions and equipment were where they'd been left behind. Those artifacts, well preserved in layers of mud and silt, are displayed in the *Cairo* Museum. The collection includes everything from mess utensils and medical equipment to ships' rigging and hardware.

Today the **Mississippi River Boat Trip Adventure Hydro-Jet Tours** depart from the Yazoo River that took the place of the Mississippi River waterfront. Owners Peggy and David Schaeffer will take you through the Yazoo River diversion canal to Goat Island, where Grant's troops made their ill-fated attempt to dig a canal and divert the Mississippi to leave Vicksburg high and dry. Where Grant failed, Mother Nature succeeded in 1876, when the river cut through its bank and drained away from Vicksburg. Years later, the Yazoo River was diverted to flow by the city and reestablish a waterfront and river traffic.

Vicksburg is 437 miles north of the Gulf of Mexico. In normal conditions, the river has a 2-to-3 mph current. You'll also see the sites of the telegraph shacks that were instrumental in warning Vicksburg of the Federals' approach by water on the hill near the river bridge and the hill by the fuel storage tanks. The jet boat tours usually last one hour. Go by early in the day to see what time tours will be leaving—times may vary somewhat.

Next door to the jet boat tours is **Harrah's,** a casino complex with gift shops, restaurants, and hotel accommodations. The casinos are all situated in giant structures that look like swimming pools. Vern played a quarter and won, I put one in and lost, so we decided to quit while we were ahead and spend our profits on soft drinks.

To get back on the Trace, we recommend taking either Highway 27 to see Rocky Springs—a worthwhile site—or Highway 61 to Port Gibson. The next loop trip begins there.

Harrah's Casino Complex is one of three riverfront casinos in Vicksburg.

❧ ACCOMMODATIONS

Anchuca—1010 First East St., Vicksburg, MS 39180; 601-631-6800.

Annabelle—501 Speed St., Vicksburg, MS 39180; 601-638-2000 or 800-791-2000.

Balfour House—P.O. Box 781, Vicksburg, MS 39180; 601-638-7113 or 800-294-7113.

Belle of the Bend—508 Klein St., Vicksburg, MS 39180; 601-634-0737 or 800-844-2308.

Cedar Grove Mansion Inn—2300 Washington St., Vicksburg, MS 39180; 601-636-1000 or 800-862-1300 (out of state) and 800-448-2820 (in state), FAX 601-634-6126.

Cherry Street Cottage—2212 Cherry St., Vicksburg, MS 39180; 601-636-7086.

The Corners—601 Klein St., Vicksburg, MS 39180; 601-636-7421 or 800-444-7421.

Duff Green Mansion—1114 First E. St., Vicksburg, MS 39180; 601-636-6968, 638-6662 or 800-992-0037.

Flowerree Cottage—2309 Pearl St., Vicksburg, MS 39180; 601-638-2704.

Grey Oaks—4142 Rifle Range Rd., Vicksburg, MS 39180; 601-638-4424.

McRaven—1445 Harrison St., Vicksburg, MS 39180; 601-636-1663.

Tomil Manor—2430 Drummond St., Vicksburg, MS 39180; 601-638-8893.

The Vicksburg—801 Clay St., Vicksburg, MS 39180; 601-636-4146 or 800-844-4146.

❧ ATTRACTIONS

Assault at Vicksburg—Two-day re-enactment; $2 adults, $1 children 6–12, each day; Campsites available; Contact the Convention and Visitors Bureau for brochure.

Ameristar Casino—4144 Washington St., Vicksburg, MS 39180; 601-638-1000; Gambling, entertainment, and dining; Twenty-four hours/day; 800-700-7456 for reservations and information.

Biedenharn Candy Company and Museum of Coca-Cola Memorabilia—1107 Washington St., Vicksburg, MS 39180; 601-638-6514; Mon.–Sat., 9 A.M.–5 P.M.; Sun., 1:30–4:30 P.M.; $1.75 adults, $1.25 under 12; Museum and soda fountain.

Grey and Blue Naval Museum—1823 Clay St., Vicksburg, MS 39180; 601-638-6500; Mon.–Sat., 9 A.M.–5 P.M.; Sun., 1–5 p.m.; $1.50 adults, $1 12 and under, $5 max. for family; Features the world's largest collection of Civil War gunboat models, paintings of naval actions, reference files of these historic fighting vessels, books, VCR tapes, and model kits.

Corner Drug Store—1123 Washington St., Vicksburg, MS 39180; 601-636-2756; Mon.–Sat. 8 A.M.–6 P.M.; Sun., 9–11 A.M.; 1800-era drug-store in a twentieth-century working pharmacy; Extensive Civil War artifacts, herbs from the Bible, antique medical instruments, and won-derful collection of old guns.

Christ Church—1119 Main St., Vicksburg, MS 39180; 601-638-5899; Donations; Tours, Mon.–Fri,. 9 A.M.—6 P.M.; Oldest public building with some original furnishings; Cornerstone laid in 1839; Held ser-vices during the siege.

Gold in the Hills—P.O. Box 1095, Vicksburg, MS 39180; 601-636-0471; $7 adults, $4 children 12 and under; Old-time melodramas for booing, cheering, throwing peanuts, and singing; Send for brochure of plays and dates.

Harrah's Casino & Hotel—1310 Mulberry, Vicksburg, MS 39180; 800-427-7247 for reservations and information; Gambling, entertainment pavilion, and hotel.

Isle of Capri Casino—3990 Washington St., Vicksburg, MS 39180; 601-636-5700, 800-THE-ISLE; Gambling, entertainment, and dining; Twenty-four hours/day.

Martha Vick House—1300 Grove St., Vicksburg, MS 39180; 601-638-7036; $5 adults, under 12 free; Mon.–Sat., 9 A.M.–5 P.M.; Sun., 1–4:30 P.M.; Vicksburg founder, Newit Vick, built this home for his daughter circa 1830; Elegant furnishings and paintings.

Mississippi River Adventures Hydro-Jet Boat Tours—(foot of Clay St.) P.O. Box 506, Vicksburg, MS 39180; 601-638-5443 or 800-521-4363; March 1–Oct. 30; Daily 40-mile, 1-hour cruises; $25 adults, $15 6–12 years, $6.50 under 6; Tour guide/pilot describes history of Vicksburg from the river; See where Grant tried and failed to "steal" the Mississippi River from Vicksburg.

The Old Court House—1008 Cherry St., Vicksburg, MS 39180; 601-636-0741; Self-guided tours, Mon.–Sat., 8:30 A.M.–4:30 P.M.; Sun., until 5 P.M. during Daylight Savings Time; $1.75 adults, grade students

I–12 $1, under 6 free, $1.25 over 65; A must-see history of Vicksburg and many great Americans in the city's most historic building constructed by slaves in 1858.

Spirit of Vicksburg—(foot of Clay St.) P.O. Box 1405, Vicksburg, MS 39180; 601-634-6059; $6 adults, $3 under 12, 3 and under free; Daily cruises, 2 P.M., 90 minutes; $19.95 dinner cruises, 7 P.M., June–Aug. and 6:30 P.M., April, May, Sept., and Oct.

Toys and Soldiers Museum—1100 Cherry St., Vicksburg, MS 39180; 601-638-1986; Tours, Mon.–Sat., 9 A.M.–4:30 P.M.; Sun. 1:30—4:30 P.M.; $2 adults, grade students 1-12 $1.50, preschool free; More than 3,000 old and new toy soldiers in a privately owned museum; Diverse collections of trains, figurines, and memorabilia; Gift shop.

U.S. Army Engineer Waterways Experiment Station—3909 Halls Ferry Rd., Vicksburg, MS 39180; 601-634-2502; Free guided tours, 10 A.M. each work day; Handicapped facilities; Largest research and development facility in U.S. Army Corps of Engineers; See scale models of Fisherman's Wharf and others.

The Vanishing Glory—717 Clay St., Vicksburg, MS 39180; 601-634-1863; Daily shows on the hour beginning 10 A.M.; $3.50 adults, $2 students, under 6 free; 30-minute slide program of the campaign and siege of Vicksburg.

Vicksburg Historic Tours—9 Crestwood Dr., Vicksburg, MS 39180; 601-638-8888; Mon.–Sun., $25 adults, $24 over 62, $12 children 6–12; Feb.–mid Nov., 3.5-hour tour of Vicksburg Military Park, old historic Vicksburg, and an antebellum home; Reservations advisable.

Vicksburg National Military Park —I-20 & Clay St., Vicksburg, MS 39180; 601-636-0583; *Cairo* Museum 601-636-2199; Visitor Center, daily, 8 A.M.—5 P.M.; 18-minute film shown every 30 minutes recounts campaign; 16-mile tour with guide in your car $15, van $20, bus $30; Cassette tape rental $4.50; Must-see battlefields and monuments; Visitor Center exhibits and artifacts from the siege of Vicksburg; Excellent book selection.

USS Cairo *Museum*—Daily, 9 A.M.–5 P.M.; $3/car, $1/person/van/bus, 16 under free, U.S. citizen over 62 free; See USS *Cairo*, first boat sunk by electrically detonated torpedo; Pictorials in museum and boat outside.

Yesterday's Children Antique Doll Museum—1104 Washington St., Vicksburg, MS 39180; 601-638-0650; Mon.–Sat., 9:30 A.M.–4:30 P.M.; $2 adults, $1 under 13; Museum and gift shop with more than 1,000 dolls from around the world.

❧ RESTAURANTS

Beechwood Restaurant and Lounge—4451 E. Clay St., Vicksburg, MS 39180; 601-636-376;. 11 A.M.–11 P.M.; 7 days/week; Lounge, 6 P.M.–until; Live entertainment, 9 P.M., Tues.–Sun.

Cedar Grove's Garden Room Restaurant—2300 Washington St., Vicksburg, MS 39180; 601-636-1000 or 800-862-1300, FAX 601-634-6126.

Delta Bistro—(Magnolia Inn) 4155 Washington St., Vicksburg, MS 39180; 601-636-5145; Breakfast, 6–10 A.M.; Dinner, 5–10 P.M.; 7 days/week; Lounge, 4–12 P.M.

Delta Point—4144 Washington St., Vicksburg, MS 39180; 601-636-5317; Lunch, Mon.–Fri., 11 A.M.–2 P.M.; Dinner, 5-10 P.M.; Sunday brunch, 11 A.M.–2:30 P.M.; Reservations preferred.

The Dock Seafood Buffet—E. Clay St., Vicksburg, MS 39180; 601-634-0450; Open 5 P.M.; 7 days/week.

Eddie Monsour's Restaurant and Lounge—1903 G Mission 66, Vicksburg, MS 39180; 601-638-1571; Lunch, Mon.-Fri., 11;30 a.m.; Dinner, Mon.-Sat., 5:30-10 P.M.

Goldie's—4127 S. Washington St., Vicksburg, MS 39180; 601-636-9839; Lunch and dinner.

Garnett's—(Holiday Inn of Vicksburg) I-20 & Hwy. 80 E, Vicksburg, MS 39180; 601-636-4551; Open 6 A.M.–10 P.M., 7 days/week.

Hacienda Don Carlos—3316 Old Halls Ferry Rd., Vicksburg, MS 39180; 601-638-0913; Mon.–Sat., 11 A.M.–10 P.M.

Harrison House Tearoom—1433 Harrison St., Vicksburg, MS 39180; 601-638-2178; Lunch, Mon.–Fri., 11:30 A.M.–2 P.M.; Tea, 2–4 P.M.; Reservations suggested.

Jacque's Cafe in the Park—(Park Inn International) 4137 I-20 Frontage Rd., Vicksburg, MS 39180; 601-638-5811; Open 5–10 P.M., 7 nights/week.

The Lucky Fisherman—(5 miles off I-20) Hwy. 61 S., Vicksburg, MS 39180; 601-634-1040; Tues.–Sun., 5–10 P.M.

Maxwell's Restaurant—4702 Clay St., Vicksburg, MS 39180; 601-636-1344 or 800-418-7379; Mon.–Sat., 11 A.M.–10 P.M.

The New Orleans Cafe—1100 Washington St., Vicksburg, MS 39180; 601-638-8182; 11 A.M.–until, 7 days/week; Happy hour, 2–7 P.M.

Old Southern Tearoom—801 Clay St., Vicksburg, MS 39180; 601-636-4005; Mon.–Sat., 7 A.M.–9 P.M.; Sun., 7 A.M. through dinner.

River Road Restaurant—Downtown; Mon.–Sat., 11 A.M.–10 P.M.

Rowdy's Family Restaurant—Hwy. 27 & Hwy. 80, Vicksburg, MS 39180; 601-638-2375; Sun.–Thurs., 11 A.M.–9:30 P.M.; Fri.–Sat., 11 A.M.–11 P.M.

Solly's—1921 Washington St., Vicksburg, MS 39180; 601-636-2020;
   Tues.–Sat., 11 A.M.–10 P.M.; Sun., 11 A.M.–9 P.M.
Sun Koon—3535 I-20 Frontage Rd., Vicksburg, MS 39180; 601-638-4941;
   Lunch, Mon.–Fri., 11:30 A.M.–2 P.M.; Dinner, Mon.–Sat., 5–10 P.M.
Tavern in the Park—3327 Clay St., Vicksburg, MS 39180; 601-638-4759;
   7 A.M.–10 P.M., 7 days/week; Happy hour, 4–7 P.M. nightly.
Top o' the River—4150 Washington St., Vicksburg, MS 39180; 601-
   636-6262; 5–9 P.M., Sun., Tues.–Thurs.; 5–10 P.M., Fri.–Sat.
Tuminello's—500 Speed, Vicksburg, MS 39180; 601-634-0507;
   Tues.–Sun.; Lounge, 4:30 P.M.; Dinner, 5 P.M.
Velchoff's Corner Restaurant & Miller's Still Lounge—1101 Washington St., Vicks-
   burg, MS 39180; 601-638-8661; Sun.–Sat., 11 A.M.–10 P.M.; Live
   entertainment on weekends.
Walnut Hills Restaurant—1214 Adams St., Vicksburg, MS 39180; 601-
   638-4910; Mon.–Fri., 11 A.M.–9 P.M.; Sun., 11 A.M.–2 P.M.

❧ SHOPPING

Harrison House Antiques—1433 Harrison St., Vicksburg, MS 39180; 601-
   638-2178; Mon.–Fri., 9 A.M.–5 P.M.; Antiques and collectibles.
Old Field Home—2108 Cherry St., Vicksburg, MS 39180; 601-636-0773;
   Antiques, collectibles, interiors, fine furniture, and accessories.

❧ FOR MORE INFORMATION

Vicksburg Convention and Visitors Bureau—P.O. Box 110, Vicksburg, MS 39181;
   800-221-3536; Contact for pilgrimage information.

17 Loop Tour IV:
Port Gibson / Grand Gulf Park / Lorman / Fayette / Church Hill

From Jackson you can exit I-20 via Mississippi Route 18 if you want to visit the tiny hamlet of Raymond. You may want to stop if history or collectible records are special interests. Otherwise take I-20 to reenter the Trace via Highway 467. Raymond is also about 3 miles off the Trace via Route 467. This intersection is approximately 5 miles south of the temporary terminus of the Natchez Trace south of Jackson.

If you went to Vicksburg, we encourage you to come back to the Trace in time to see Rocky Springs. From Vicksburg you can get back on the Trace via I-20 or miss about 25 miles of the parkway by using Highway 27, just northeast of the city, to reconnect with the Trace near mile marker 58.

The Battle of Raymond was fought 1¼ miles southwest of town on May 12, 1863. The courthouse, a colonnaded two-story white building built in 1857–59 by the Weldon brothers with a skilled slave-labor crew, served as a Confederate hospital after the Battle of Raymond.

The collection of vintage records in the **Little Big Store,** in the old depot, is a music lover's delight. Two rooms contain row after row of albums ranging from rhythm and blues to hard rock, country-western to classical. Highway 467 returns you to the Natchez Trace Parkway.

Visitors will find several reasons to stop for a visit at the Rocky Springs site, about 25 miles south of Raymond via the Natchez

Cotton was the basis for the economy of the "Old South" prior to the arrival of the boll weevil.

Trace Parkway. Rocky Springs was actually a rural community with origins as early as the 1790s. The spring drew travelers from the Natchez Trace.

The most notorious events in Rocky Springs' history relate to the connection of a local tavern, known as the Red House, with the infamous thieves and murderers in the Harpe and Mason gangs. Legend has it that one of the gangs had a hideout nearby and that a murder took place near the spring. The Harpe brothers, who had come to the West from North Carolina, lived for a time in Knoxville, Tennessee, before terrorizing travelers up and down the length of the Natchez Trace. Their crimes were particularly atrocious, often involving brutal murders and grisly disposal of the bodies by gutting them, filling the abdominal cavities with stones, and sinking them in nearby swamps or streams. They have been credited with bashing the skull of a crying toddler against the wall at the King's Tavern in Natchez. (Micajah, or Big Harpe, is reputed to have said the only thing he regretted was brutally killing one of the Harpe infants.) The Harpes were also accused of murdering a fellow traveler in a tavern because he snored too loudly. Another traveler was lashed to his horse and the horse beaten until it was driven off a cliff. Even their fellow outlaws at the hideout at Cave-in-Rock in Illinois thought the Harpes went too far and ran them out. Big Harpe was eventually captured and beheaded in northwest Kentucky.

Mason's gang robbed on the Trace and on the river, frequently leaving signs claiming credit for their deeds. Eventually a $2,000 reward was offered for Mason's capture, dead or alive. A head purported to be his was presented for the bounty at the circuit court in the old town of Greenville, just north of Natchez. As events unfolded, one of the men who had brought in the head was identified as Wiley Harpe, the notorious Little Harpe of the Harpe gang, by a scar beneath his left breast. He was subsequently hanged and beheaded.

Today the crumbling remains of a cistern mark the site of the Red House. The peace of the farming community following the capture of the Harpes was abruptly broken in May of 1863 when Gen. U. S. Grant provisioned more than 40,000 troops from an area that

Services are still held regularly at the Rocky Springs church.

supported only 2,500 citizens on a daily basis. The community was again devastated in 1878 when yellow fever claimed the lives of several citizens of the area; but the final blow was dealt when the boll weevil destroyed the cotton crop. Only heaps of rubble, remains of cisterns, and the brick church, erected in 1837, remain today. In fact, services are still conducted at the church.

There are twenty-two campsites and restrooms available at **Rocky Springs Campground** and several trails here are part of the Natchez Trace National Scenic Trail. The trail north of Rocky Springs begins at the campground and extends 6 miles through terrain that reportedly includes quicksand hazards, so be especially alert. Look for a staging area at the northern end of the trail, on the exit to Utica near milepost 60. You'll also find a section of trail south of Rocky Springs, including a 2.5-mile trail south to Owens Creek that begins behind the picnic area. Be forewarned: this section of the trail crosses the creek several times before reaching the visitors parking area at Owens Creek.

The day we visited Owens Creek, children were playing in the cool water and squealing with delight. Several large steppingstones cross the creek, for those of you who are able to forego the pleasures of wading or at least dangling your toes. Although the trail ends at a gravel road just south of Owens Falls, horseback riders can proceed to Bayou Pierre. For more information, contact the Rocky Springs Ranger Station at 601-535-7142.

At the Grindstone Ford marker a trail through the woods leads to a wide section of the Old Trace. Although the signs proclaim this area is wheelchair accessible, there were huge logs blocking the entrance to the path through the woods the day we visited. An ice storm had devastated this area in late winter, several months before our July visit, so the logs may only have been temporary indications that the paths were not yet cleared of all the storm-damaged trees.

As you continue along the Natchez Trace Parkway, you'll see the signs for exiting to Port Gibson, the City Too Beautiful to Burn. Originally known as Gibson's Landing, the county seat of Claiborne County was chartered in 1803. The community grew up around a seasonal landing established on the Bayou Pierre. The town originally

Cotton fields required long hours of back-breaking labor beneath the sweltering Mississippi sun.

prospered as a frontier settlement. In time, some of the flatboats that landed here were used to construct fine homes and churches. As you enter Port Gibson from the Trace on Highway 18, turn left onto Church Street to visit the famous First Presbyterian Church with its upward-pointing index finger. The Reverend Zebulon Butler was well known for this pulpit gesture. His parishioners honored him with a wooden replica atop the steeple of their church when it was built in 1859. Eventually a metal likeness replaced the wooden hand.

The famous frontier preacher Lorenzo Dow also called Port Gibson home for a time. In fact, Port Gibson has been referred to as the city of churches; there are eight on Church Street alone.

The Port Gibson Pilgrimage Association invites you to visit beautifully restored antebellum homes each spring. Included on the tour are two of Port Gibson's bed and breakfast accommodations, **Oak Square** and **Gibson's Landing.** Both are located on Church Street, which is a lovely, shady street with wide sidewalks that invite

Oak Square Bed and Breakfast offers southern hospitality to Port Gibson visitors.

you to get out of your car and stroll along the first National Historic District in Mississippi. Gibson's Landing, a three-story 1832 Federal home, boasts a spiral staircase ascending to attractively restored suites. First-floor accommodations offer Jacuzzis.

Oak Square is Port Gibson's largest mansion. This neoclassical home is set amid towering oaks, for which it is named. We stopped for a chat with Mr. Lum, the present owner, who offers hospitality to visitors in a guest house on the grounds. He and his daughter explained to us that Oak Square is host to living history events each spring during the Spring Pilgrimage weekend. A traditional maypole with twin circles of revelers, a period fashion show, a maiden's fan dance, and carriage tours are just a sampling of what you can expect.

If you find yourself willing to spend a little more time in Port Gibson, we suggest you proceed down Church Street to the Gibson house. This lovely brick structure was built in 1805 and now houses the **Visitor Information Center.** The staff are most helpful in providing maps, directions, and tips on which parts of the Battlefield Tour are best left for dry-weather viewing.

While looking over your maps, you may want to stop for a bit of lunch. We suggest the **Old Depot Restaurant and Lounge,** on South Market Street, billed as the restaurant "too good to miss in the town too beautiful to burn." Located in the restored train depot, they offer a lunch buffet with fried chicken, hamburger steak, smothered chicken, au gratin potatoes, mustard greens, lima beans, squash, cornbread, soup, salad, and dessert for around $5. Lighter entrées include chef, seafood, and chicken salads. Dinner entrees include steaks, seafood, fried catfish, prime rib, and po' boy sandwiches from $5.95 to $9.99. The service was good, the food was tasty, and a nonsmoking section was available.. They also feature domestic and imported beers, wine, and cocktails.

JB's also serves lunch. The day we visited, they featured chicken and dumplings and were in the process of cutting up okra from their garden. Folks, it just doesn't get fresher than that! Their prices are very reasonable. Don't expect anything fancy at JB's—just good home cooking and plenty of it. In fact, when we first drove by we thought it was a service station that someone had converted to living quarters.

Grant's Place Restaurant, on Church Street, also features home cooking—we had our choice of lima beans, chicken either stewed or fried, macaroni and cheese, greens, and cornbread; they also serve sandwiches. Open Monday through Saturday from 10 A.M.–9 P.M. and Sunday 10 A.M–5 P.M. Meals range from $2.50 to $4. Grant's wasn't fancy, but the food was good.

Next, turn onto Main Street and proceed through the business district. At the corner of Main and Carroll, a state historical marker explains that the first shot fired at the Battle of Port Gibson during Grant's advance from Bruinsburg on May 1, 1863, was 4 miles west of town. Grant had decided to cross the river at Bruinsburg on April 30 after the bombardment of the Grand Gulf defenses failed to provide a landing site for Union troops. Rather than proceed toward Vicksburg on the Bruinsburg Road, he moved most of his 17,000 troops through the Mississippi night over the Rodney Road, hoping to arrive before the Confederates burned the bridges over Bayou Pierre. A skirmish ensued when a Confederate outpost was discovered around midnight near the Shaifer house on Widows Creek. At dawn the Union troops began to advance along the Rodney Road toward Martin E. Green's brigade and along the Bruinsburg Road toward Tracy's Alabama brigade. After twelve hours of furious fighting, the outnumbered Confederates were driven from the battlefield along Rodney Road.

Gen. Edward D. Tracy was among 60 Confederates killed. Another 340 were wounded and 387 went missing out of 8,000 Confederates in action. The Union forces lost 131 killed, 719 wounded, and 25 missing from among 23,000 engaged in battle here. Legend tells us that in lieu of leaving behind occupying forces in the city he called "too beautiful too burn," General Grant had some of Port Gibson's leading citizens and fair young ladies held hostage in Vicksburg to keep the folks back home in line.

While you're in town, be sure to stop by the **Mississippi Cultural Crossroads,** a nonprofit educational and cultural organization at the corner of Market and Fair streets. The friendly folks here will be delighted to take you next door and show you locally made quilts for sale. One quilter, Hystercine Rankin, has been designated a

Master Artist by the Mississippi Arts Commission. She often uses scenes of daily life as in her Sunburst Quilt, which was inspired by the sight of the sun rising into a cloud bank; but she may be just as likely to use pure practicality, as in her Britches Quilt, made of recycled scraps of hand-me-down jeans. At any rate, she considers her quilting to be a strictly utilitarian undertaking, designed to keep her family warm. Prices range from $75 for a crib quilt to $600 for an intricate queen-size quilt. Other beautiful quilts for $125–$250 were being prepared for a show.

The Cultural Crossroads also produce a publication called *I Ain't Lying*, which is the result of area children's interviewing family members and neighbors, then coming back and recording the cultural histories.

Across the street you'll find a civil rights exhibit, including photography and artifacts, at the Matt Ross Administration Building. **City Hall** also has a public exhibit of photographs, from the Allen Collection, called Picturing Our Past. Fifty photographs have been selected from more than one thousand plate-glass negatives of images taken between 1906 and 1911 by Leigh Briscoe Allen. Scenes of Port Gibson's busy unpaved streets, music-making, river baptisms, and cotton picking are all represented.

To get to the **Grand Gulf Military Park** follow signs for the Grand Gulf Tour by turning off Church Street onto Walnut Street. You'll pass over the bridge over Bayou Pierre on your way to the park. You'll pass the entrances to the Grand Gulf Nuclear Station on your left before reaching the entrance to the Grand Gulf Military Park, on your right. The Battle of Grand Gulf took place on April 29, 1863, and is diagrammed in a case showing the movement of Union gunboats. The battle began at 7:50 A.M. and ended at 1:30 P.M. the same day. The Union gunboats could not silence the Confederate defenses at Grand Gulf and so were unable to provide a landing area for Grant's troops. Grant went ashore at Bruinsburg in the largest amphibious landing in American history until the Normandy invasion during World War II. The military park offers a campground, restrooms, and a museum with artifacts from the Civil War, Indian artifacts, geological samples, fossils, geodes, mastodon bones (including a molar

The Catholic church at Grand Gulf Military Park is one of the restored buildings in this one-time boomtown.

Grand Gulf was a Confederate strong-
hold during the Civil War. Many artifacts surround the park's museum.

that's as large as your head), tools and implements from the 1700s
and 1800s, remnants from Windsor Ruins, period costumes, rifles
from the 1800s, and a unique rocking chair with rockers fore and aft
called the Shaifer Chair.

The original jail for Grand Gulf is behind the museum. The two
jail cells are metal and intimidating, and we're told that they sat outside with their human contents at the mercy of the scorching Mississippi sun. You'll also find firetrucks, carriages, and wagons including a
Conestoga wagon, a Studebaker ambulance built in 1862 (the only
one known verified by the Smithsonian to have survived the Civil
War), a Confederate caisson used to haul ammunition, a pirogue, and
a Parrott cannon used by the Union, which was rescued from Hollywood, where it was being used as a movie prop.

The campground hugs the hill and offers shady sites for tent
camping. There are also RV sites at the edge of the upper camping
sites. The lower campsites are nearer the bathhouse. There is an RV
dump site also. The park closes at dark for day use.

Across the road from the entrance is a short road that takes you
directly to the Mississippi River. Although there's no fishing in the
park, you can fish in the river. On the left side of the road leading to
the river, you'll see a post displaying high-water marks through the
years. In 1927 the all-time high of 56.2 feet was reached. Parking is
available at the end of the road. Before you is the Mighty Mississippi.

This firetruck, once part of the thriving community of Grand Gulf, is now
in the park's museum.

If you continue straight rather than turn right into the park or left to reach the river, you'll eventually come to the Fort Cobun site, which has a walking tour of the fort area. Be careful driving up—the road comes to an abrupt turn as you top the hill. We thought it best if you enter from the right-hand side and drive straight back to the park rather than try to follow the loop shown on the Grand Gulf Tour map, unless you clarify the directions at the park. We had some trouble following the map and wound up in someone's driveway at the top of the hill overlooking the Mississippi.

Unlike the peaceful mill scene shown here, the Mighty Mississippi tore away fifty-five city blocks of Grand Gulf between 1855 and 1860.

To visit additional battlefield markers and the **Windsor Ruins,** proceed on Main Street and take a right on Carrol Street. The road veers to your left before becoming the Rodney Road, and 1.2 miles later you'll encounter a "Y." If you stay to your right, you'll be on Bruinsburg Road.

Due to decreasing river trade, Bruinsburg declined steadily after the war. The former site is now private property. In many areas, the route of Grant's march has been left fairly undisturbed except by time.

Rodney Road lies to your left at the Y junction. Confederate troops were stationed down both of these roads to block Grant's advance. Stay to your right on State Route 552 to visit Point Lookout, approximately 3 miles from the Y, overlooking Bayou Pierre.

Rodney Road was of strategic importance during the Civil War. The city of Rodney missed being the state capital by a few votes.

The magnificent Windsor Ruins survived the conflagration of the Civil War only to be reduced to ashes by a careless cigarette.

The log cabin on the site is a reconstruction of a Presbyterian church built in 1801. This was also the north anchor of General Tracy's Confederate brigade during the Battle of Port Gibson. Now property of the state, the site is under the supervision of the Grand Gulf State Park. A dirt road leads up to the log cabin from either side of the sign. The cabin consists of one room about twenty feet square. Today a short path leads to a precipitous drop at the edge of the cane. These same cane-filled ravines prohibited the Confederates from reinforcing each other without marching back to the Y junction.

Approximately 6.5 miles down Mississippi Highway 552, you'll see the sign for Windsor Ruins. Union soldiers rested in the shade here on the afternoon before the Battle of Port Gibson.

Windsor was built in 1859 by Smith Coffee Daniel II, who died of tuberculosis two weeks after the start of the Civil War. Records tell us he built an innovative cisternlike plumbing system to collect water from the roof and store it in two copper tanks until it was diverted to marble tubs within the house. The mansion had four floors, and the top floor housed a fine ballroom with a cupola looking toward the Mississippi. Unfortunately, the magnificent structure survived the Civil War only to burn to the ground on February 17, 1890, when a careless guest left a smoldering cigarette near combustible materials. No one was killed in the blaze, but the home and most of its contents were destroyed. Only twenty-three of the original Corinthian columns mutely remind us of the elegance contained here long ago.

Most of the land surrounding Windsor is now part of **Canemount Plantation Bed and Breakfast,** which is about 4 miles from Windsor Ruins down Highway 552.

Canemount Plantation Bed and Breakfast, built in 1855, presently sits amid six thousand working acres.

Canemount Plantation, which contains a wildlife sanctuary, was built in 1855 and is a fine example of Italianate architecture. Wilma, one of the helpful and friendly staff, greeted us and directed us to our accommodations in the Pond House, where we found fresh flowers, a bottle of wine, cheese, and fruit waiting for us. The refrigerator was stocked with soft drinks. We had a living room, a bedroom with a king-size bed, and a bath with a Jacuzzi.

There's a small swimming pool behind the sun room, if you'd like to stretch your muscles after the day's journey. We decided on a morning swim instead so James, another staff member, could take us on a two-hour jeep safari where we spotted deer, flocks of wild turkeys, and evidence of the wild boars that roam the vast acreage that comprises Canemount Plantation today. Dinner began with delicious sausage-stuffed quail, green beans, and garlic grits as only Miss Georgia, chef extraordinaire, can fix them and wound up with carrot cake, a glass of wine, and good conversation. Vernon says that staying with owners Ray John and Rachel Forrest is a lot more like visiting friends than staying at a bed and breakfast.

Breakfast was fresh fruit, coffee, fruit juice, and blueberry pancakes with bacon. Canemount offers the outdoors enthusiast oppor-

One of Mississippi's oldest businesses, the Lorman Country Store, began operation in 1875.

tunities to view wildlife, tour the game preserve, and participate in a Daniel Boone-style hunt due to their herd-management practices. Not to be left without options, fishermen can visit their privately stocked lake.

Exit the Natchez Trace Parkway at U.S. 61 and head south, or continue east on Mississippi 552 from Canemount to visit another worthwhile stop for adventurers. The **Old Country Store,** at Lorman, was established in 1875 and looks it. The ceilings are fourteen feet high, and the front porch is wide enough for you to "set a spell" while you enjoy some old-fashioned hoop cheese or homemade ice cream. Inside you'll also find souvenirs like regional history books, cookbooks, Shankstowne sunbonnets, calico, and hardware, as well as a free museum overflowing with mementos of days gone by. The Breithaupt family welcomes you from 8 A.M. to 6 P.M. weekdays and Sundays from noon to 6 P.M., except Christmas and Easter.

Continue east on 552 directly across from the Old Country Store to visit **Rosswood Plantation.** This 1857 mansion was completed by David Schroder, the architect of Windsor. It has been completely restored and is available for tours or bed and breakfast accommodations. All rooms are in the mansion and feature canopy beds, private baths, fireplaces, color TVs, and phones. A heated pool and spa await guests along with a full plantation breakfast.

Backroaders should continue on 61 South to visit Fayette. You'll be able to find tourist information readily at the Little House by turning at the courthouse intersection (a right turn if you're heading north).

Fayette is the site of the Medgar Evers Homecoming every June, usually the first weekend. Charles Evers, the brother of the slain civil rights activist, still lives in town and operates the **Soul Food Cafe,** where he serves breakfast and lunch. We're told you can sometimes find pig lips being served, if you're interested in a real adventure. (We didn't have the opportunity to try them, we're sorry to say.)

Robell's Restaurant, at 211 East Main, is open for breakfast from 6–9 A.M., lunch from 11 A.M.–1:30 P.M., and dinner after 2 P.M., if you're interested in traditional fare.

You may return to the Natchez Trace Parkway via Highway 553 from Fayette, but you'll probably want to visit **Springfield Plantation,** just 1 mile west of the entrance to the parkway. Legend has it that Andrew Jackson married Rachel Donelson Robards here in 1791. Springfield has not undergone the same extensive restoration and remodeling as most of the bed and breakfast sites we've visited. Most of Springfield's interior, including the magnificent mantels and woodwork, is original. It was built by Thomas Marston Green in 1786–91 and was one of the first mansions in the Mississippi Valley boasting a full colonnade. Springfield is still a working plantation.

You may want to consider traveling on the 553 loop through historic Church Hill to visit additional plantation homes and the **Cedars Bed and Breakfast.** The present owners have recently renovated the 1830 structure; it was once the home of actor George Hamilton, who sold it to the Hare Krishnas. (It has since had two other owners.) There are ponds for fishing and nature trails on the 176-acre estate.

You can obtain additional information about sites that are open to the public on this drive at Springfield. If you take this route to return to the Natchez Trace via 553, watch for the signs to Emerald Mound.

If you decide not to continue on 553, return to the Parkway, where Coles Creek will be your next stop. A cool, lazy stream, picnic tables, and restrooms invite you to linger.

Mount Locust was built by John Blommart in 1779 to meet the requirements of the land grant extended by the British, who controlled the area at the time. By 1781, Blommart was one of the wealthiest men in the Old Natchez District. His fortunes reversed, however, when he led an unsuccessful rebellion against the Spanish, who confiscated his land and put him in prison.

The next owner was a man named Ferguson, who established Mount Locust as an inn for Kaintucks (frontiersmen) traveling the Natchez Trace. Mount Locust hosted Gen. Andrew Jackson, among others. Although Ferguson dreamed of establishing a town to be named Union near Mount Locust, it failed to be chosen as the county seat and did not prosper.

After Ferguson's death, his widow, Paulina, the mother of seven children, married James Chamberlain, Mount Locust's overseer. In addition to her seven children by Ferguson, Paulina and James had four sons by the time he left in 1810. She remained at Mount Locust, raising her family and running the inn and the farm until her death in 1849.

By 1810, nearly 10,000 travelers had found their way to the Natchez Trace, but soon the steamboats were arriving regularly at Mississippi port towns and the inn no longer catered to travelers but to wealthy vacationers from Natchez.

Several additions were made to the house, but it was occupied by members of the Chamberlain family until its purchase by the National Park Service in 1937. It is the only surviving inn of all those that existed along the Natchez Trace from the late 1700s to the mid-1820s. The restoration was done from 1955 to 1956, and approximately 20 percent of the original materials remain. The park service has a unique interpreter at this site—ranger Eric Chamberlain, the great-great grandson of James and Paulina Chamberlain; he was born in one of the upstairs bedrooms.

Eric possesses a wealth of information and will answer visitors' questions about construction of the house, its history, and the delightful fragrance of sweet olive trees that drifts across the summer breezes. The site closes at 5 P.M., so be sure to allow yourself time for a walk about the grounds before you leave.

Turpin Creek also offers a picnic area and a chance to stretch your legs a bit before proceeding to Emerald Mound, 1 mile west of the parkway. There are several houses and a small market along the road leading to the mound, so follow the signs. Emerald Mound is worth seeing.

To get there, turn off the parkway at mile marker 10.3. It is the second largest Indian temple mound in the United States. A path leads you to the top, where you are 35 feet higher than the parking lot. The mound is 770 feet long and 435 feet wide. Built between 1300 and 1600 by the ancestors of the Natchez Indians, the monument began as a small hill and was transformed into a site for rituals.

Historic Jefferson College was the first educational institution in the Mississippi Territory. It is located on Highway 61, 6 miles east of Natchez. Visitors are invited to tour the exhibition buildings and grounds from 9 A.M. to 5 P.M. daily, and 1 to 5 P.M. on Sundays. A nature trail passes St. Catherine Creek. Restrooms are available in Prospere Hall.

Remain on Highway 61 into Natchez. The southern terminus of the parkway is incomplete at this writing and expected to be completed by the end of this century.

ACCOMMODATIONS

Canemount Plantation—Rt. 2, Box 45, Lorman, MS 39096; 601-877-3784 or 455-2150; Daily, 9 A.M.–5 P.M.; Guided tours.

The Cedars Bed & Breakfast—Rt. 2, Box 298, Church Hill, MS 39120; 601-445-2203, FAX 445-2372.

Gibson's Landing—P.O. Box 195, Port Gibson, MS 39150; 601-437-3432.

Oak Square Plantation—1207 Church St., Port Gibson, MS 39150; 601-437-4350 or 437-5300.

Rosswood Plantation Bed & Breakfast Inn—Lorman, MS 39096; 601-437-4215 or 800-533-5889; Tours and gift shop.

ATTRACTIONS

Claiborne County Historical Tours—Residences, churches, and historical places of significance dating back to 1810.

Grand Gulf Military Park—Rt. 2, Box 389, Port Gibson, MS 39150; 601-437-5911; $1.50 adults, $1 seniors, and 75¢ for students; Open year-round, sunrise-sunset; Museum, Mon.–Sat., 8 A.M.–noon, 1–5 P.M.

Mississippi Cultural Crossroads—507 Market St., Port Gibson, MS 39150; 601-437-8905 or 437-3203; Free; Mon.–Fri., 8 A.M.–5 P.M.; Quilting and traveling African and European American quilt exhibits.

Old Country Store—P.O. Box 217, Lorman, MS 39096; 601-437-3661.

Port Gibson City Hall—1005 College St., Port Gibson, MS 39150; 601-437-4234; The Allen Collection, exhibit of fifty photographs of the rural South taken the first decade of the twentieth century.

Springfield Plantation—Rt. 1, Box 201, Fayette MS 39069; 601-786-3802; Year-round tours.

RESTAURANTS

Grant's—Hwy. 61 N., Port Gibson, MS 39150; 601-437-0079; Mon.–Fri., 6 A.M.–9 P.M.; Sat., 10 A.M.–9 P.M.; Sun., 10 A.M.–6 P.M.

J.B.'s Restaurant—313 Market St., Port Gibson, MS 39150; 601-437-3429; Mon.–Sat., 7:30 A.M.–7 P.M.

Robell's Restaurant—211 E. Main, Fayette, MS 39069; Open 6-9 A.M; Lunch, 11 A.M.–1:30 P.M.; Dinner, 2 P.M.

The Old Depot Restaurant & Lounge, Ltd.—S. Market St., Port Gibson, MS 39150; 601-437-4711; Mon.–Sat., 11 A.M.–until.

The Soul Food Cafe—E. Main, Fayette, MS 39069.

SPECIAL EVENTS

Spring: Annual 1800s Spring Festival—P.O. Box 491, Port Gibson, MS 39150; 601-437-4351; Dances, lawn games, maypole, artisans, craftsmen, tribute to inventor of the Bowie knife, collectors, musicians, exhibits, and a variety of "shows."

FOR MORE INFORMATION

Jefferson County Tourism—Box 7, Fayette, MS 39069; 601-786-3003.

Port Gibson Chamber of Commerce—P.O. Box 491, Port Gibson, MS 39150; 601-437-4351; Ask for free self-guided tour map.

18 Natchez: Mississippi's First City

Natchez is the end of the Trace for modern travelers, but for nearly two centuries, during the 1700s and 1800s, it was the beginning. Mile marker 8.1 is the temporary terminus; Highway 61 takes visitors into the city. Plans are being made for the Trace to continue to the old Fort Rosalie site, on the Mississippi River. Completion date is scheduled for the turn of the century.

In many ways, Natchez is the most sophisticated city you'll visit on your journey along the Mississippi corridor of the Natchez Trace, partly because of the extraordinary number of elegant bed and breakfasts located in many of the former townhouse mansions of wealthy plantation owners and businessmen. Natchez also has unusually good restaurants, especially for such a small town, and they represent tastes ranging from Continental to Cajun, catfish to pasta.

More than six hundred historic structures adorn Mississippi's oldest city. Perhaps the main reason Natchez seems so singular is the heritage that results from the flags of five nations having flown over it since the Natchez Indians were driven from their homeland by the French at Fort Rosalie in 1730. Natchez has the exotic flavor of New Orleans but maintains its unique small-town charm.

Visitors find Natchez delightful in springtime, when the azaleas and dogwoods are in bloom; heavenly in summer and fall, when the fragrant gardenia, magnolia, and sweet olive are flowering; and splendid when the camellias blossom during the winter holiday season. You can ride through its historic streets in a horse-drawn carriage,

Mississippi River Bridge as seen from Natchez Under-the-Hill at sunset.

rent a bicycle for a day's touring, travel in an air-conditioned double-decker tour bus, or stroll along while visiting the many specialty gift and antiques shops. Do you get the feeling we love Natchez? It's a fact, and we think you will too.

Before we take you to visit some of the city's highlights, we'll briefly recall some of significant events in the colorful past of Natchez.

The Frenchman Jean Baptiste Le Moyne, sieur de Bienville, built Fort Rosalie in 1716 near the Grand Village of the Natchez Indians. The Grand Village was built in stages, probably beginning in the thirteenth century. By the time the French arrived, it was the ceremonial center for the tribe. Bienville believed no threat was posed by the peaceful Natchez tribe; the French had allied with the Choctaw to the north against their mutual foes, the Chickasaw.

Bienville was no longer in charge at Fort Rosalie when the Natchez Indians learned that the new French commander, the sieur de Chopart, was planning to demand that they abandon their tribal lands, including the ceremonial grounds. The angry Natchez led the French to believe an attack was imminent by their supposed Choctaw friends. The French enlisted the help of the Natchez to defend the settlement, even arming a number of the Natchez warriors. As they waited with the French for the Choctaw attack that never came, the Natchez turned on them with a vengeance.

The carefully planned massacre erupted on November 28, 1729, when more than five hundred French men, women, and children were killed. The news traveled quickly through the horrified French colonies at New Orleans and Mobile. The French reestablished their alliance with the Choctaw, and the retaliation against the fleeing Natchez was swift and severe. A few may have escaped to the safety of the Chickasaw, Creek, or Cherokee villages to the north, but the nation of the Natchez was destroyed forever.

The abandoned site at Fort Rosalie gradually returned to wilderness. During this time, control of the land at Natchez passed into British hands at the conclusion of the Seven Years' War, while Spain established dominion over New Orleans. The British began to seek land grants and gradually established settlements in the area. In the meantime, the colonists were becoming increasingly rebellious in the east and the American Revolution began.

In 1779, Spain declared war on England, and the Natchez District was seized. The Spanish encouraged the people of Natchez to stay as settlers if they wished, and the stage was set for political intrigue as former British subjects took Spanish loyalty oaths on North American soil following the American Revolution.

Although Natchez was a center of culture and commerce, it was also known as the Barbary Coast of the Mississippi. At one time it was reputed to be the home of more millionaires than any other city in the United States, but the majority of the Natchez Trace travelers were never invited to the mansions high on the bluffs.

Although it is now part of the Deep South, you should remember that Natchez was once the southern terminus of the first Wild West our country was to possess. Commerce gradually developed as settlers from Tennessee, Ohio, Indiana, and Kentucky brought flour, lard, butter, candles, millstones, wagons, iron, furs, and livestock to market on flatboats traveling down the Tennessee and Ohio rivers to markets at Natchez, on the Mississippi River. The flatboats were usually sold for the lumber they contained before the Kaintucks, as these boatmen came to be known, headed north on the Natchez Trace with their hard-earned profits in their pockets. They often frequented the establishments of Natchez Under the Hill, where gamblers, harlots, and thieves waited to divest them of their earnings before they began the long overland journey home through the lawless wilderness beyond Bayou Pierre.

During the 1790s, the Natchez District was receiving a steady stream of Americans with few pretensions of loyalty to Spain. Among these hardy travelers were Rachel Donelson Robards and Andrew Jackson from Nashville. The lovely Rachel was estranged from her husband, Lewis Robards of Kentucky, and fled Nashville to stay with the Abner Green family in Natchez in 1790.

Andrew Jackson was familiar with Natchez, having previously established business contacts and purchased some property at Bruinsburg. He was also acquainted with Rachel and had been a boarder in her mother's home in Nashville.

This stone marker denotes the beginning of the Kaintucks' trek home to Tennessee and beyond.

We are told they were married in August 1791 at Springfield, the mansion of Thomas Marston Green, Jr., believing a divorce had been obtained by Robards in Virginia. Their love story has been the subject of numerous books and at least one movie. (See chapter 2 for additional information.)

By 1798 the United States was in undisputed possession of the western outpost and began to seek ways to strengthen the ties between the eastern states and the newly established Mississippi Territory. Efforts to enhance communication included the establishment of a post office in Natchez. Postriders carried the mail between Nashville and Natchez. According to James Crutchfield's *The Natchez Trace, A Pictorial History*, postriders who left Nashville on Saturday evening were expected to arrive in Natchez ten days and four hours later. In 1801 a project was undertaken to improve the Natchez Trace, or Post Road, as it was sometimes called.

Despite these and other efforts, concerns eventually developed because of rumors of a conspiracy led by Aaron Burr, the former vice president of the United States, to seek western secession and invade Mexico. Burr was arrested in Natchez, and legend says a hearing was held beneath the Burr Oaks at Jefferson College in order to accommodate the huge crowd that convened for the trial. He was acquitted by the jury, and Natchez celebrated his vindication. Burr attempted to persuade a young lady of his acquaintance, Madeline Price, to leave Natchez with him. She refused, and Burr left for the coast alone, only to be arrested again and taken to Richmond for trial. He was once again exonerated, and many historians believe the charges had been orchestrated by his enemies.

In 1811 the first steamboat reached Natchez, and the city became even more important as a center of commerce for river traffic. Many northern and eastern businessmen and their families came to Natchez and prospered. As a result, many of the mansions in Natchez were owned by Union sympathizers, who found themselves in difficult situations when Mississippi became the second state to secede from the Union. You will hear many of their stories when you tour homes in the area. Although the flag of the fifth nation, the Confederacy, flew over Natchez, the loyalties of many of its citizens were clearly divided. This may be the reason Natchez surrendered so quickly when Union gunboats visited the town on the bluffs.

You'll find few distinctions these days between Natchez Under-the-Hill and the mansions above—they are all pleased you've come to Natchez, and you'll receive a gracious welcome wherever you go!

At this writing, the southern terminus is 8 miles from Natchez. By the end of this century, the proposed parkway will take you to the Mississippi River and the site of Fort Rosalie, the first European settlement in the state. As you exit the Natchez Trace Parkway today at its southern terminus on State Route 61, you'll pass the privately owned Traceway Campground, on your right, on your way into Natchez.

Outstanding accommodations are available in Natchez, whether you're camping or staying in modern motels or antebellum bed and breakfasts. Reservations for more than twenty-five bed and breakfast accommodations can be arranged through Natchez Pilgrimage Tours or with individual bed and breakfasts. The offices of Natchez Pilgrimage Tours are located at the corner of Canal and State streets. You can also make arrangements at this location for carriage rides, double-decker bus tours, and tickets for Spring and Fall Pilgrimage

Horsedrawn carriages provide visitors with a relaxing tour of Natchez.

The Double Decker Tour Bus gives visitors not only a tour of Natchez but also background information and history of the sites.

Built in 1792, Linden contains an
extensive collection of heirlooms.

Look familiar? The front door at
Linden was the model used for Tara
in the movie *Gone With the Wind.*

tours. There are many excellent choices, but we'd like to share a few of
our favorites with you.

Turn left off Melrose onto Connor Circle to visit **Linden,** a Federal plantation-style home built in 1792. The present owner, Jeanette
Feltus, has been extending her personal brand of southern hospitality
to guests for more than twelve years. Linden has been in her family
since 1849, and an impressive array of Federal-style furniture dating
back to the 1820s was actually used in this house by her ascendants.
Her children are the sixth generation to have lived in the two-hundred-year-old home.

When you get there, you may recognize Linden's front door. It
was the model used for Tara in the movie *Gone With the Wind.*

As Feltus takes visitors on tours through the rooms, she adds
personal anecdotes that help them fully appreciate daily life at Linden for her ancestors. Many additions have been made through the
years, but one of the most enjoyable is the ninety-eight-foot shut-
tered gallery, or porch, that spans the length of the house. Breakfast
is served here.

Our first breakfast was a Continental affair—not the breakfast,
which was plantation-style eggs, grits, ham, and biscuits, but our

tablemates, who were visiting from Germany, Italy, and France. Throughout the days we explored Natchez, the lilt of foreign accents added a cosmopolitan air that seemed unusual in such a small town. No one seemed quite certain how these European connections have developed, but you'll find them readily apparent when you visit.

Our lodgings were very comfortable, thanks to a beautiful king-size four-poster canopy bed, individual thermostat controls, and accommodating private bath.

Monmouth Plantation is rated among the top-ten romantic places in the United States by *USA Today*.

Monmouth Plantation, a member of the Small Luxury Hotels of the World, is just around the corner from Linden, on John A. Quitman Boulevard.

Monmouth, a two-story Federal-style brick mansion set on thirty-one acres, was purchased by native New Yorker John Quitman for $12,000 in 1826, when he was twenty-seven years old. He became famous for his boldness in battle during the Mexican War of 1846 and rose to the rank of general. He supported the South and the lifestyle of his adopted region including the owning of slaves. Quitman was an attorney who served as governor of Mississippi and a U.S. congressman. As governor he tried unsuccessfully to get Mississippi to leave the Union as early as 1850. He died at Monmouth of a condition known as the national hotel disease, an ailment similar to the Legionnaires' of modern times.

When the Civil War came to Natchez, Union soldiers camped on the grounds, pillaged the house, and cut down the massive oak trees for firewood. The house was not destroyed after Quitman's daughters pledged their loyalty to the United States even though their brother was serving in the Confederate army. By the 1900s, the mansion had fallen into disuse, and the grounds were littered and overgrown. It was rescued in the late 1970s by the current owners, Ron and Lani Riches, who are from Southern California and have shown a great respect for this house and its former owner, John Quitman, through careful restoration and thoughtful accumulation of items related to Quitman.

A publication entitled *Monmouth Plantation, A Dream in Time,* which chronicles the house, its history, and the Riches' labor of love, is available for a nominal fee. Monmouth has been designated a

You can dream the night away in this queen-size full tester bed when you stay at Monmouth.

Monmouth sits among twenty-six landscaped acres.

National Historic Landmark and rated one of the top ten most romantic places in the United States by *Glamour* magazine and *USA Today* and one of the top twelve inns in America by *Country Inns*. Does that give you an idea of the magic they've been able to weave here?

Mr. Quitman's bedroom has a particularly lovely queen-size full tester bed, but all the available rooms are quite elegant. The grounds were beautiful in Quitman's day and remain so today. On twenty-six beautifully landscaped acres, you'll find a gazebo overlooking a lovely garden pond, a wisteria arbor with perennials in front, a rose garden, water lilies, a lotus pond, and garden cottages off by themselves. Guests may use cane poles for fishing in the pond. Hidden charms are tucked around every bend: Behind the pond a sign directs you to landscape designer Larry Stewart's walking trail through a magnolia grove.

For overnight guests breakfast includes grits, eggs, link sausage or ham, biscuits, jam, fresh fruit, and cereal. You can also visit Monmouth by candlelight—for a gourmet five-course dinner available by reservation!

Glen Auburn is convenient to downtown Natchez.

The **Glen Auburn,** at 300 South Commerce, is a good choice if you're interested in doing a walking tour of Natchez. This elegant Victorian mansion is on the National Register of Historic Places but has introduced such modern conveniences as Jacuzzis into its original French Second Empire features. A swimming pool offers respite from the sultry summer nights, and a traditional southern breakfast is served.

Just down the street you'll find **T.A.S.S. House Bed and Breakfast,** at 404 South Commerce. We met the owners, Robert and Lela Costa, one beautiful day when the crepe myrtles were blooming, and we had to know what T.A.S.S. stood for. He replied (with a twinkle in his eye), "Tea, antiques, sherry, and sass." You'll get some of each if you visit Lela and Robert in their lovely Greek Revival home.

An alternative for a downtown location is the **Guest House Historic Hotel,** at the corner of Pearl and Franklin. It offers eighteen guest rooms (including handicapped accessible) with private baths, cable TV, telephone, and lovely antique furnishings. Registration includes a complimentary bottle of wine on arrival, and it's on the

T.A.S.S. House—Tea, Antiques, Sherry, and Sass.

Weymouth Hall has an outstanding collection of antique furnishings.

downtown trolley stop. It also offers AARP discounts and has a AAA three-diamond rating that is well deserved. The building is two stories high and does not have an elevator, so you may want to request a first-floor room if stairs present a problem for you.

For those wanting to stay in a bed and breakfast on a limited budget, we found the one above the Country Treasures specialty shop, at 206 Washington Street, to be the least expensive in Natchez.

If you don't mind being out of the immediate downtown area, three other interesting choices come to mind. **Weymouth Hall,** just north of downtown on Cemetery Road, stands high on the loess bluff overlooking the Mississippi River.

Weymouth Hall is participating in a massive stabilization effort to prevent further deterioration of the bluff; the operation requires tons of more stable soils to be mixed with the unstable loess that comprises most of the bluffs along this area. If the concept is successful at Weymouth Hall, and so far it has been, it may benefit others experiencing problems with slope stabilization. Inside Weymouth Hall you'll find an outstanding collection of antique furnishings by masters like John Belter, Charles Baudoine, and P. Mallard, as well as fine

Weymouth Hall, situated high on a loess bluff, overlooks the Mississippi River.

porcelains. The guest rooms, which open to recessed porches over-looking the Mississippi, have private entrances.

The second choice, the **Briars,** is south of the immediate down-town area on Irving Lane, just across the US 84 and 98 bypass (also known as John R. Junkin Drive). Built around 1814, the Briars was the home of Varina Howell when she married Jefferson Davis in 1845 in a simple ceremony in the parlor. Her beauty at nineteen was legendary—she was often called the Rose of Mississippi. Davis was forty-five and a West Point graduate with a bright future ahead of him. Sixteen years later he became the president of the Confederacy and their lives changed forever.

This bed and breakfast has received the AAA four-diamond award. The spacious bedrooms offer private baths, king or queen-size beds, and cable TV. The nineteen-acre estate enjoys a fantastic view of the Mississippi River from the observation point. In the spring-time a dazzling display of more than one thousand azaleas graces the gardens.

Our personal favorite is last on our list of bed and breakfast accommodations. **Oakland Plantation,** 8 miles south of Natchez on the historic Lower Woodville Road, reminded us of home (not that we live in a plantation home). It seemed like home because we could hear the tree frogs and crickets and thousands of other critters mak-ing their night sounds—and that's all we could hear!

There were fresh flowers—lantana and honeysuckle—both in our room and outside the window. We live in the country and love it, and that's exactly where Oakland is. We also love dogs, and so do the Peabodys, who own Oakland. They even allow their guests to bring their well-behaved pets to visit!

You can play tennis on the Oakland courts (Mrs. Peabody will give lessons if you'd like; she's a U.S. Professional Tennis Association instructor) or roam around the 360-plus acres. The Peabodys will gladly give you a map with sketches showing the trail system they've developed or you can fish from a nearby pond.

If that's not enough to get you to Oakland, let us tell you about the houses—that's right, there are two of them. The bed and breakfast is in a two-story brick house, built in 1785 by Abner Green, that is

The bed and breakfast at Oakland Plantation was built in 1785 and is thought to be the oldest residence in the state.

This and other massive oak trees were the inspiration for the name Oakland.

the oldest brick home in the state. In many ways it seemed more like a house you'd expect to find in New England, not in Natchez.

Its appearance is Federal style, and the millwork around the massive fireplace in our room was in keeping with the same lines. In 1790, when Andrew Jackson brought Rachel Robards to Natchez, she stayed with the Green family for five months, both at Oakland and at Springfield.

At one time Oakland was owned by a former slave on the plantation, Alexander Mazique. He bought the property at auction on January 2, 1891. His Choctaw wife, Clara, lived here until her death in 1951. It was virtually abandoned until it was purchased by the Peabodys in 1955.

The "big house" is plantation style and has beautiful cypress mantels and floors. The antiques the Peabodys have collected through the years are most interesting. One of our favorite pieces isn't the oldest or even the most expensive—it's Mr. Peabody's grandfather's grandfather clock. Just like in the childhood song, "never to run again," although nothing can be found wrong with it.

A full country-style breakfast featuring fresh biscuits is served.

Although these bed and breakfasts are our favorites, there's simply not enough room to tell you all the good things the others have to offer. We don't think you can go wrong in Natchez—except by not going!

You'll find there are some great restaurants in Natchez as well. We sampled a good cross section, but more are opening every day for you to enjoy. Here are our current favorites.

The **Natchez Landing,** at Natchez Under-the-Hill, has a menu that includes steaks, pork ribs, smoked chicken, smoked beef plate, appetizers, barbecued shrimp, fried shrimp and grilled and fried catfish—in English, French, German, and Italian! In any language the mustard greens, catfish nuggets, and ribs were great. There's also a full service bar and a nonsmoking area. They offer a delicious bread pudding with bourbon sauce for dessert.

Dining is casual at Natchez Landing overlooking the Mississippi River.

Dining is casual, overlooking the Mississippi below the edge of the bluff. Only a few businesses remain at the site of Natchez Under-the-Hill. The bank here is also suffering from instability problems, causing the street to be a little narrower than it used to be and the parking a little harder to find. The ribs alone are worth the hunt for a parking space, but if there's room for a cold beer on the porch out front overlooking the river, it's worth walking quite a distance for!

We also suggest dinner at **Pearl Street Pasta.** The restaurant has a small, intimate setting with the soothing sounds of violins audible in the background. They offer a variety of delicious pasta dishes. All entrées are served with a fresh green salad and hot garlic bread. The house salad dressing is a sweet herbal vinaigrette. We thoroughly enjoyed a glass of white wine and a plate of locally celebrated Pearl Street Pasta Chicken in white sauce with pearl onions and steamed baby carrots on the side. The chef claims the chicken was simply seasoned with lemon and pepper but we've tried it since and there have to be other ingredients that make the chicken so delectable. The dessert choices vary, but they all taste like Mom just baked them—because she did. The owner's mother really does make all the desserts, and Mom really knows how to bake! Lunch is Monday through Saturday from 11:30 A.M. to 2 P.M. Dinner is served seven nights a week from 6 to 10 P.M.

Once an outlaws' hangout, today Natchez Under-the-Hill is a popular tourist destination.

If you want a truly delicious plate of prime rib—we're talking the best we've ever tasted—visit **King's Tavern,** at 619 Jefferson Street. Yvonne Scott and John Peterson have hit upon a seasoning and a technique for hickory grilling that yields the most succulent, divine piece of prime rib imaginable.

The tavern was built before 1789 and is believed to be the oldest building in Natchez. The site was on the Old Natchez Trace and served as a mail and stagecoach station. The first U.S. mail was distributed from the tavern in 1803.

The restored primitive two-story structure of brick, poplar, and cypress resembles the blockhouses of the American frontier days.

While you're there, get the staff to tell you about the resident apparition, Madeleine. Better yet, maybe there will be a manifestation while you're there. Don't worry—she never tries to harm anyone even though she was reputed to have been murdered and walled up in the chimney.

Liza's, at 657 South Canal Street, specializes in contemporary regional cuisine and is the current favorite dinner destination for most of the people we met who live in Natchez. It's open Tuesday through Sunday, from 5:30 to 10.30 P.M.

Clara Nell's Deli, at 609 Franklin Street, is a good lunch or early dinner choice if you're browsing the antique shops on Franklin. Clara Nell will serve you homemade soups, deli sandwiches, salads, and desserts. You can also buy deli meats and cheeses by the pound if you're heading back up the Trace and want to picnic along the way. Try the black-eyed pea salad or Greek salad with your sandwich for a change of pace.

We also enjoyed the food at **Scrooge's Old English Pub and Restaurant,** at 315 Main Street. The luncheon special was a delicious grilled chicken dish, and the house salad dressing was a Thousand Island type with a little touch of horseradish for zip. An interesting collection of nineteenth-century Natchez photographs by Earl Norman lines the walls. He had a photographic studio upstairs from 1925 until his death in 1951. A very successful renovation of this mid-1860s building creates a pleasant dining environment from 11 A.M. to 11 P.M. The menu includes surf-and-turf items. Our only criticism was the absence of a smoke-free area for diners.

In addition to the historic homes tours, there are several local attractions that may be of interest to you. The **Office of Historic Natchez Foundation,** at 108 South Commerce, has displays of the Natchez Collection and displays pertinent to the history of the area. The Natchez Collection, as director Ron Miller explained to us, are home furnishings that originate from the styles of antiques in the historic houses of Natchez. The display items are not for sale but may be ordered from your local retailer, who represents the licensed manufacturers of the collection.

The **Bike Center,** on Main Street, is open Tuesday through Friday from 10 A.M. to 5:30 P.M. and Saturday from 10 A.M. to 3 P.M. Bike rentals are from one to three hours, three to five hours, and all day. No rentals to children under twelve.

There are many specialty gift shops in the downtown area and a large number of antiques shops as well. Franklin Street is considered antiques row, but there are numerous shops throughout the downtown area. Mrs Killelea's shop, **Brown Barnett Dixon's Antiques and Fine Gifts,** had silver, china, and oriental rugs. She told us a story of "Sweet Auntie" Byrnes, who lived at Ravennaside. Sweet Auntie had a party once a year for the children of Natchez and brought down MoonFlower, an exquisite fairy doll, from the treetops as if she really were a fairy. She was quite a character who, while decked out in a big hat, was driven around by a chauffeur. She was loved by the community, but she became very well known for her work with the Natchez Trace Association, serving as president of the association for more than thirty years.

The **Lady Luck Casino Riverboat** is docked just down the hill from Natchez Landing. There are ubiquitous slot machines asking for 25 cents to $5 a pull. There's also roulette and a poker parlor. A quiet restaurant serving sandwiches and shrimp is at the northern end of the boat with a view of the river but no exit for walking outside around the promenade.

The **Old South Winery,** at 65 South Concord Avenue, continues a family tradition established in the 1800s—making fine muscadine table wines. Tours and tastings occur daily until 6 P.M.

The Grand Village of the Natchez, on Jefferson Davis Boulevard, is open from 9 A.M. to 5 P.M. Monday through Saturday and 1:30 to

Muscadine grapes evenutally become fine table wines at the Old South Winery.

This reconstructed Indian dwelling is part of the Grand Village of the Natchez.

5 P.M. on Sundays. A museum houses displays concerning the Natchez Indians. Check out the mound site here and a reconstruction of a Natchez dwelling.

Natchez National Historical Park comprises three units: Melrose, William Johnson, and Longwood. The Melrose Estate is located at One Melrose-Montebello Parkway. House tours are conducted daily from 9 A.M. to 5 P.M. Fees are charged.

John McMurran, the law partner of Gen. John Quitman, was born in Pennsylvania and met Quitman in law school. He joined Quitman in Natchez in 1826, married Mary Louisa Turner, and moved with her to Melrose in 1845. They spent the dangerous hot summer months in Europe or the Northeast and returned to Natchez in the winter. They sold Melrose in 1866, and John died the same year. Mary lived at her parent's home, Woodlands, until her death. The eighty-acre property contains the Melrose Mansion and several outbuildings, including a re-created slave residence, a stable, and a carriage house.

The **William Johnson Complex,** at 210 State Street, is undergoing restoration. Known as the Barber of Natchez, William Johnson was a freedman because his mother, Amy, had been freed. On January 21, 1820, Amy's owner, William Johnson, addressed an eloquent

Melrose Estate, a Greek revival home built in 1845, is representative of the town homes of wealthy plantation owners.

petition to the Mississippi General Assembly, then in session at Natchez, asking the body to free Amy's son, William. They could not emancipate him because he was underage and was unable to execute a bond. He was freed at the age of eleven, became a barber, and thrived in the local community until his death in 1851.

Longwood, on Lower Woodville Road, is a gorgeous octagonal house visited by many people. This is a not-to-miss site that remains unfinished to this day, even tools having been left behind when workmen fled to their northern homes at the outbreak of the Civil War.

Dr. Nutt, the builder, wanted to move his family inside the safety of the house and wait out the war. In order to do that, he had to put down rough cypress as temporary flooring instead of the slate he had originally planned. Today you still walk on those "temporary" floors. A series of mirrors funnels the light downstairs. The piano arrived before the blockades were erected, and the crate it arrived in is still upstairs. Most of the furniture belongs to the family, but there are a few pieces that were given to the home. The fireplaces are of Italian marble—there were to be twenty-six throughout the house. The outside walls are twenty-seven inches thick, but the inside walls are seventeen inches with a five-inch air space for heating and cooling purposes.

Longwood, the unusual octagonal home built by Dr. Nutt, remains unfinished to this day.

A view from the center of Longwood into the unfinished dome.

Over the dining-room table is a punkah (you may know it as a "shoofly" fan). A cord was pulled by slave children, swinging the fan back and forth. Flytrap jars were another bug eliminator used before screens were invented, and Longwood has a selection of unique fly-trap jars.

Our guide on a journey through Natchez on the double-decker bus provided much historical background on the city. One of the tips we gleaned was that the plantations were north of town and the homes in Natchez were the plantation owners' town houses. Two clues on how to date a home built before 1850: If there are more than twelve panes of glass in a window, or if there are two front doors with the roof pitching over the front porch, the house was probably built before 1850.

The **Burn,** at 712 North Union, was restored by Catherine Miller, who started the Natchez Pilgrimage. This elegant 1834 home offers seven rooms for overnight guests and is a favorite destination of many visitors.

The architect of **Auburn,** located on Duncan at Auburn Avenue, was Levi Weeks. He came to Natchez after being acquitted of the murder of his fiancée in New York. He had been defended by Aaron Burr and Alexander Hamilton, who would later fight a famous duel.

ACCOMMODATIONS

Many motel chains are in the Natchez area.

The Briars Inn—31 Irving Ln., Natchez, MS 39120; 601-446-9654 or 800-634-1818.

The Burn—712 N. Union St., Natchez, MS 39121; 601-442-1344 or 800-654-8859.

Camellia Gardens—506 S. Union St., Natchez, MS 39120; 601-446-7944.

Clifton Heights—212 Linton Ave., Natchez, MS 39120; 601-446-8047.

Dorsey House—305 N. Pearl St., Natchez, MS 39120; 601-442-5845.

Dunleith—84 Homochitto St., Natchez, MS 39121; 601-446-8500 or 800-443-2455.

Elgin—Elgin Rd. off Hwy. 61 S., Natchez, MS 39120: 601-446-6100 or 800-647-6742.

Glen Auburn—300 S. Commerce St., Natchez, MS 39120; 601-442-4099 or 800-833-0170.

Glenfield—6 Providence Rd., Natchez, MS 39120; 601-442-1002 or 800-442-2366.

Governor Holmes House—207 S. Wall St., Natchez, MS 39120; 601-442-2366.

The Guest House Historical Hotel—210 N. Pearl St., Natchez, MS 39120; 601-442-1054 or 800-442-1054.

Harper House—201 Arlington Ave., Natchez, MS 39120; 601-445-5557 or 800-571-8848.

Highpoint—215 Linton Ave., Natchez, MS 39120; 601-442-6963 or 800-283-4099.

Hope Farm—147 Homochitto St., Natchez, MS 39120; 601-445-4848 or 800-647-6742.

Lansdowne—Martin Luther King, Jr., Rd., Natchez, MS 39120; 800-647-6742.

Linden—1 Linden Pl., Natchez, MS 39120; 601-445-5472 or 800-2LINDEN.

Monmouth—36 Melrose Ave., Natchez, MS 39120; 601-442-5852 or 800-828-4531.

Mount Repose—Martin Luther King, Jr., Rd., Natchez, MS 39120; 800-647-6742.

Oakland Plantation—1124 Lower Woodville Rd., Natchez, MS 39120; 601-445-5101 or 800-824-0355.

Oakwood—Upper Kingston Rd., Natchez, MS 39120; 601-445-4738 or 205-636-5178.

Pleasant Hill—310 S. Pearl St., Natchez, MS 39120; 601-442-7674 or 800-621-7952.

Ravennaside—601 S. Union at Ravenna Ln., Natchez, MS 39120; 601-442-8015.

Riverside—211 Clifton Ave., Natchez, MS 39120; 601-446-5730.

The Russell House—404 N. Union St., Natchez, MS 39120; 601-445-7499 or 800-256-4667.

Shields Town House—701 N. Union St., Natchez, MS 39120; 601-442-7680 or 800-647-6742.

Sweet Olive Tree Manor—700 Orleans St., Natchez, MS 39120; 601-442-1401 or 800-256-4667.

T.A.S.S. House—404 S. Commerce St., Natchez, MS 39120; 601-445-4663 or 601-446-9917.

Texada—222 S. Wall St., Natchez, MS 39120; 601-445-4283 or 800-647-6742.

Wensel House—206 Washington St., Natchez, MS 39120; 601-445-8577.

Weymouth Hall—1 Cemetery Rd., Natchez, MS 39120; 601-445-2304.

White Wings—311 N. Wall St., Natchez, MS 39120; 601-442-2757 or 601-445-6025.

Wigwam—307 Oak St., Natchez, MS 39120; 601-442-2600 or 800-862-1300.

The William Harris House—311 Jefferson St., Natchez, MS 39120; 601-445-2003 or 601-446-8464.

Natchez Eola Hotel—110 N. Pearl St., Natchez, MS 39120; 601-445-6000 or 800-888-9140.

❧ ATTRACTIONS

Natchez Museum of Afro-American History and Culture—307 A Market St.; For
   more information about ten sites on the "Black Heritage Tour" call
   800-647-6724.

William Johnson House—210 State St.; Johnson was a prominent free African-
   American who chronicled life in antebellum Natchez through his
   diaries and will; Natchez National Historical Park, P.O. Box 1208,
   Natchez, MS 39121; 601-442-7047.

Fort Rosalie—504 S. Canal St.; First European settlement in Mississippi;
   8 A.M.–4 P.M.; Natchez National Historical Park, P.O. Box 1208,
   Natchez, MS 39121; 601-442-7047.

Melrose Estate—1 Melrose-Montebello Pkwy.; 80-acre site of the McMurran
   residence and family farm established in 1845; Free admission to
   grounds 9 A.M.–4 P.M.; Tour charges vary with $4 maximum; Natchez
   National Historical Park, P.O. Box 1208, Natchez, MS 39121; 601-
   442-7047.

Grand Village of the Natchez Indians— 400 Jefferson Davis Blvd., Natchez, MS
   39120; 601-446-6502; History and archaeology of the Natchez Indians
   indicate the mounds on the banks of St. Catherine Creek is the site of
   their Grand Village; A walking tour of artifacts, exhibits, Indian house,
   plazas, and mounds; Free; Mon.–Sat., 8 A.M.–5 P.M.; Sun., 1:30–5 P.M.

Double-Decker Bus Tour—Hourly departure from Canal St. Depot parking
   lot; $10, children half fare; See fifty antebellum homes and churches on
   a narrated tour of Natchez; 601-446-6631.

Walking Tour—104 S. Wall St., Natchez, MS 39120; 601-442-8666 or
   800-345-2352; Fifty-minute tours of historic Natchez begin at
   10:30 A.M. and 1:30 P.M. daily from covered platform at the Canal
   Street Depot; $5 adults, children free.

Old South Winery—65 S. Concord Ave., Natchez, MS 39120; 601-
   445-9924; Open until 6 P.M. daily; Muscadine vineyards, processing,
   bottling, and tasting on site of eleven wines.

Lady Luck Casino—21 Silver St., Natchez, MS 39120; 800-722-5825;
   Riverboat gambling.

❧ RESTAURANTS

King's Tavern—619 Jefferson St., Natchez, MS 39120; 800-256-KING;
   Lunch, Mon.–Sat., 11:30 A.M.–2 P.M.; Dinner, 5 P.M.–10 P.M.;
   7 days/week; Lounge, 4 P.M.–until.

Pearl Street Pasta—105 S. Pearl St., Natchez, MS 39120; 601-442-9284;
Mon.–Sat., lunch; Dinner, 7 nights/week.

Clara Nell's Downtown Deli—609 A Franklin St., Natchez, MS 39120;
601-445-7799; Mon.–Fri., 8:30 A.M.–6 P.M.; Sat., 10 A.M.–3 P.M.;
Delivery available.

The Natchez Landing, Ltd.—Natchez Under-the-Hill, Natchez, MS 39120;
601-442-6639; Lunch, Sat.–Sun,. 11:30 A.M.; Dinner, 5–10 P.M.;
Menus in English, French, German, and Italian.

Liza's Contemporary Cuisine—657 S. Canal St., Natchez, MS 39120; 601-
446-6368; Tues.–Sun., 5:30–10:30 P.M.

The Carriage House—401 High St., Natchez, MS 39120; 601-445-5151;
Lunch, 11 A.M.–2:30 P.M.; Dinner only during Pilgrimage, 5:30–9 P.M.

The Wharf Master's House—Silver St., Natchez Under-the-Hill. 601-
445-6025; Lunch, Sat.–Sun., 12–4 P.M.; Dinner, 5–10 P.M.;
7 days/week.

Cock of the Walk—200 N. Broadway, Natchez, MS 39121; 601-446-8920;
Lunch and dinner.

Fat Mama Tamales—500 S. Canal St., Natchez, MS 39120; 601-442-4548;
Open daily; eat in or take out.

Mammy's Cupboard—555 Hwy. 61 S., Natchez, MS 39120; 601-445-8957;
Tues.-Sat., Sun. afternoons.

The Fare—109 N. Pearl St., Natchez, MS 39120; 601-442-5299;
Mon.–Sat., 7:30 A.M.–3 P.M.; Breakfast, lunch, catering.

Scrooge's—315 Main St., Natchez, MS 39120; 601-446-9922; Mon.–Sat.,
11 A.M.- 11 P.M.; Dinner after 5 P.M.

Monmouth Plantation—John A. Quitman Pkwy., Natchez, MS 3912; 601-
442-5852; Tues.–Sat., 7:30 P.M.; Reservations required.

Doug's Restaurant—410 Main St., Natchez, MS 39120; 601-446-7193;
Daily lunch buffet, 6 A.M.–2 P.M.

✄ SHOPPING

The Antiquarian—624 Franklin St.

Antiques, J. E. Guerico—701 Franklin St.

As You Like It—410 N. Commerce St.

Audubon Gallery—103 S. Broadway

Boll Weevil's & Daniels' Basketry—Canal St. Depot

Brown Barnett Dixon's Fine Gifts—511–515 Main St.

Capricorn Gallery LTD—403 Main St.

The Cook's Corner—412 Main St.
Country Bumpkin—502 Franklin St.
Country Treasures—206 Washington St.
Darby's Antiques & Southern Uniques—410 Main St.
Historic Natchez Collection—108 S. Commerce St.
H. Hal Garner Antiques and Interiors—10-614 Franklin St.
Heritage Antiques—526 Franklin St.
Lower Lodge Antiques—716 Franklin St.
Molasses Flats Antiques—200 Main St.
Natchez Antiques and Collectibles—522–524 Franklin St.
Netterville Jewelry—617 Franklin St.
Rarity Collector—511–515 Main St., upstairs
The Rendezvous Antiques—104 S. Canal St.
Santa's Station—215 Main St.
Sharp Designs and Works of Art—703 Franklin St.
Simonton Antiques—631 Franklin St.
Southern Antiques and Collectibles—106 S. Canal St.
Storyville Antiques—706 Franklin St.
T.A.S.S. House Antiques—111 N. Pearl St.
The Wilkins House Antiques—300 N. Commerce St.
Franklin Street Marketplace—4 E. Franklin St.
Canal Street Depot and Market—Canal at State St.
Magnolia Mall—D'Evereux Dr.
Morgantown Mall—Hwy. 61 N.
Natchez Mall—John R. Junkin Dr.
Trace Town Mall—Seargent S. Prentiss Dr.

⅋ SPECIAL EVENTS

February: Krewe of Alpheus Mardi Gras—parade and costume ball. Krewe
of Phoenix—Parade and grand ball.
March: Natchez Spring Pilgrimage—Visit antebellum homes; Nightly entertainment; The Natchez Pow Wow—Celebration of Indian and non-
Indians, featuring music, dancing, and crafts.
April: Swine Days on the Mississippi—Barbecue cook-off and street dance.
May: Natchez Opera Festival—Celebration of all types of music for all
ages; T. C. Jordan Professional Golf Tournament—Watch some of the
nation's best golfers compete.

June: The Natchez Library Celebration—Yearly event focusing on the literature and history of the area; Adams County Sheriff's Rodeo—Two days of rodeo fun; Floozie Contest—Floozies sashay from the *Mississippi Queen* and *Delta Queen* steamboats to the Wharf Master's House at Natchez Under-the-Hill.

July: Natchez Bicycle Race—Annual event of races, a ride through history, balloon glow, and street dance.

August: River Road Food Festival—Cajun and New Orleans-style foods experienced at the Natchez Eola Hotel.

September: Magnolia Storytelling Festival—Series of workshops and performances emphasizing the importance of storytelling to our history and culture; The Copper Magnolia Festival—Crafts fair, storytelling, food, music, and carriage rides.

October: Fall Pilgrimage—Parade of historic homes, nightly entertainment; Pioneer Day at Jefferson College—Demonstration of pioneer ways, buckskinning, butter and bread making, outdoor cooking, fiddling, and handiwork; Great Mississippi Balloon Race—Music, food, street dance, and seventy-balloon, four-flight race, with rides and attractions for the smaller balloon enthusiasts; Ghost Tales around the Campfire at Jefferson College—Spooky campfire stories.

November: The Pilgrimage Garden Club Annual Antiques Forum—Perfect for antiques lovers; Broadway Bash Chili Cook-Off—Chili tasting, crafts, and live entertainment, to benefit the Natchez Children's Home.

December: A Victorian Christmas in Natchez—Candlelight tours of historic homes, carriage rides, and Christmas carols.

✐ FOR MORE INFORMATION

Historic Natchez Foundation—P.O. Box 1761, Natchez, MS 39121; 601-442-2500 or 800-445-2510, FAX 601-442-2525.

Natchez Convention & Visitors Bureau—P.O. Box 1485, Natchez, MS 39121-1485; 601-446-6345 or 800-647-6724, FAX 601-442-0814.

Natchez National Historical Park—P.O. Box 1208, Natchez, MS 39121; 601-442-7047.

Southwest Mississippi Resource Conservation and Development—114 Industrial Park Rd., Brookhaven, MS 39601-2148; 601-833-5539, FAX 601-835-0054.

Natchez Pilgrimage Tours—P.O. Box 347, Natchez, MS 39121; 601-446-6631 or 800-647-6742.

19 *Tennessee Outdoor Recreation*

From Middle Tennessee through the northwestern corner of Alabama to southwestern Mississippi, you have outdoor recreational opportunities galore, including fishing, camping, hunting, bicycling, hiking, horseback riding, canoeing, swimming, picnicking, strolling along nature trails and historical paths, and golf.

Most of these activities are accessible on or just off the Natchez Trace. As you drive, you will see nature trail signs, but there are hiking trails at some sites, such as Meriwether Lewis Park. All are marked, and some have paved sections.

Water activities—canoeing, swimming, and fishing—are somewhat limited on the Trace, but you don't have to go far to find plenty of places to wet a line or float your boat.

For hunting and golf you must exit the Trace. Wildlife Management Areas in each state offer public hunting, and public golf courses are listed below.

Largemouth bass is the most pursued species in Tennessee's waters.

BIKING

Bikers are welcome to pedal the entire Trace; the parkway was built with this in mind. There are side trips that may interest you in each state. Many bikers prefer to travel from north to south through Tennessee because, in spite of its many hills, it is generally a downhill trek. Two areas off the Trace that welcome bikers:

DAVID CROCKETT STATE RECREATIONAL
   PARK
P.O. Box 398
Lawrenceburg, TN 38646

MERIWETHER LEWIS PARK
Hwy. 20 and Natchez Trace
Hohenwald, TN 38462
615-680-4025

❧ CAMPING

Campsites, resort inns, and RV sites on Pickwick Lake near Pickwick Dam. Nature trails, swimming, playground, picnicking, and many other amenities; wheelchair accessible.

PICKWICK LANDING STATE RESORT PARK
P.O. Box 15
Pickwick, TN 38365
901-689-3135 for information

Camping, swimming, playgrounds, nature trails, tennis, and interpretive center.

DAVID CROCKETT STATE RECREATIONAL
   PARK
P.O. Box 398
Lawrenceburg, TN 38646
615-762-9408

Camping (twenty-two sites) with hookups and bathhouse at Bellis Botel below Pickwick Dam.

BELLIS BOTEL
Botel Rd.
Pickwick Dam, TN 38372
901-925-4787

There are ninety sites near the dam, with bathhouse; open year-round.

US TVA RESERVATION
Hwy. 128
Pickwick Dam, TN 38365
901-925-4346

RV and tent camping on the Trace in the Meriwether Lewis Park. Facilities include RV pads, primitive sites, bathhouses, restrooms, picnicking, nature trails, museum, and interpretive markers.

MERIWETHER LEWIS PARK
Hwy. 20 and Natchez Trace
Hohenwald, TN 38462
615-680-4025

A commercial RV park near Columbia has sixty-five sites with hookups and dump station, bathhouse, swimming pool; open year-round.

TRAVELER'S RV PARK
1792 Bear Creek Rd.
Columbia, TN 38401

The following four campgrounds are on Percy Priest Lake. Call for information.
   Anderson Rd. Campground has thirty-seven public sites with bathhouse (May–Sept.); 615-361-1980.
   Cook Campground has fifty-seven public sites with bathhouse (May–Sept.); 615-889-1096.
   Poole Knobs Campground has 125 public sites with bathhouse; 615-459-6948.
   Seven Points Campground has sixty public sites with bathhouse; 615-889-5198.
   Hermitage Landing, also on Percy Priest Lake, has two hundred private sites. The facility offers hookups, dump station, bathhouse, grocery; open year-round.

HERMITAGE LANDING
1001 Bell Rd.
Hermitage, TN 37076
615-889-7050

Nashville KOA Kampground and Holiday

Nashville Travel Park are between Percy Priest and Old Hickory lakes. KOA has 460 private sites will full facilities.

NASHVILLE KOA KAMPGROUND
2626 Music Valley Dr.
Nashville, TN 37214
615-889-0282

Holiday Nashville Travel Park has 238 private hookup sites.

HOLIDAY NASHVILLE TRAVEL PARK
2572 Music Valley Dr.
Nashville, TN 37214
615-889-4225

Two camping areas on Old Hickory Lake: Shutes Branch has eighty-four sites, 615-754-4847, open May–Sept.; and Cedar Creek has fifty-six sites, 615-754-4947, open April–Oct.

Contact Corps of Engineers for a list of all its campgrounds and maps for its lakes.

U.S. ARMY CORPS OF ENGINEERS
Public Affairs Office
P.O. Box 1070
Nashville, TN 37202-1070
615-736-7161

CANOEING

The Harpeth, Buffalo, and Duck rivers flow very close to the Trace; in fact, you cross the Buffalo and Duck rivers on the Trace.

A Harpeth River canoe launch site is just a few miles north of the Trace terminus, at the Highway 100 bridge. Look for the entrance on

Canoeing is a fast-growing sport. Tennessee has several navigable streams crossing the parkway.

the southeast side of the bridge; open from sunup to sundown. This Class I scenic river takes you some 50 miles to its mouth on the Cumberland River.

Fishing is fair: black bass, bream, and catfish are the most prevalent species in the upper reaches. The closer you get to the mouth, the more species are available.

The Duck River runs under the Trace just south of the Gordon House and Ferry site. A short trail leads from the Gordon House to the river. There is no easy canoe access there, but east toward Columbia on State Route 7 there is an entry point at Chickasaw Trace Park.

The Duck meanders about 57 miles from the park to Centerville, then another 45 miles to the

Tennessee River. This slow stream is about sixty feet wide, has pretty scenery, and has some hazards in the form of dead falls and strainers.

Farther south, at Metal Ford, is a convenient place to launch your canoe and fish the Buffalo River. The most popular float river in Tennessee because of its beauty and fishing, Metal Ford, with its shallow depths, is about as far upstream as you would like to launch.

It's about 50 miles to Flatwoods from Metal Ford. There are a number of canoe liveries and campgrounds in Flatwoods. From Flatwoods to its mouth on the Duck River is more than 60 miles.

FLATWOODS CANOE BASE
Rt. 4, Box 612B
Flatwoods, TN 37096
615-589-5661

BUFFALO RIVER CANOE RENTAL
Rt. 4, Box 510
Flatwoods, TN 37096
615-589-2755

BUFFALO RIVER CANOEING
18 W. Linden
Hohenwald, TN 38461
615-796-5596

RIVER RAT CANOE RENTAL
4361 Hwy. 431
Columbia, TN 38401
615-381-2278

🐟 FISHING

Percy Priest, Old Hickory, and Cheatham lakes (managed by the Corps of Engineers) are all within a fifteen-minute drive or less of downtown Nashville. Stripers, hybrids, stripe (white bass),

Lakes along the parkway are often accessible to boats, large and small.

largemouth, smallmouth, Kentucky bass, bream, crappie, catfish, walleye, sauger, and saugeye swim these waters. The twenty-five-pound world-record walleye came from Old Hickory.

Percy Priest is a hill-land reservoir with steep points, humps, flats, and deep coves. The bottom is sand, gravel, and mud. This nutrient-rich lake keeps producing large numbers of bass in spite of the fishing pressure.

Old Hickory and Cheatham lakes are reservoirs on the Cumberland River and almost always have some current. If you like river fishing, try the upper ends of these lakes; if you like wide, deep coves, you will want to fish near their dams. Old Hickory has much wood cover along the main channel flats, whereas Cheatham is narrower and swifter with fewer flats.

The seagoing stripers have become a favored fish species for anglers wanting a true trophy fish. Stripers in Old Hickory exceed fifty pounds; those in Percy Priest and Cheatham run about twenty to thirty pounds. The hybrid, a cross between the saltwater striper and freshwater stripe, has gained favor over the striper for its hard fight. The hybrid might weigh between ten and twenty pounds and is stocked only in Percy Priest Lake.

All three lakes have good to excellent largemouth bass angling. Larger bass are in Cheatham Lake. Priest has the largest smallmouth and Kentucky bass populations.

Pickwick Dam tailwaters (headwaters of Kentucky Lake), located 13 miles south of Savannah, Tennessee, has the best sauger fishing in the state. From the dam downstream for several miles also has wonderful smallmouth angling.

Above the dam on Pickwick lake, smallmouth is the most popular species sought by anglers. The lake also has sauger, crappie, largemouth bass, bream, and catfish.

Of the three states traversed by the Trace, Tennessee has the most fishing opportunities. You could easily spend your vacation fishing here without wetting your hook in the same waters twice.

Detailed information about fishing is available in *Two Dozen Fishin' Holes—A Guide to Middle Tennessee,* by Vernon Summerlin. For an autographed, postpaid copy, send $12.50 to

VERNON SUMMERLIN
5550 Boy Scout Rd.
Franklin, TN 37064

For maps and lists of camping, fishing, picnicking, swimming, and hunting opportunities contact

U.S. ARMY CORPS OF ENGINEERS
Public Affairs Office
P.O. Box 1070
Nashville, TN 37202-1070
615-736-7161

For state fishing and hunting regulations and maps of local Wildlife Management Areas and lakes, contact

TENNESSEE WILDLIFE RESOURCES
    AGENCY
P.O. Box 40747
Nashville, TN 37204
615-781-6622

Laurel Hill Lake, in Laurel Hill Wildlife Management Area, is a frog jump to the east off the Trace at milepost 370. Fishing and hunting are available here.

The lake has all three black bass, bream, crappie, catfish, and walleye. It is open year-round and is managed by the Tennessee Wildlife Resources Agency.

GOLFING

PICKWICK LANDING STATE RESORT PARK
P.O. Box 15
Pickwick, TN 38365
901-689-3135 for park information
901-689-3129 for reservations

HARPETH HILLS GOLF—2424 Old Hickory Blvd., 615-862-8493; eighteen holes.
McCABE GOLF—100 46th Ave. N., 615-862-8491; twenty-seven holes.

Golfers follow the links in all weather in all seasons.

RADNOR LAKE STATE NATURAL AREA
1160 Otter Creek Rd.
Nashville, TN 37220
615-373-3467

Percy and Edwin Warner parks have extensive trails and include the original terminus of the Old Natchez Trace.

There is easy access from Highway 100 west of Nashville, Old Hickory Boulevard, and Belle Meade Boulevard.

Large wild cave with wildlife and wildflowers; hiking trails, picnic, and wildflower tours; also Civil War history; open year-round; free.

SOUTHPORT SALTPETER CAVE
2171 Mack Benderman Rd.
Culleoka, TN 38451
615-379-4404

Nature trails among 5,345 acres of reclaimed land close to Monsanto Manufacturing. Now wetlands, the area includes wildlife observation areas, abundant wildlife, and waterfowl.

TENNESSEE WILDLIFE OBSERVATION
    AREA-MONSANTO PONDS
Monsanto Rd., Hwy. 50 W.
Columbia, TN 38401
615-388-2155 (Chamber of Commerce)

TED RHODES GOLF—2400 Metrocenter Blvd., 615-862-8463; eighteen holes.

TWO RIVERS GOLF—3150 McGavock Pike; 615-889-2675; eighteen holes.

WARNER GOLF—Forrest Park Dr., 615-352-9958; nine holes.

⤳ HIKING

A nature trail around scenic Radnor Lake in southwest Nashville; bird-watching and interpretive center.

Meriwether Lewis Park has hiking in conjunction with the Lewis grave and museum at mile marker 385.9.

MERIWETHER LEWIS PARK
Hwy. 20 & Natchez Trace
Hohenwald, TN 38462
615-680-4025

✑ HORSE TRAILS

Horseback riding along the Trace is governed by
federal regulations that state (in part): "the use
of horses or pack animals outside of trails,
routes or areas designated for their use is prohibited and the use of horses or pack animals on
a park road is prohibited except: (1) where such
travel is necessary to cross to or from designated
trails, or areas, or privately owned property, and
no alternative trails or routes have been designated; or (2) when the road has been closed to
motor vehicles."

This means that horseback riding is prohibited along the entire length of the Trace except on
established trails. At the present there are only
four horse trails developed along the Trace.

Trailers are permitted on the Trace when used
noncommercially to transport horses. Make sure
your trailer meets state traffic regulations for
lights, brakes, length, and load.

In Tennessee there is one 25-mile horse trail,
Garrison Creek Trail, that loops south on the
eastern side and back on the western side of the
Trace at Garrison Creek, mile marker 427.5.
Access is also available at Highway 7 near mile-
post 415.6.

The following private stable has trails:

This is one of the horse trails running parallel to the Trace
from Garrison Creek.

KINDERHOOK LIVERY STABLE
Kirby White Rd.
Santa Fe, TN
615-682-3969

Horseback-riding resort near Waynesboro:

BUFFALO RIVER TRAIL RIDE
P.O. Box 591
Waynesboro, TN 38485

✑ HUNTING

Public hunting information is available at Tennessee Wildlife Resources Agency. Ask for

Wildlife Management Area (WMA) locations, maps, and seasons.

Cheatham WMA northwest of Nashville; 615-792-4510; Small and big game and turkey.

Eagle Creek WMA near Waynesboro; 615-781-6622; Small and big game.

Laurel Hill WMA, adjacent to Trace with Trace exit, or enter via Hwy. 64; About 15 miles west of Lawrenceburg; 615-762-2079; Small and big game and turkey.

❧ NATURE TRAILS

The following are places to stretch your legs and see a bit of nature and/or history. Pick up a copy of the Natchez Trace Parkway map for all the reference points, mile markers, and routes along the Trace from Nashville to Natchez. The National Park Service/U.S. Department of the Interior provides a variety of free maps.

Garrison Creek, at mile marker 427.6, is a combination horse and hiking trail for 24.5 miles.

Gordon House, at mile marker 407.7, takes you over a bridge into the woods and down to the edge of the Duck River; Interpretive markers tell you of the terrain.

Jackson Falls, at mile marker 404.7, is a steeply descending nine-hundred-foot trail to Jackson Falls in a severely eroded landscape.

The Duck River Overlook, also at mile marker 404.7, hiking trail is 2,100 feet long; connects with Baker Bluff Overlook to the north, at milepost 405.2

Old Trace Trail, at mile marker 403.7, is a 2,000-foot walk over the old Trace.

Fall Hollow Waterfall, at mile marker 391.9, is a short hike of 630 feet to the waterfall overlook; an unofficial trail takes you down the steep hillside to the base of the falls.

Meriwether Lewis, at mile marker 385.9, has 2.3 miles of trails between the Lewis gravesite and Little Swan picnic area; about half of the trail is the Old Trace.

Metal Ford, at mile marker 382.8, is a pleasant walk beside the Buffalo River with interpretive markers.

Glen Rock Branch, from mile marker 365.1 to 364.5, is a 1-mile trail along a fast-flowing stream that connects two picnic areas.

Sweetwater Branch, at mile marker 363.0, shows the struggle for survival in a poor habitat via twenty-four interpretive stops along 2,500 feet of trail.

❧ FOR MORE INFORMATION

For tourist information, maps, and brochures contact the following:

NASHVILLE AREA CHAMBER OF
    COMMERCE
161 Fourth Ave. N.
Nashville, TN 37219
615-259-4700

NASHVILLE CONVENTION AND VISITORS
    BUREAU
161 Fourth Ave. N.
Nashville, TN 37219
615-259-4700

TENNESSEE TOURIST DEVELOPMENT
P.O. Box 23170
Nashville, TN 37202
615-741-2158
Ask for free *Travel Tennessee—The Official Vacation Guide.*

20 *Alabama Outdoor Recreation*

Alabama Mountain Lakes Association is head-quarters for abundant information about all of North Alabama. Contact Susann Hamlin at

ALABAMA MOUNTAIN LAKES ASSOCIATION
P.O. Box 1075
Mooresville, AL 35649-1075
205-350-3500 or 800-648-5381

❧ BIKING

See also Camping and Nature Trails sections in this chapter.

A 2.6-mile jogging/biking trail winds around the Tennessee Valley Authority (TVA)/Muscle Shoals reservation. For more information, contact

DIRECTOR OF INFORMATION
TENNESSEE VALLEY AUTHORITY
400 Commerce Ave.
Knoxville, TN 37902
800-362-9250 (in TN)
800-251-9242 (in other Tennessee Valley
   states)

❧ CAMPING

Wilson Dam/Muscle Shoals Reservation Area has two camping areas. Contact Director of Information at TVA.

Veterans Memorial Park offers an eighteen-hole disc golf course, six tennis courts, softball, baseball, football, soccer, an amphitheater, twenty-two campsites, five pavilions, RV facilities, bathhouses, washers and dryers, and public telephones. Open-air picnic tables and fireplaces in the pavilions. Park and camping year-round. Camping fees: $8 trailers, $5 tents, and $6 senior citizens.

FLORENCE PARK AND RECREATION
   DEPARTMENT
P.O. Box 2040
Florence, AL 35630
205-760-6416

Bear Creek Development Authority has six campgrounds. The address is Bear Creek Development Authority, P.O. Box 670, Russellville, AL 35653.

RV and tent camping with full facilities, hiking, and biking:

Elliott Branch Campground, 205-332-9804
Horseshoe Bend Campground, 205-332-
   4392
Piney Point, 205-332-4392
Williams Hollow Campground, 205-332-
   4392

RV and tent camping with full facilities and biking:

> Slickrock Campground, 205-332-9809
> Twin Forks Campground, 205-332-4392

McFarland Park, along the Tennessee River, has RV and tent camping with full facilities including biking and hiking. There is a long stretch of clear bank for fishing and launching ramps are nearby.

> PARK & RECREATION DEPT.
> P.O. Box 2040
> Florence, AL 35630
> 205-760-6416

Another camping facility in Florence with full facilities and tennis:

> VETERANS MEMORIAL PARK
> P.O. Box 2040
> Florence, AL 35630
> 205-760-6416

DISMALS CANYON CAMPGROUND

Campgrounds are open from March 1 to December 31. Ten developed RV and tent sites with electrical hookups and dump station; cabins also for rent. Primitive camping is available and can accommodate up to thirty. Dismals Canyon is a registered national landmark with natural canyon, waterfalls, and nature trail. This is a must-see! (See also Canoeing and Hiking sections in this chapter.)

⚓ CANOEING

Bear Creek Canoe Run (canoe livery and rentals for Bear Creek).

This swimming hole is at the head of the waterfall that leads you into the Dismals Canyon where summertime temperatures are fourteen degrees cooler than those above ground.

> DISMALS CANYON
> Rt. 3, Box 281
> Phil Campbell, AL 35581
> 800-808-7998

Bear Creek Floatway: One of Alabama's premier canoeing floatways stretches for 26 miles through some of the most rugged and scenic terrain in the state. The water varies from Class I–VI rapids. A $2 daily permit per person is required, with access at designated points only. Public access, however, is available from Hwy. 5 to Hwy. 241, 2 miles. Alabama water law requires purchasing the right for the public to float on Bear Creek. The river is open to travel but the banks are private property. You can float, fish, and swim, but the riverbanks are off limits unless it's an emergency.

From Mill Creek access downstream, TVA has acquired the same public rights as above 241 bridge, plus wider scenic easements and right of the public to be on a fifty-foot-wide strip on either bank of the creek for walking, sunbathing, bank fishing, and the like.

No camping is allowed anywhere along Bear Creek.

For additional information call TVA, 205-386-2222 or Bear Creek Development Authority, 205-3332-4392

The Lower Bear Creek Canoe Trail has a 34-mile Class I stretch in a serene and pastoral setting and is well suited for beginning canoeists. Upstream access is near Red Bay from Hwy. 24; 50 miles to Tishomingo State Park and another 64 miles to Bishop Bridge, near the Alabama/Mississippi state line. May to October is the most popular canoeing season.

BEAR CREEK DEVELOPMENT AUTHORITY
P.O. Box 670
Russellville, AL 35653
205-332-4392

RUSSELLVILLE/FRANKLIN COUNTY
     CHAMBER OF COMMERCE
P.O. Box 44
Russellville, AL 35653
205-332-1760

FISHING

Wilson Dam and Lake: Begun in 1918 as part of a World War I munitions project, Wilson Dam has enough concrete to make a sidewalk two feet wide around the earth. This engineering feat contains one of the world's highest single-life locks of one hundred feet. Open year-round, tours are available of the turbines and inner working of this 629,840-kilowatt structure, which is a national historical landmark.

Wilson Lake is the home of the former world-record smallmouth bass. The lake is deep with underwater points and bars, sharp drop-offs, and well-defined channel. Crappie; smallmouth, largemouth, and spotted bass; catfish; bream; and sauger are the predominant species.

The tailwaters hold large numbers of small-mouth bass over four pounds. Stripe, sauger, and catfish are also caught here in good numbers.

For maps and information:

CHAMBER OF COMMERCE OF THE SHOALS
104 S. Pine St.
Florence, AL 35630
205-764-4661

COLBERT COUNTY TOURISM AND CON-
     VENTION BUREAU
P.O. Box 440
Tuscumbia, AL 35674
205-383-0783 or 800-344-0783

DIRECTOR OF INFORMATION
TENNESSEE VALLEY AUTHORITY
400 Commerce Ave.
Knoxville, TN 37902
800-362-9250 (in TN)
800-251-9242 (in other Tennessee Valley
     states)

Pickwick Lake is another superb smallmouth lake and ranks as one of the South's best trophy smallie lakes. Pickwick's rocky bottom is an ideal habitat for this bass. Other attributes: sunken islands, constant water flow, shallow cover, and well-defined channel with an abundance of threadfin shad for forage. Sauger, bream, white bass, crappie, catfish, and largemouth and spotted bass share the waters with the prized smallmouth.

For maps and information:

CHAMBER OF COMMERCE OF THE SHOALS
104 S. Pine St.
Florence, AL 35630
205-764-4661

COLBERT COUNTY TOURISM AND CON-
    VENTION BUREAU
P.O. Box 440
Tuscumbia, AL 35674
205-383-0783

Bear Creek Lakes: Little Bear, Big Bear, Upper Bear, and Cedar Creek lakes are stocked with largemouth, smallmouth, and spotted bass, hybrid striped bass, crappie, and channel catfish. All four lakes have shallow and deep water offering a variety of fishing conditions with more abundant shallow cover in Cedar Creek Lake. Boating, camping, picnicking, and swimming are available. Fishing all year, and boat launches open twenty-four hours.

The Bear Creek Development Authority operates and manages fifteen public-use areas around the 250 miles of shoreline on the four lakes. Five camping areas with a total of two hundred campsites. Most sites have electrical and water hookups.

Bear Creek Dam: Beach, picnic area, overlook, boat ramp, and tailwater fishing.

Cedar Creek Dam: Boat ramp and tailwater fishing.

Little Bear Dam: Fishing pier with facilities for the handicapped.

Dates: April 1–October 15. Camping area gates close at 10 P.M. and open at 7 A.M.; Admission: $2 per day; camping rates vary from $5.50 to $10 per night.

BEAR CREEK DEVELOPMENT AUTHORITY
P.O. Box 670
Russellville, AL 35653
205-332-4392

RUSSELLVILLE/ FRANKLIN COUNTY
    CHAMBER OF COMMERCE
P.O. Box 44
Russellville, AL 35653
205-332-1760

GOLFING

An eighteen-hole public golf course is located in Florence. It has clubs and carts for rent, a pro shop, and a microwave sandwich/snack bar.

MCFARLAND PARK AND GOLF COURSE
200 McFarland Dr.
P.O. Box 2040
Florence, AL 35630

Look for the nine-hole public golf course in Tuscumbia on Woodmont Drive.

SPRING CREEK GOLF COURSE
P.O. Box 407
Tuscumbia, AL 35674

HIKING

Dismals Canyon: Known for its mysterious twinkle-in-the-dark worms called Dismalites, the canyon has been declared a National Historic Site by the National Geological Society. Located near Phil Campbell, the area is one of the oldest untouched tracts of forest east of the Mississippi River and features some exotic plants not native to Alabama. A natural bridge, unusual rock formations, waterfalls, a swimming area, and campgrounds are some of the attractions of the Dismals. The canyon has perhaps the most unusual hiking available in the state.

The Dismals also hold pieces of history. After killing Alexander Hamilton in a duel, former vice-president Aaron Burr reportedly hid out for many months at an ancient Indian campsite within the Dismals. Several outlaw gangs, including the James gang, used the area as a hideout.

President Andrew Jackson held Indians in the confines of the canyon before their forced march over the Trail of Tears to the Oklahoma Territory.

Daily admission: $4.50 adults, $2.50 12 and younger. Tent site $13.50 and up. RV site with hookups and dump station $17.50. Canoe rates whole day $35, and half-day $25.

DISMALS CANYON
Clint and Beverly Franklin
Rt. 3, Box 281
Phil Campbell, AL 35581
800-808-7998

RUSSELLVILLE/FRANKLIN COUNTY
    CHAMBER OF COMMERCE
P.O. Box 44
Russellville, AL 35653
205-332-1760

HUNTING

Hunting, biking, and horseback riding available at the following WMAs:

Lauderdale Wildlife Management Area, near Waterloo.

Thomas Wildlife Management Area, near Florence.

Seven Mile Island Wildlife Management Area, near Cherokee.

Contact the Alabama Department of Conservation and Natural Resources for fishing and hunting regulations and information about the above WMAs.

ALABAMA DEPARTMENT OF CONSERVATION & NATURAL RESOURCES
    64 N. Union St.
    Montgomery, AL 36130
    205-242-3486

These Alabama hunters in Tennessee River backwaters wait in a duck blind for game to appear.

Coon hunters who have loved their faithful dogs will appreciate the Coon Dog Cemetery, near Tuscumbia. More than 100 coon dogs have been buried here in marked graves since Labor Day 1937, when Key Underwood laid his famous dog, Troop, to rest. Only tried and true coon dogs are allowed to be buried here. One marker reads, "Black Ranger—He was good as the best and better than the rest." Each Labor Day a celebration is held in the park with picnicking, bluegrass bands, buck dancing, and a liars contest.

For details on the celebration, contact Colbert County Tourism and Convention Bureau, P.O. Box 440, Tuscumbia, AL 35674; 205-383-0783.

Directions: 7 miles west of Tuscumbia on US 72, turn left on Alabama Hwy. 247 and travel about 12 miles; turn right and follow the signs.

❧ NATURE TRAILS

The following are places to stretch your legs and see a bit of nature and/or history. Pick up a copy of the Natchez Trace Parkway map for all the reference points, mile markers, and routes along the Trace from Nashville to Natchez. The Park Service provides a variety of maps free.

Rock Spring, at mile marker 330.2, offers 22 interpretive stops along its 2,200-foot trail from meadow to bottom land to hillside.

Colbert Ferry, at mile marker 327.3, is high on a bluff overlooking the Tennessee River. There is a steep path to the river through dense woods.

Buzzard Roost Spring, at mile marker 320.3, has a short trail down to the spring that supplied Levi Colbert's stand.

Freedom Hills Overlook, at mile marker 317.0, has a quarter-mile trail that leads to the highest point on the parkway in Alabama, an 800-foot elevation.

The following are in the 2,400-acre Wilson Dam/Muscle Shoals reservation, along the Tennessee River. Enter the reservation at the southern end of Wilson Dam to try out six trails with a total of 10 miles.

South Port Historical Trail: 1.3 miles of paths with nine stops to view Civil War breastworks, stonework of the Civilian Conservation Corps, an 1840 bridge, an 1851 cemetery, a laboratory from which scientists battled malaria and yellow fever in the Tennessee Valley, and other sites.

Old First Quarters Small Wild Area: A 1-mile trail through a twenty-five-acre mini-wilderness to view and photograph wildlife.

Rockpile Trail: This strenuous trail's length varies 2.7 to 3.6 miles. You climb up and down limestone bluffs to get a good view of Wilson Dam and its tailwaters.

Muscle Shoals Energy Trail: It uses a portion of the Rockpile Trail.

Gunnery Hill Fitness Trail: An .8-mile trek with numbered, illustrated exercise stations where you can test your physical abilities and have fun.

Jogging/Bicycling Trail: A 2.6-mile path winds around the reservation.

For more information on Wilson Dam trails, see TVA address in the Biking section of this chapter.

21 *Mississippi Outdoor Recreation*

The following two sources can answer most of your questions, provide you with maps and brochures, and point you in the right direction regarding outdoor recreational opportunities. (Other contact information for the places described here can be found throughout the chapter.)

MISSISSIPPI DEPT. OF WILDLIFE, FISHERIES
    AND PARKS
P.O. Box 451
Jackson, MS 39205-0451
601-362-9212

MISSISSIPPI DEPT. OF WILDLIFE, FISHERIES
    AND PARKS
Office of Parks
P.O. Box 23093
Jackson, MS 39225-3093
800-GO-PARKS (800-467-2757) or 601-
    364-2140

To get you started in Mississippi, the following is a sampling of what the state has to offer. This list is not meant to be complete but enough to keep you active while traveling the Trace.

Cypress Swamp provides an idea of what it was like to travel the lowlands of the Trace a hundred years ago.

ᔥ BIKING

Mississippi rules for bicycling:

1. Move with traffic. Stay on right side of street near curb.
2. No more than two abreast when riding on streets or highways. Two abreast may not take up more than one lane.
3. Illegal to hitch a ride on a moving vehicle.
4. Use turn signals.
5. Leave the street for emergency vehicles.
6. Pass on the left of all vehicles.
7. A light must be used on the front of all bicycles at night, with a red light or reflector on rear of bicycle.

Campsites are set aside for bikers and hikers only.

Bikers may order information including a bicycling map from

THE NATCHEZ TRACE PARKWAY
RR 1, NT-143
Tupelo, MS 38801
601-680-4025

and/or information on planning a bicycle tour of Mississippi from

INDIAN CYCLE FITNESS AND OUTDOOR
125 Dyess Rd.
Ridgeland, MS 39157
800-898-0019

Motorized and nonmotorized trails within 2,500 acres:

TRACE STATE PARK
Rt. 1, Box 254
Belden, MS 38826
601-489-2958

Bikers and hikers camping only near entrance of Maintenance Center, just south of Kosciusko's Museum/Information Center. Look for entrance on your right before you reach the gates to the maintenance area.

ᔥ CAMPING

J. P. Coleman State Park offers twenty cabin units, three suites, and fifty-seven camping pads 13 miles north of Iuka, off Rt. 25 on Pickwick Lake.

J. P. COLEMAN STATE PARK
Rt. 5, Box 504
Iuka, MS 38852
601-423-6515

Tishomingo State Park, at mile marker 303.0, offers six cabins, group camping for 142 people, tent camping, sixty-two camping pads, swimming, nature trails, canoeing, and multiuse playing field.

TISHOMINGO STATE PARK
P.O. Box 880
Tishomingo, MS 38873
601-438-6914

Lake Lamar Bruce, 1.5 miles northeast of Saltillo, offers fishing, boat rental, ramps, camping, and bathhouse; 601-869-209.

Tombigbee State Park, 6 miles southeast of Tupelo off Rt. 6, offers lakeside group camp for 200, meeting room, seven cabins, and twenty camping pads.

TOMBIGBEE STATE PARK
Rt. 2, Box 336-E
Tupelo, MS 38801
601-842-7669

Elvis Presley Lake and Campground has 350-acre lake in 850-acre park. Primitive sites (no utilities) and full-service sites available. Located 2.5 miles northeast of Hwy. 78 and Veteran's Blvd. intersection. Swimming, boating, fishing, hiking, and water-skiing also available.

ELVIS PRESLEY LAKE AND CAMPGROUND
Rt. 4, Box 387 E
Tupelo, MS 38801
601-841-1304

Natchez Trace RV Complex between mile markers 251 and 252 (Pontotoc Road exit) is open year-round and offers four hundred feet of the Trace, full pull-through hookups, showers and restrooms, LP gas, nine-hole putting green, and free Continental breakfast.

NATCHEZ TRACE RV COMPLEX
P.O. Box 2564
Tupelo, MS 3803
601-767-8609

Trace State Park, located 10 miles east of Pontotoc off Rt. 6, offers twenty-five camping pads with water and electricity, six cabins, tent camping, swimming, water-skiing, fishing, boat rental, and motorized and nonmotorized trails in its 2,500 acres.

TRACE STATE PARK
Rt. 1, Box 254
Belden, MS 38826
601-489-2958

Davis Lake exit, at mile marker 243.1 and 4 miles from the Trace, offers camping; fishing for bass, bream, catfish, and crappie; boat rental; canoeing and tubing; cabins; and nature trails; 601-285-3264.

Choctaw Lake Recreation Area (near Ackerman) offers twenty-seven campsites with electrical hookups, thirty-five sites with tables and grills (one is handicapped accessible), and two group shelters; 601-285-3264.

Jeff Busby, at mile marker 193.1, has eighteen primitive sites, picnic tables, exhibit shelter, and overlook at top of Little Mountain. Jeff Busby site is the only store and gas station on the Trace; 601-387-4365.

Kosciusko: Bikers and hikers primitive camp facility; see Biking section, this chapter.

Holmes County State Park, about 18 miles

Comfortable campsites, like this one at Davis Lake, are common along the Natchez Trace Parkway.

River Valley Supply District. Contact them for brochures and information about Timberlake, Goshen Springs, Coal Bluff, and Low Head campgrounds. These campgrounds range from Spillway Road on the eastern end of the dam, along the eastern shore to the north end of lake, and on the Pearl River.

PEARL RIVER VALLEY SUPPLY DISTRICT
P.O. Box 12750
Jackson, MS 39236
601-354-3448 or 856-6574

Goshen Springs Campground: 601-829-2751
Timber Lake Campground: 601-922-9100
Coal Bluff Campground: 601-654-7726
Low Head Dam: 601-654-9359

west of Kosciusko on Rt. 12 or 4 miles south of Durant off I-55, Exit 150, offers tent camping, twelve cabins, and twenty-eight camping pads, two fishing lakes, archery range, skating rink, and nature trail.

HOLMES COUNTY STATE PARK
Rt. 1, Box 153
Durant, MS 39063
601-653-3351

Ross Barnett Reservoir: The Trace runs parallel to the lake, with scenic views. You can reach the lake from the Trace via Highway 43, which crosses it about two-thirds of the way up. Exit at mile marker 113.0 to reach Spillway Road and travel across the dam.

There are private campgrounds around the lake. The reservoir is owned and operated by Pearl

The tailwaters of Ross Barnett Reservoir let anglers experience a change from lake fishing.

There are about twenty public launching ramps on Ross Barnett Reservoir and the Pearl River, four full-service marinas, and three fishing piers. The pier at Rankin Boat ramp (eastern end of dam) is handicapped accessible.

LeFleur's Bluff State Park offers thirty camping pads, tent camping, bathhouse, sanitation dump station, fishing, playground, boat ramps, nature trail, swimming pool, clubhouse, picnic areas with grills, three large pavilions, four tennis courts, and camp store.

LeFleur's Bluff State Park
2140 Riverside Dr.
Jackson, MS 39202
601-987-3985

Edwards area: Askew's Landing Campground has more than forty hookups around lake with fishing, canoeing, and nature trails.

Askew's Landing Campground
Rt. 2, Box 353
Edwards, MS 39066
601-852-2331

Rocky Springs, at mile marker 54.8, has twenty-two campsites, picnic tables, interpretive trail through old town site, and hiking trail on the Old Trace.

Grand Gulf Military Monument Park has camping, cabins, bathhouses, and nature trail.

Grand Gulf Military Monument Park
Rt. 2, Box 389
Port Gibson, MS 39150
601-437-5911

Vicksburg area: Indian Hills Campground, 7 miles east of Vicksburg on I-20, has sixty-two campsites, bathhouse, store, and nearby golf and tennis.

Indian Hills Campground
P.O. Box 168
Vicksburg, MS 39180
601-638-5519

Leisure Living Campground, on Eagle Lake 13 miles north of Hwy. 61, west on 465W 15 miles, has thirty campsites with full hookups; 601-279-4259.

River City RV Park has sixty-six level pads (all pull-through), full hookups, picnic tables, swimming pool, playground, game room, and laundry.

River City RV Park
211 Miller St.
Vicksburg, MS 39180
601-631-0388

Vicksburg KOA Battlefield Campground has eighty sites with full hookups, laundry, store, playground, and swimming pool.

Vicksburg KOA Battlefield Campground
4407 I-20 Frontage Rd
Vicksburg, MS 39180
601-636-2025

Clear Creek Campground, 10 minutes east of Vicksburg near I-20, has thirty-five full hookups and ten with water, store, laundry, showers, game room, LP gas, and FAX service; 601-638-5519.

Natchez Trace State Park, 10 miles north of

Natchez off US 61 at Stanton, offers twenty-one tent camping areas, cabins, nature trail, and picnic area.

NATCHEZ TRACE STATE PARK
230-B Wickcliff Rd.
Natchez, MS 39120
601-442-2658

Whispering Pines Travel Trailer Park, on Hwy. 61 N. half a mile north of Natchez, offers full hookups and showers; 601-442-3624.

Plantation Park Campground, on Hwy. 61 S. 3.4 miles from Hwy. 84-61 junction, has full hookups, showers, and swimming pool; 601-442-5222.

✺ CANOEING

J. P. Coleman State Park: Bear Creek Float Trip.

Tishomingo State Park offers eight-mile float trip down Bear Creek, April through mid-October. Everything provided, two trips daily at 9 A.M. and 1 P.M.

Tombigbee State Park
Trace State Park
Davis Lake
Ross Barnett Reservoir (see Pearl River Valley Supply District address)
Grand Gulf Military Monument Park
Natchez Trace State Park

✺ FISHING

J. P. Coleman State Park (1,400 acres on Pickwick Lake) offers fishing, camping, canoeing, swimming, boating, boat rentals, skiing, picnicking,

pool, minigolf, cabins with kitchenettes, six motel-like units, fifty-seven camping pads, RV hookups, potable water, tables, and grills, as well as a full-service marina catering to all water sports. Restaurant open during the summer. Reservations recommended.

Tennessee-Tombigbee Waterway runs south from Pickwick Lake via Yellow Creek through Mississippi into Alabama. This slack-water (imperceptible current) stream is shallow and narrow, and wakes can be a hazard to small craft. Get the brochure "Boating on the Tenn-Tom" if you plan to use this waterway. It contains rules, points of interest along its 448-mile course, maps with marinas, ports, locks and dams, fishing, and more. Request it from

TENN-TOM WATERWAY DEVELOPMENT
    AUTHORITY
P.O. Drawer 671
Columbus, MS 39703
601-328-3286

Tishomingo State Park, at mile marker 304, offers fishing, boat rental, canoeing, and tubing.

Bay Springs Lake has 7,000 surface acres with bass, bream, catfish, and crappie fishing. On the Tenn-Tom Waterway, it is 8 miles long and has five major creeks. Exit Trace at mile marker 293.4.

Tombigbee State Park has bass, bream, crappie, and catfish; boat rental, ramps, and canoeing.

Lake Lamar Bruce, 1.5 miles northeast of Saltillo, offers fishing, boat rental, ramps, camping, and bathhouse; 601-869-209.

Trace State Park has fishing, ramps, and boat rentals. Trace Lake is 600 acres, stocked with

Boats aren't necessary to enjoy fishing. Many fish species feed and make their homes within a few feet of the bank.

Ross Barnett Reservoir: 50 square miles of fishing and boating north of Jackson. Four marinas offer boat and motor rental, fishing, and sailing supplies.

Edwards area: Askew's Landing Campground has a lake stocked with bass, crappie, bream, and catfish. Ideal for canoes and jonboats.

Grand Gulf Military Monument Park offers backwater fishing with some alligators.

Vicksburg has several fishing areas. Eagle, Chotard, Tennessee, Albermarle, and other oxbow lakes are north of the city, east off Hwy. 61. Fish the Yazoo and Mississippi rivers by launching your boat at the foot of Clay Street, or fish along the bank.

Natchez Trace State Park probably offers the best largemouth fishing in the state. The 250-acre lake has standing timber amid the confluence of four streams, which produces many bass over eight pounds. Concession, boat rentals, and camping.

Natchez is on the Mississippi River; fishing abounds.

redear (shellcracker), bluegill, crappie, catfish, and bass.

Elvis Presley State Park has a 350-acre lake with bream, bass, crappie, and catfish.

Davis Lake has bass, bream, crappie, and catfish.

Choctaw Lake Recreation Area (near Ackerman): This one-hundred-acre lake offers fishing for bream, catfish, bass, and crappie; one fishing pier; boating; canoeing; swimming/beach; hiking; camping; group shelters; and hunting on nearby Tombigbee National Forest lands. Off Hwy. 15, 2 miles south of Ackerman; 601-285-3264.

CHOCTAW COUNTY ECONOMIC
  DEVELOPMENT
P.O. Box 737
Ackerman, MS 39735
601-285-3778

❧ G O L F: Public Courses

Tupelo:
  AMORY GOLF CLUB
  P.O. Box 276
  Hwy. 25 N.
  Amory, MS 38821
  601-256-9454
  (Nine holes, pro shop)

BEL AIR PARK
P.O. Box 1419
Country Club Rd.
Tupelo, MS 38802
601-841-6446
(Nine holes, pro shop)

THE MEADOWS, INC.
Rt. 7, Box 224
Tupelo, MS 38801
601-840-1985
(Nine holes, pro shop)

Starkville:
MISSISSIPPI STATE UNIVERSITY
P.O. Box 6070
Old Hwy. 82
Starkville, MS 39759
601-352-3028
(Eighteen holes, pro shop)

Jackson:
GROVE PARK
1800 Walter Welch Dr.
Jackson, MS 39213
601-982-9728
(Nine holes, open year-round)

SONNY GUY MUNICIPAL
3200 Woodrow Wilson Dr.
Jackson, MS 39209
601-960-1905
(Eighteen holes, pro shop, open year-round)

LEFLEUR'S BLUFF GOLF COURSE
1205 Lakeland Dr.
Jackson, MS 39216

601-987-3998 or 987-3923
(Nine holes, driving range, pro shop)

EAGLE RIDGE GOLF COURSE
P.O. Box 1145
Hinds Community College, Hwy. 18 S.
Raymond, MS 39154
601-857-5993
(Eighteen holes, pro shop)

ROBIN HOOD LAKE RESORT
P.O. Box 1735
1000 Lake Rd.
Brandon, MS 39043
601-825-8343
(Eighteen holes, pro shop)

Vicksburg:
CLEAR CREEK GOLF COURSE
1566 Tiffentown Rd.
Vicksburg, MS 39180
601-638-9395
(Eighteen holes, pro shop)

Natchez:
DUNCAN PARK
57 Duncan Park Rd.
Natchez, MS 39120
601-442-5955
(Nine holes, pro shop)

WINDING CREEK GOLF COURSE
505 S. Commerce St.
Natchez, MS 39121
601-442-6995
(Eighteen holes, pro shop)

ᑲ HIKING

J. P. Coleman State Park has a 13-mile trail system.

Tishomingo State Park (milepost 302.8).

Trace State Park has many trails (25 miles) around the lake.

Choctaw Lake Recreation Area (near Ackerman): 3-mile hiking trail adjacent to one-hundred-acre lake; 601-285-3264.

Jeff Busby (milepost 193.1) hiking trail leads to one of the highest points on the Natchez Trace; Little Mountain Trail is 1 mile long.

Rocky Springs (milepost 54.8) has about 4 miles of trails; you can hike down the Old Trace to Owens Creek Waterfall (milepost 52.4), 1.5 miles down the parkway.

Owens Creek Trail (milepost 52.4) offers a 5- or 10-mile hike.

Grand Gulf Military Monument Park.

Old Trace Trail, at Coles Creek, is 3.5 miles long from milepost 16.8 to Highway 553, milepost 20.0.

ᑲ HORSE TRAILS

See Tennessee section on horse trails for federal regulations regarding horses on the Natchez Trace.

Tupelo Horse Trail: A 3½-mile trail located northwest of Tupelo within the Trace boundaries; Access from the parkway at Highway 6 (milepost 259.7 or 260.0), east on Highway 6 to Thomas St. (second traffic light), north on Thomas St. to Jackson St., west on Jackson and under the Trace

These horseback riders are making their way from Owl Mounds toward Davis Lake.

overpass; Paved parking on right but no water, restrooms, or camping.

Tombigbee Horse Trail: An elongated figure-eight trail, 9 or 15 miles in length is located almost entirely on the Tombigbee National Forest next to the Trace. Access is available through Witch Dance (milepost 233.2), 6 miles south of Highway 32 and 4 miles off Highway 8. Southwest of Tupelo, 23 miles in Track Tombigbee Ranger District. Camping, water, and restrooms.

WITCH DANCE HORSE TRAIL
Rt. 1, Box 98A
Ackerman, MS 39735
601-285-3264

Lonesome Pine Horse Trail: A 15-mile, one-way trail located northeast of Jackson within the Trace boundaries. Access from the parkway at Highway 43 (milepost 114.9). Gravel parking space is limited. No water, restrooms, or camping.

Trace State Park Trails (not on the Trace): Near Tupelo, off Hwy. 6 in Pontotoc County. Six trails (25 miles) with lodging and stables available.

TRACE STATE PARK TRAILS
Rt. 1, Box 254
Belden, MS 38826
601-489-2958

Houston:

CRAZY HORSE RANCH TRAIL RIDES
Natchez Trace Parkway at Witch Dance
(by appointment only)
601-831-9494

Quail hunting is an old southern tradition. A good bird dog is necessary to locate the bobwhite that flies only when you are about to step on it.

ᝐ HUNTING

For license information, call 800-5-GO-HUNT.

Private: Canemount Plantation has hunting for the connoisseur—trophy deer, boar, and turkey.

CANEMOUNT PLANTATION
Rt. 2, Box 45
Lorman, MS 39096
601-445-2150, 887-3784, or
800-423-0684

The following Wildlife Management Areas (WMAs) are open to the public:

Chickasaw WMA: Near Houston; 27,259 acres; large and small game and waterfowl; camping.

CHICKASAW WMA
Rt. 4, Box 60-B
New Albany, MS 38652
601-364-2123, 568-7400, or 534-9235

Choctaw WMA: Near Ackerman; 24,314 acres; large and small game and waterfowl; camping.

CHOCTAW WMA
Rt. 1
Ackerman, MS 39735
601-364-2123 or 285-3569

Copiah County WMA: Near Port Gibson; 6,500 acres; large and small game.

Copiah County WMA
Rt. I, Box 8
Pattison, MS 39144
601-364-2123 or 277-3508

Divide Section WMA: Near Iuka; 12,000 acres; large and small game and waterfowl.

Divide Section WMA
Rt. I, Box 618
Golden, MS 38827
601-364-2123 or 423-1455

Pearl River WMA: Near Canton; 6,000 acres; large and small game and waterfowl; camping; bathhouse; wildlife tours.

Pearl River WMA
Rt. 3, Box 248
Canton, MS 39046
601-364-2123 or 856-5140

Sandy Creek WMA: Near Natchez; 16,407 acres; large and small game and waterfowl; camping.

Sandy Creek WMA
P.O. Box 215
Meadville, MS 39653
601-364-2123 or 384-2658

National Wildlife Refuge (NWR) hunting: Noxubee NWR: Near Starkville; 42,000 acres; large and small game and waterfowl; camping; fishing; boat ramp; nature trail.

Rt. I, Box 84
Brooksville, MS 39739
601-364-2123 or 323-5548

St. Catherine's Creek NWR: Near Natchez; deer (archery) and small game.

St. Catherine's Creek NWR
P.O. Box 18639
Natchez, MS 39122
601-442-6696

Tara WMA: Near Vicksburg; lodging; guided hunts.

NATURE TRAILS

The following are places to stretch your legs and see a bit of nature and/or history. Pick up a copy of the Natchez Trace Parkway map for all the reference points, mile markers, and routes along the Trace from Nashville to Natchez. The Park Service provides a variety of maps free.

Tishomingo, at mile marker 302.8, has trails throughout the park.

Tenn-Tom Waterway, at mile marker 293.2, lets you walk along the canal.

Donivan Slough, at mile marker 283.3, tells the story of a slough via twenty-two interpretive stops along the 1,660-foot trail.

Dogwood Valley, at mile marker 275.2, has twelve interpretive stops along the 1,000-foot path.

Confederate Gravesites trail, at mile marker 269.4, is 1,400 feet long and has one interpretive stop.

Tupelo Park Headquarters/Beech Springs, at mile marker 266.0, offers a 2,830-foot trek with eighteen interpretive stops

Chickasaw Village, at mile marker 261.8, has twenty-two interpretive stops along the 1,200-

Cole Creek nature trail takes you into a mixed forest. You can see where the swamp is giving way to a hardwood forest.

foot trail depicting Indian uses of plants. You have the option of hiking 4.6 miles to Old Town Overlook, near the Tupelo Visitors Center, with ten interpretive stops.

Trace State Park: Jason M. Stewart Nature Trail, along western edge of lake; many other trails.

Bynum Mounds, at mile marker 232.4, is a leisurely walk among Indian mounds.

Jeff Busby, at mile marker 193.1, has 1,900-foot trail and twenty-eight interpretive stops depicting plants used as food by Indians and settlers; a 1-mile hike from campground to summit.

Cole Creek, at mile marker 175.6, reveals the changes from swamp to mixed hardwood forest along its seven-hundred-foot trail; ten interpretive stops.

Hurricane Creek, at mile marker 164.3, is one thousand feet long; eleven interpretive stops.

Myrick Creek/Beaver Dam, at mile marker 145.1, takes you one thousand feet among old beaver dams and changing environment; nine interpretive stops.

Upper Choctaw Boundary, at mile marker 128.4, has Southern Pines nature trail of nine interpretive stops along the seven-hundred-foot trail.

Cypress Swamp, at mile marker 122.0, has a 2,200-foot trail; twenty-two interpretive stops.

Rocky Springs, at mile marker 54.8, offers a 1½-mile trek or a 10-mile trek to Owen Creek area.

Windsor Ruins, near Port Gibson, MS.

Bullen Creek, at mile marker 18.4, has twenty-three interpretive stops along a 1,100-foot trail.

Mount Locust, at mile marker 15.5.

Emerald Mound, at mile marker 10.3.

Grand Village of the Natchez State Historic Site at Natchez, MS.

22 *Tips for Bicyclists*

The Natchez Trace Parkway is a wonderful place for cycling. The speed limit is 50 miles per hour for automobiles and strictly enforced; the traffic is generally light; and the road travels through some beautiful country. Cyclists travel the Trace year-round, but spring and fall offer exceptional scenery and pleasant weather without the extremes of the other seasons.

Because much of the Trace passes through rural areas, planning for food and rest stops becomes important. Here are some tips that may be helpful if you're planning to cycle the Trace.

These bikers traveled from St. Louis to experience the 16-mile trek through Vicksburg National Military Park and to view the battlesites and monuments.

The entire Natchez Trace Parkway is for biking, all 450 miles of it. It's easier pedaling from north to south because that direction is down hill!

We recommend beginning at the intersection of Highway 96 and the Natchez Trace Parkway outside Franklin, because the northern terminus at Nashville has not been completed.

✺ DAY ONE

Your first stop is for lunch in Leipers Fork. Overnight accommodations are also nearby at Namaste Bed and Breakfast, for those of you who started in Nashville or points beyond.

Until completion of the northern terminus in the summer of 1996, the total distance from the intersection on Highway 96 to your first overnight stop, at Swan View Motel in Hohenwald, will be approximately 50 miles. To reach Swan View, exit at milepost 391.1, take Highway 412 west toward Hohenwald. The motel and adjacent restaurant are one mile on the left. An alternative site for campers is the Meriwether Lewis State Park.

✺ DAY TWO

Second day's lunch stop is in Collinwood at the Old Depot Cafe, Keith's Country Triangle, or Pat's Place, about 35 miles from Highway 412. Overnight stop is at Easterwood Bed and Breakfast in Cherokee, Alabama, a distance of approximately 35 miles from Collinwood. Exit Highway 72 and go east into Cherokee. Turn right at the center of town and travel four blocks to the Easterwood. The Wooden Nickle Restaurant is a good place for dinner.

Alternative lodging at Tishomingo State Park, cabins or camping, is about 15 miles beyond Highway 72 to Cherokee. Exit milepost 303.9 and go 3.5 miles to park headquarters.

✺ DAY THREE

Third day's stop, 45 miles from Tishomingo, is at Trace Inn in Tupelo. Exit milepost 260.1, and the motel is on Highway 6 adjacent to the parkway. There are no restaurants between Tishomingo and Tupelo.

An alternative for an overnight stop is Davis Lake Campground, approximately 60 miles from Tishomingo. Exit at milepost 243.1 and go 4 miles west.

❧ DAY FOUR

For your fourth day's lunch, stop at Houston, 20 miles from Davis Lake. Exit milepost 229.7, follow Highway 8 for 4 miles west into Houston. Your overnight stay at Harmon House Bed and Breakfast in Houston is 35 miles from Tupelo. Looking ahead from Houston, it's about 45 miles to Jeff Busby Campground and 55 miles to French Camp Bed and Breakfast; both Jeff Busby and French Camp are along the Trace.

❧ DAY FIVE

Fifth day's lunch stop is Kosciusko. There's a small campground outside Kosciusko for bicyclists only, and the Redbud Inn Bed and Breakfast is in town. Exit milepost 159.8 and follow Mississippi Highway 31 into town. Motels are on the bypass to your right.

Here is a "bikers only" campsite just south of the Kosciusko Museum and Information Center.

Your overnight stop in Jackson is 55 miles away from Kosciusko. Exit milepost 102.4 adjacent to Ridgeland Crafts Center. It's 3.5 miles south on Highway 51 to Best Western Jackson or Hampton Inn. Alternative: Ratliff Ferry Campground (45 miles from Kosciusko), north of town on the Pearl River—much less traffic here.

Eventually you will have to exit the parkway to pass through Jackson, because the Trace is incomplete here, so pick your route carefully.

❧ DAY SIX

Sixth day's lunch stop is on the road with an overnight stay in Port Gibson, 58 miles from getting back on the Trace south of Jackson. Oak Square or Gibsons Landing Bed and Breakfast are in Port Gibson.

❧ DAY SEVEN

Seventh day, cycle into Natchez, 40 miles south of Port Gibson. Many bed and breakfasts, motels, and restaurants await you.

For additional information, see the chapter heading for the community you'll be visiting, and contact the National Park Service for bicycling information.

NATIONAL PARK SERVICE
Natchez Trace Parkway
Rt. I, NT 143
Tupelo, MS 38801
601-842-1572

Index

Cathy and Vernon Summerlin live quietly in the country near Leipers Fork, Tennessee.

Cathy, when she gets time away from performing duties as a registered nurse at Vanderbilt Medical Center, loves to travel and garden. *Traveling the Trace* is her first step toward a new career as a travel writer.

Vernon is an award-winning outdoor writer, columnist, and photographer. He is the publisher and editor of *Tennessee Angler* magazine, producer of *Tennessee Angler Radio*, a freelance writer and photographer, and a television field host. His articles have appeared in many outdoor magazines, including *Field & Stream*, *Outdoor Life*, and *Bassmaster*. His first book was *Two Dozen Fishing Holes—A Guide to Middle Tennessee*.